About This Book

Why is this topic important?

Continuing education and development lie at the very heart of any successful organization. Time and time again, studies show that the best organizations, those that deliver better-than-average return on investment, also happen to be the ones with the highest commitment to training and development. Moreover, training has become a powerful ally in the war for talent. Job seekers frequently cite a strong commitment to development as one of the principal reasons for joining or remaining with an organization.

What can you achieve with this book?

In your hands is a working toolkit, a valuable source of knowledge for the training professional. Offering entirely new content each year, the Pfeiffer Training *Annual* showcases the latest thinking and cutting-edge approaches to training and development, contributed by practicing training professionals, consultants, academics, and subject-matter experts. Turn to the *Annual* for a rich source of ideas and to try out new methods and approaches that others in your profession have found successful.

How is this book organized?

The book is divided into four sections: Experiential Learning Activities (ELAs); Editor's Choice; Inventories, Questionnaires, and Surveys; and Articles and Discussion Resources. All the material can be freely reproduced for training purposes. The ELAs are the mainstay of the *Annual* and cover a broad range of training topics. The activities are presented as complete and ready-to-use training designs; facilitator instructions and all necessary handouts and participant materials are included. Editor's Choice pieces allow us to select material that doesn't fit the other categories and take advantage of "hot topics." The instrument section introduces reliable survey and assessment tools for gathering and sharing data on aspects of personal or team development. The articles section presents the best current thinking about training and organization development. Use these for your own professional development or as lecture resources.

About Pfeiffer

Pfeiffer serves the professional development and hands-on resource needs of training and human resource practitioners and gives them products to do their jobs better. We deliver proven ideas and solutions from experts in HR development and HR management, and we offer effective and customizable tools to improve workplace performance. From novice to seasoned professional, Pfeiffer is the source you can trust to make yourself and your organization more successful.

Essential Knowledge Pfeiffer produces insightful, practical, and comprehensive materials on topics that matter the most to training and HR professionals. Our Essential Knowledge resources translate the expertise of seasoned professionals into practical, how-to guidance on critical workplace issues and problems. These resources are supported by case studies, worksheets, and job aids and are frequently supplemented with CD-ROMs, websites, and other means of making the content easier to read, understand, and use.

Essential Tools Pfeiffer's Essential Tools resources save time and expense by offering proven, ready-to-use materials—including exercises, activities, games, instruments, and assessments—for use during a training or team-learning event. These resources are frequently offered in looseleaf or CD-ROM format to facilitate copying and customization of the material.

Pfeiffer also recognizes the remarkable power of new technologies in expanding the reach and effectiveness of training. While e-hype has often created whizbang solutions in search of a problem, we are dedicated to bringing convenience and enhancements to proven training solutions. All our e-tools comply with rigorous functionality standards. The most appropriate technology wrapped around essential content yields the perfect solution for today's on-the-go trainers and human resource professionals.

Pfeiffer
www.pfeiffer.com   *Essential resources for training and HR professionals*

The Pfeiffer Annual Series

The Pfeiffer Annuals present each year never-before-published materials contributed by learning professionals and academics and written for trainers, consultants, and human resource and performance-improvement practitioners. As a forum for the sharing of ideas, theories, models, instruments, experiential learning activities, and best and innovative practices, the *Annuals* are unique. Not least because only in the *Pfeiffer Annuals* will you find solutions from professionals like you who work in the field as trainers, consultants, facilitators, educators, and human resource and performance-improvement practitioners and whose contributions have been tried and perfected in real-life settings with actual participants and clients to meet real-world needs.

The Pfeiffer Annual: Consulting
Edited by Elaine Biech

The Pfeiffer Annual: Leadership Development
Edited by James Noel and David Dotlich

The Pfeiffer Annual: Management Development
Edited by Robert C. Preziosi

The Pfeiffer Annual: Training
Edited by Elaine Biech

Michael Allen's 2008 e-Learning Annual
Edited by Michael Allen

Call for Papers

How would you like to be published in the *Pfeiffer Training* or *Consulting Annual*? Possible topics for submissions include group and team building, organization development, leadership, problem solving, presentation and communication skills, consulting and facilitation, and training-the-trainer. Contributions may be in one of the following three formats:

- Experiential Learning Activities

- Inventories, Questionnaires, and Surveys

- Articles and Discussion Resources

To receive a copy of the submission packet, which explains the requirements and will help you determine format, language, and style to use, contact editor Elaine Biech at Pfeifferannual@ aol.com or by calling 757-588-3939.

Elaine Biech, EDITOR

The *2008*
Pfeiffer
ANNUAL

TRAINING

Pfeiffer
A Wiley Imprint
www.pfeiffer.com

ISBN-13: 978-0-7879-9628-4
ISSN: 1046-333-X

Acquiring Editor: Martin Delahoussaye
Director of Development: Kathleen Dolan Davies
Developmental Editor: Susan Rachmeler
Production Editor: Dawn Kilgore
Editor: Rebecca Taff
Manufacturing Supervisor: Becky Morgan
Editorial Assistant: Julie Rodriquez
Interior Design and Technical Art: Leigh McLellan Design

Printed in the United States of America

Printing   10 9 8 7 6 5 4 3 2 1

Contents

Experiential Learning Activities

**Topic is change focused

Editor's Choice

Inventories, Questionnaires, and Surveys

Articles and Discussion Resources

Preface

In last year's *Annual* I wrote, "Wouldn't it be wonderful if we could publish an entire *Annual* for 2008 that focuses on change?" Well, we decided to give it a chance. And here it is! *The 2008 Training and Consulting Annuals* focused on change! The *Training Annual* boasts sixteen change submissions, and the *Consulting Annual* presents ten change submissions.

This is the first time the *Annuals* have focused on one topic. Please let us know what you think. But why change? Change is everywhere. It is multiplying, and at a faster and faster rate of speed than ever before.

Let me summarize the example provided in last year's *Annuals*. In the 1700s, a stagecoach traveled comfortably at ten miles an hour. The steam engine was invented in the 1800s and could carry people almost twenty miles an hour. The rate had doubled in one hundred years. Less than a century later, airplanes flew one hundred miles an hour, quadrupling the rate of speed. In less than fifty years, manned planes such as the SR-71 and the X-15 (rocket) were flying in excess of Mach 3 (Mach 3 is three times the speed of sound, over two thousand miles an hour). Today you can out-fly the sun, having breakfast in New York and then again in San Diego the same morning—not that you would want to!

Consider knowledge—the business most of us are in. How quickly does current world knowledge change? In the past, knowledge doubled from 1 AD to 1500, or in 1,500 years. It doubled again from 1500 to 1800, in three hundred years. It doubled again from 1800 to 1900, in one hundred years. By 1940 the doubling rate was every twenty years. And by 1970, it was seven years. Today it is estimated that knowledge doubles every one or two years. It is predicted that by 2020 our collective body of knowledge will double every seventy-two days. For example, I "googled" (a new word—another sign of change) "organizational change" and the search uncovered 52,130,000 sites. The number of sites will have changed—perhaps doubled—by the time you read this!

We are certainly an information-rich society. Over 1,000,000 new websites are created every day. One weekly edition of *The New York Times* contains more information than the average person was likely to come across in a lifetime in the 17th Century.

What does this mean to you personally? Do you know someone who is in college? It is estimated that half the facts learned in engineering while in college will be obsolete five years after graduation. Half of what is learned in computer science will be outdated in just two years. And the same is true in nearly every field because information is changing, accelerating at an almost incomprehensible rate.

The accelerating rate of information is directly related to the accelerating rate of change. This means more decisions and an increased number of choices. Have you tried to make a simple purchase for your home lately? Technology has changed, requiring many more decisions than you had just a few years ago. How many decisions did you have to make when you purchased a telephone fifteen years ago? Probably very few. How many decisions do you need to make today when you purchase a telephone? What about a television set?

- *Telephone:* Land line or cell? Caller ID? Digital answering? Speaker phone? Voice-activated dialing? Camera phone? Internet capable? BlueTooth capable? Video and music capable? GPS? PDA combination? Text messaging? Picture messaging? Which carrier? What plan? How many minutes? Free minutes? Carrier-to-carrier plan? Family plan? Replacement phones? Warranties? Insurance? Ringer choices? Battery life? Headset? Charger? Car charger? Other accessories? And most important, what color?

- *Television:* Flat screen? Plasma? HD? HD-ILA? Digital? DLP? LCD? Rear projection? Traditional? Resolution? Dual HDMI high-definition input? 3HDMI? Built-in DVR? Recording time? Screen size? Accessory compatibility? Built-in VCR or DVD? Integrated PC input? Stereo? Home theater? Speaker system? Surround sound? Direct TV? Satellite?

And there will be many more changes between the time I write this and you read it. Changing something as personal and as simple as a telephone may require weeks of research, with changes occurring right before your eyes.

Like your personal life, organizational life is changing. Driven by global competition, shifting workforce demographics, customer requirements, regulatory pressures, technology advancements, stockholder expectations, and a host of other events, organizations must produce rapid change. The organization may be looking for change to adjust its mission, transform its identity, improve the quality of products or services, or decrease the amount of time it takes to get product to market.

We live in changing times. There is no doubt about it. The increased amount and rate of information has placed organizations on ever-accelerating paths of change. Dedicated to the topic of change, the *Annuals* can help you manage the change in your organizations.

The 2008 Pfeiffer Annual: Training includes a wonderful array of tools to help you with change. The centerpiece of this volume is Vince Miller's article in the Editor's Choice section that provides the history of the training profession. Vince is a walking archive of training history and was the 1974 ASTD national president. It is a pleasure to travel with him on this historical journey of how the training industry has changed.

Other musts in this volume are the articles by Peter Garber about turbulent change of the future and Mel Silberman about changing attitudes, plus thirteen others. We are honored to have ELAs from two dignitaries: Leonard Goodstein and Thiagi. These two activities alone are worth the cost of the *Annual!*

The *Consulting Annual* also includes change management tools. Check out the ELAs by two well-known authors: Karen Lawson and Bob Preziosi. We are honored to have Karl Albrecht's submission about how unrealistic expectations can derail change and Mitchell Lee Marks' article about employee adaptation and change. Both provide interesting reading and thoughtful concepts to help you with the changes you and your organization face.

It's been said that "innovation" is the new change. Did Apple change from being a computer company to an entertainment company? Or did Apple "innovate"? I'll leave you to ponder the difference. In the meantime, dig into this exciting and practical volume of the *Pfeiffer Annuals!*

What Are the Annuals?

The *Annual* series consists of practical materials written for trainers, consultants, and performance-improvement technologists. We know the materials are practical, because they are written by the same practitioners who use the materials.

The *Pfeiffer Annual: Training* focuses on skill building and knowledge enhancement and also includes articles that enhance the skills and professional development of trainers. The *Pfeiffer Annual: Consulting* focuses on intervention techniques and organizational systems. It also includes skill building for the professional consultant. You can read more about the differences between the two volumes in the section that follows this preface, "The Difference Between Training and Consulting: Which Annual to Use."

The *Annuals* have been an inspirational source for experiential learning activities, resource for instruments, and reference for cutting-edge articles for thirty-six years. Whether you are a trainer, a consultant, a facilitator, or a bit of each, you will find tools and resources that provide you with the basics and challenge (and we hope inspire) you to use new techniques and models.

Annual Loyalty

The Pfeiffer *Annual* series has many loyal subscribers. There are several reasons for this loyalty. In addition to the wide variety of topics and implementation levels, the *Annuals* provide materials that are applicable to varying circumstances. You will find instruments for individuals, teams, and organizations; experiential learning activities to round out workshops, team building, or consulting assignments; ideas and contemporary solutions for managing human capital; and articles that increase your own knowledge base, to use as reference materials in your writing, or as a source of ideas for your training or consulting assignments.

Many of our readers have been loyal customers for a dozen or more years. If you are one of them, we thank you. And we encourage each of you to give back to the profession by submitting a sample of your work to share with your colleagues.

The *Annuals* owe most of their success, though, to the fact that they are immediately ready to use. All of the materials may be duplicated for educational and training purposes. If you need to adapt or modify the materials to tailor them for your audience's needs, go right ahead. We only request that the credit statement found on the copyright page (and on each reproducible page) be retained on all copies. Our liberal copyright policy makes it easy and fast for you to use the materials to do your job. However, if you intend to reproduce the materials in publications for sale or if you wish to reproduce more than one hundred copies of any one item, please contact us for prior written permission.

If you are a new *Annual* user, welcome! If you like what you see in the 2008 edition, you may want to consider subscribing to a standing order. By doing so, you are guaranteed to receive your copy each year straight off the press and receive a discount off the cover price. And if you want to go back and have the entire series for your use, then the *Pfeiffer Library*—which contains content from the very first edition to the present day—is available on CD-ROM. You can find information on the *Pfeiffer Library* at www.pfeiffer.com.

I often refer to many of my *Annuals* from the 1980s. They include several classic activities that have become a mainstay in my team-building designs. But most of all, the *Annuals* have been a valuable resource for over thirty years because the materials come from professionals like you who work in the field as trainers, consultants, facilitators, educators, and performance-improvement technologists, whose contributions have been tried and perfected in real-life settings with actual participants and clients to meet real-world needs.

To this end, we encourage you to submit materials to be considered for publication. We are interested in receiving experiential learning activities; inventories, questionnaires, and surveys; and articles and discussion resources. Contact the Pfeiffer Editorial Department at the address listed on the copyright page for copies of our guidelines for contributors or contact me directly at Box 8249, Norfolk, VA 23503, or by email at pfeiffer annual@aol.com. We welcome your comments, ideas, and contributions.

Acknowledgments

Thank you to the dedicated, friendly, thoughtful people at Pfeiffer who produced the *2008 Pfeiffer Annuals:* Kathleen Dolan Davies, Martin Delahoussaye, Dawn Kilgore, Susan Rachmeler, and Rebecca Taff. Thank you to Lorraine Kohart of ebb associates inc, who assisted our authors with the many submission details and who ensured that we met all the deadlines.

Most important, thank you to our contributors, who have once again shared their ideas, techniques, and materials so that trainers and consultants everywhere may benefit. Won't you consider joining the ranks of these prestigious professionals?

Elaine Biech
Editor
July 2007

The Difference Between Training and Consulting
Which Annual to Use?

Two volumes of the *Pfeiffer Annuals*—training and consulting—are resources for two different but closely related professions. Each *Annual* serves as a collection of tools and support materials used by the professionals in their respective arenas. The volumes include activities, articles, and instruments used by individuals in the training and consulting fields. The training volume is written with the trainer in mind, and the consulting volume is written with the consultant in mind.

How can you differentiate between the two volumes? Let's begin by defining each profession.

A *trainer* can be defined as anyone who is responsible for designing and delivering knowledge to adult learners and may include an internal HRD professional employed by an organization or an external practitioner who contracts with an organization to design and conduct training programs. Generally, the trainer is a subject-matter expert who is expected to transfer knowledge so that the trainee can know or do something new. A *consultant* is someone who provides unique assistance or advice (based on what the consultant knows or has experienced) to someone else, usually known as "the client." The consultant may not necessarily be a subject-matter expert in all situations. Often the consultant is an expert at using specific tools to extract, coordinate, resolve, organize, expedite, or implement an organizational situation.

The lines between the consulting and training professions have blurred in the past few years. First, the names and titles have blurred. For example, some external trainers call themselves "training consultants" as a way of distinguishing themselves from internal trainers. Some organizations now have internal consultants, who usually reside in the training department. Second, the roles have blurred. While a consultant has always been expected to deliver measurable results, now trainers are expected to do so as well. Both are expected to improve performance; both are expected to contribute to the bottom line. Facilitation was at one time thought to be a consultant skill; today trainers are expected to use facilitation skills to train. Training one-on-one was a trainer skill; today consultants train executives one-on-one and call it "coaching." The introduction of the "performance technologist," whose role is one of combined trainer and consultant, is a perfect example of a new profession that has evolved due to the need for trainers to use more "consulting" techniques in their work. The "performance consultant" is a new role supported by the American Society for Training and Development (ASTD). ASTD has shifted its focus from training to performance improvement.

As you can see, the roles and goals of training and consulting are not nearly as specific as they once may have been. However, when you step back and examine the two professions from a big-picture perspective, you can more easily differentiate between the two. Maintaining a big-picture focus will also help you determine which *Pfeiffer Annual* to turn to as your first resource.

Both volumes cover the same general topics: communication, teamwork, problem solving, and leadership. However, depending on your requirement and purpose—a training or consulting need—you will use each in different situations. You will select the *Annual* based on *how you will interact with the topic, not on what the topic might be.* Let's take a topic such as teamwork, for example. If you are searching for a lecturette that teaches the advantages of teamwork, a workshop activity that demonstrates the skill of making decisions in a team, or a handout that discusses team stages, look to the Training *Annual.* On the other hand, if you are conducting a team-building session for a dysfunctional team, helping to form a new team, or trying to understand the dynamics of an executive team, you will look to the Consulting *Annual.*

The Training Annual

The materials in the Training volume focus on skill building and knowledge enhancement, as well as on the professional development of trainers. They generally focus on controlled events: a training program, a conference presentation, a classroom setting. Look to the Training *Annual* to find ways to improve a training session for ten to one thousand people and anything else that falls in the human resource development category:

- Specific experiential learning activities that can be built into a training program;

- Techniques to improve training: debriefing exercises, conducting role plays, managing time;

- Topical lecturettes;

- Ideas to improve a boring training program;

- Icebreakers and energizers for a training session;

- Surveys that can be used in a classroom;

- Ideas for moving an organization from training to performance; and

- Ways to improve your skills as a trainer.

The Consulting Annual

The materials in the Consulting volume focus on intervention techniques and organizational systems, as well as on the professional development of consultants. They generally focus on "tools" that you can have available just in case: concepts about organizations and their development (or demise); and about more global situations. Look to the Consulting *Annual* to find ways to improve consulting activities from team building and executive coaching to organization development and strategic planning:

- Skills for working with executives;

- Techniques for solving problems, effecting change, and gathering data;

- Team-building tools, techniques, and tactics;

- Facilitation ideas and methods;

- Processes to examine for improving an organization's effectiveness;

- Surveys that can be used organizationally; and

- Ways to improve your effectiveness as a consultant.

Summary

Even though the professions and the work are closely related and at times interchangeable, there is a difference. Use the following table to help you determine which *Annual* you should scan first for help. Remember, however, that there is some blending of the two and either *Annual* may have your answer. It depends . . .

Element	Consulting	Training
Topics	Teams, Communication, Problem Solving	Teams, Communication, Problem Solving
Topic Focus	Individual, Department	Corporate, Global
Purpose	Skill Building, Knowledge Transfer	Coaching, Strategic Planning, Building Teams
Recipient	Individuals, Departments	Usually More Organizational
Organizational Level	All Workforce Members	Usually Closer to the Top
Delivery Profile	Workshops, Presentations	Intervention, Implementation
Atmosphere	Structured	Unstructured
Time Frame	Defined	Undefined
Organizational Cost	Moderate	High
Change Effort	Low to Moderate	Moderate to High
Setting	Usually a Classroom	Anywhere
Professional Experience	Entry Level, Novice	Proficient, Master Level
Risk Level	Low	High
Professional Needs	Activities, Resources	Tools, Theory
Application	Individual Skills	Usually Organizational System

When you get right down to it, we are all trainers and consultants. The skills may cross over. A great trainer is also a skilled consultant. And a great consultant is also a skilled trainer. The topics may be the same, but how you implement them may be vastly different. Which *Annual* to use? Remember to think about your purpose in terms of the big picture: consulting or training.

As you can see, we have both covered.

Introduction
to *The 2008 Pfeiffer Annual: Training*

The 2008 Pfeiffer Annual: Training is a collection of practical and useful materials for professionals in the broad area described as human resource development (HRD). The materials are written by and for professionals, including trainers, organization-development and organization-effectiveness consultants, performance-improvement technologists, facilitators, educators, instructional designers, and others.

Each *Annual* has three main sections: Experiential Learning Activities; Inventories, Questionnaires, and Surveys; and Articles and Discussion Resources. A fourth section, Editor's Choice, has been reserved for those unique contributions that do not fit neatly into one of the three main sections, but are valuable as identified by the editorial staff. Each published submission is classified in one of the following categories: Individual Development, Communication, Problem Solving, Groups, Teams, Consulting, Facilitating, Leadership, and Organizations. Within each category, pieces are further classified into logical subcategories, which are identified in the introductions to the three sections.

The Training *Annual* and the Consulting *Annual* for 2008 have a slightly different focus from past years. Both emphasize the topic of change, a topic that permeates our organizations and pervades all that we do as professionals in the learning and consulting arena.

The series continues to provide an opportunity for HRD professionals who wish to share their experiences, their viewpoints, and their processes with their colleagues. To that end, Pfeiffer publishes guidelines for potential authors. These guidelines are available from the Pfeiffer Editorial Department at Jossey-Bass, Inc., in San Francisco, California.

Materials are selected for the *Annuals* based on the quality of the ideas, applicability to real-world concerns, relevance to current HRD issues, clarity of presentation, and ability to enhance our readers' professional development. In addition, we choose experiential learning activities that will create a high degree of enthusiasm among the participants and add enjoyment to the learning process.

Our contributor list includes a wide selection of experts in the field: in-house practitioners, consultants, and academically based professionals. A list of contributors to the *Annual* can be found at the end of the volume, including their names, affiliations, addresses, telephone numbers, facsimile numbers, and email addresses. Readers will find this list useful if they wish to locate the authors of specific pieces for feedback, comments, or questions. Further information on each contributor is presented in a brief biographical sketch that appears at the conclusion of each article. We publish this information to encourage "networking," which continues to be a valuable mainstay in the field of human resource development.

We are pleased with the high quality of material that is submitted for publication each year and often regret that we have page limitations. In addition, just as we cannot publish every manuscript we receive, you may find that not all published works are equally useful to you. Therefore, we encourage and invite ideas, materials, and suggestions that will help us to make subsequent *Annuals* as useful as possible to all of our readers.

Introduction
to the Experiential Learning Activities Section

Experiential learning activities ensure that lasting learning occurs. They should be selected with a specific learning objective in mind. These objectives are based on the participants' needs and the facilitator's skills. Although the experiential learning activities presented here all vary in goals, group size, time required, and process, they all incorporate one important element: questions that ensure learning has occurred. This discussion, led by the facilitator, assists participants to process the activity, to internalize the learning, and to relate it to their day-to-day situations. It is this element that creates the unique learning experience and learning opportunity that only an experiential learning activity can bring to the group process.

Readers have used the *Annuals'* experiential learning activities for years to enhance their training and consulting events. Each learning experience is complete and includes all lecturettes, handout content, and other written material necessary to facilitate the activity. In addition, many include variations of the design that the facilitator might find useful. If the activity does not fit perfectly with your objective, within your time frame, or to your group size, we encourage you to adapt the activity by adding your own variations. You will find additional experiential learning activities listed in the "Experiential Learning Activities Categories" chart that immediately follows this introduction.

The 2008 Pfeiffer Annual: Training includes fourteen activities, in the following categories:

Individual Development: Sensory Awareness

Change Partners: Experiencing the Impact of Change, by Beverly J. Bitterman

Individual Development: Self-Disclosure

Ten Things: Overcoming Resistance to Change, by Jean Barbazette

Individual Development: Diversity

International Candies: Exploring Cultural Expectations,
by Dianne Hofner Saphiere

Black Sheep: Dealing with Diversity, by Peter R. Garber

Communication: Awareness

**Changing Places, Facing Changes: Understanding Feelings Evoked
by Change, by Deborah Spring Laurel

Problem Solving: Generating Alternatives

**Creativity: Producing Change Through Chaos, by Robert Alan Black

Groups: Competition/Collaboration

Who Am I? Challenging the Team, by Robert Alan Black

Collaborative Tales: Using Reflective Analysis, by Edwina Pio

Teams: Roles

**Tools for Change: Identifying Your Role on the Change Team,
by Donna Goldstein and Dennis Collins

Teams: Problem Solving/Decision Making

Corporate Box: Learning to Listen, by Mark Rose and Greg Robinson

Consulting, Training, and Facilitating: Facilitating: Blocks to Learning

**Alphabet Soup: Building Skills to Deal with Change, by Cher Holton

Leadership: Ethics

Tic Tac: Deciding What to Do, by Kathleen Finch

Organizations: Vision, Mission, Values, Strategy

**Clouded Visions: Avoiding the Perils of Prediction, by Leonard D. Goodstein

Organizations: Change Management

**Forty-Five: Reacting to Workplace Change,
by Sivasailam "Thiagi" Thiagarajan

To further assist you in selecting appropriate ELAs, we provide the following grid
that summarizes category, time required, group size, and risk factor for each ELA.

**Topic is change focused

Category	ELA Title	Page	Time Required	Group Size	Risk Factor
Individual Development: Sensory Awareness	Change Partners: Experiencing the Impact of Change	11	45 to 55 minutes	10+	Moderate
Individual Development: Self-Disclosure	Ten Things: Overcoming Resistance to Change	17	60 minutes	2 to 200	Moderate
Individual Development: Diversity	International Candies: Exploring Cultural Expectations	23	35 minutes	10 to 100	Low
Individual Development: Diversity	Black Sheep: Dealing with Diversity	31	60 minutes	Any	High
Communication: Awareness	Changing Places, Facing Changes: Understanding Feelings Evoked by Change	37	2 hours	Groups of 4	Moderate
Problem Solving: Generating Alternatives	Creativity: Producing Change Through Chaos	43	75 to 90 minutes	Any	Moderate
Groups: Competition/ Collaboration	Who Am I? Challenging the Team	49	30 minutes	Groups of 5	Low
Groups: Competition/ Collaboration	Collaborative Tales: Using Reflective Analysis	55	60 minutes	8 to 36	Moderate
Teams: Roles	Tools for Change: Identifying Your Role on the Change Team	63	40 to 50 minutes	7 to 10	Low
Teams: Problem Solving/ Decision Making	Corporate Box: Learning to Listen	67	60 to 90 minutes	12 to 50+ who work together	Low to Moderate
Consulting, Training, and Facilitating: Facilitating: Blocks to Learning	Alphabet Soup: Building Skills to Deal with Change	73	30 to 60 minutes	Unlimited	Low
Leadership: Ethics	Tic Tac: Deciding What to Do	79	90 minutes	3 to 15	Moderate
Organizations: Vision, Mission, Values, Strategy	Clouded Visions: Avoiding the Perils of Prediction	89	60 to 90 minutes	10 to 50	Low
Organizations: Change Management	Forty-Five: Reacting to Workplace Change	95	30 to 50 minutes	10 to 100, best with 15 to 30	Moderate to High

Experiential Learning Activities Categories

Change Partners
Experiencing the Impact of Change

Activity Summary

An activity that uncovers emotions typically experienced in change situations and helps people understand how these emotions influence their reactions to change.

Goals

- To experience a variety of emotions and reactions resulting from change.

- To determine what is needed to maintain energy and a positive atmosphere during a change initiative.

- To identify the shared responsibility of management and employees in a change situation.

Group Size

A minimum of 10 participants participating in an organizational change initiative of some type.

Time Required

45 to 55 minutes.

Materials

- A watch with a second hand or a timer.

- Flip chart and markers or a whiteboard if the room is small enough.

Physical Setting

A room with chairs around a U-shaped table or several round tables. Six to eight square feet per participants in pairs.

Facilitating Risk Rating

Moderate.

Process

1. Explain that the group is going to experience a change that they will all be able to participate in equally. Ask them to pick partners. Depending on other goals you may have for the training, ask that they select someone they do know or someone they do not know well.

2. Give the following instructions:

   You will have exactly 1 minute to study your partners and to notice everything you can about them.

3. Call time and ask participants to turn their backs to their partners. Once everyone has turned around, have them change three superficial physical things about themselves. Give them 1 minute to do this.
   (5 minutes.)

4. Time them for 1 minute and watch the room. You want to create a little urgency, but also to give enough time to allow most to finish. Say, "OK, time's up. When I say 'begin,' turn around and take turns identifying what is different about your partner. Go back and forth until you have noticed the three changes that each of you made."

5. Observe the room and notice:

   • How the group is reacting.

   • Whether all are participating.
   (5 minutes.)

6. Call time and ask them to turn their backs to each other again and change three more things about themselves in the next minute. Expect groans and resistance. Notice what happens.
   (5 minutes.)

7. Again, call time and have them identify the three things that have changed about their partners. Give them slightly less time than before and call time. Without time for discussion, have them turn their backs to each other again and change three more things. Expect more resistance this time. Notice people's reactions. Give them about 45 seconds this time. Call out, "Time's up," when some are still changing.

   (5 minutes.)

8. Again, have them identify what is different about their partners.

   (5 minutes.)

9. Depending on the group size, you can debrief the experience with the whole group or you can pose questions that they can discuss in small groups and then share highlights with the larger group. Use the following questions to get started:

   - What was your first reaction to the request to change three things about yourself?

   - Did your reaction to the task change as you went into the second and third rounds? If so, what made the difference?

   - Who enjoyed the challenge each time?

   - What were you thinking that helped you to enjoy it? (Here you are looking for thoughts that lead to emotion. To enjoy the exercise, one may see it as a game, a competition, or an opportunity to be creative, for example.)

   - Who felt frustrated by the challenge to keep changing?

   - What were you thinking that resulted in your frustration? (Thinking that leads to frustration could be wanting to get it right and not look foolish or the pressure of digging more deeply to think of things to change.)

   - Who felt angry?

   - What were you thinking that made you feel angry? (Look for violation of rights thoughts like "This is a waste of time," "It's beneath me," "I don't have enough options for all the changes you want me to make.")

   - Who already put everything back the way it was? (Expect laughter at this. And make the point that, without reinforcement, change is difficult to maintain. We want to get back to the status quo.)

- What would have made it easier for you to do the exercise? (Anticipate answers having to do with sharing what was going to happen, knowing they should have worn more jewelry, having more time, and so forth.)

- What have you noticed about other people's reactions to the same experience? (Highlight answers that reflect understanding that people react differently to change and that the change agents need to take that into consideration.)

- How were your reactions during the exercise similar to or different from your reactions to changes your organization is making now or has made in the past? (Some will say that they felt many of the same emotions, so point out that often people have patterns of reactions to change—anger, avoidance, dismissal, and so on.)

- If you were in charge, how would you set up an organizational change to get the best results? (Here you are looking for a desire to involve those impacted, communication requests, lifelines for those who may have their employment impacted, and similar ideas.)

  (20 minutes.)

10. In closing, reinforce the idea that we all have habitual thinking patterns and that these come out under stressful change conditions. We might be aware, for instance, that we are cautious about changing or resistant to the very idea. If that is the case, having an awareness of how we react gives us an opportunity to choose a different way of thinking that might work better for us in a given circumstance.

11. Also make the point that it is both the responsibility of those initiating a change and those participating in the change to communicate their needs. Understanding the various ways people react and what people need in times of change opens the way for better communication and smoother change initiatives.

12. Express the thought that sometimes, when working with other people and seeking their buy-in, it is faster to take more time to plan than it is to speed through and find that the change didn't really stick.

Variation

For a longer debriefing, pose a variety of change scenarios and place participants in small groups to discuss them. Scenarios need to be relevant to the group involved and could include some of the following:

- Launching a new product

- Merging with another company

- Adding a new shift

- Downsizing

- Reorganizing

- Cutting an old product

- Changing longstanding procedures

Some questions to consider might be:

- What would be some expected reactions to the change?

- How do you expect specific groups to react? (Different departments, employees with different longevity, etc., may react differently to the same news, depending on whether they see it as a threat or an opportunity.)

Submitted by Beverly J. Bitterman.

Beverly J. Bitterman, *owner of Beverly Bitterman and Associates, is an executive and team coach. She is an experienced facilitator who creates environments in which groups are comfortable communicating about issues, uncovering and removing barriers to high performance, and taking concrete action to move forward on projects. She works with individuals in the areas of forgiveness and life balance. Ms. Bitterman delivers the Trimetrix assessment instrument, teaches facilitation and communication skills for the University of South Florida Continuing Education Department, and has held several offices for the Nashville, Tennessee, chapter of ASTD.*

Ten Things
Overcoming Resistance to Change

Activity Summary

An activity that helps people identify barriers to making successful and effective changes.

Goals

- Reduce the resistance of staff to a planned change.

- Reduce employee anxiety around a proposed change.

Group Size

Any size from 2 to 200.

Time Required

60 minutes.

Materials

- Flip chart.

- Felt-tipped markers.

Physical Setting

Sufficient room for participants to stand and work in pairs.

Facilitating Risk Rating

Moderate.

Process

1. Ask all participants to stand up, find partners, and face their partners. If there is an uneven number of trainees, ask three people to form a triad, or you could be someone's partner.

2. Tell participants they are going to make some changes in their physical appearance and that their partners will have to determine what has changed. *(5 minutes.)*

3. Say that the purpose of making these changes will be discussed following the activity.

4. Tell partners that they will have 60 seconds to memorize every aspect of their partners' appearance. Later they will be asked to make a few small changes, and they will have to identify what's different. (*Note:* 60 seconds is a long time to stare at another person. Some will become uncomfortable, but do *not* cut the time short. Being uncomfortable looking at another's performance is one of the learning points of this activity.) *(2 minutes.)*

5. Ask the partners to turn their backs to each other and make *five* changes in their physical appearance. They can be very small or obvious ones. Most participants figure out they can take items off, add items to their appearance, or move objects without prompting. Allow enough time for everyone to make the changes. *(5 minutes.)*

6. *Before you tell the partners to face each other,* tell them that they will now take turns identifying the others' changes. Give these further instructions:

   • If your partner does not guess correctly, do *not* tell him or her what was incorrect at this time.

   • After you have taken turns guessing, do *not* put yourself back to the way you were before.

   Tell them to turn around and take turns identifying the changes the other person has made.

7. After they have had enough time to guess each other's changes, tell them to turn their backs to each other again. Now ask them to make ten changes from the way they appear right now. (*Note:* If this request is too "high risk" for some participants, suggest that they can put five back and think of five new changes. *Do not give participants this hint unless they become very resistant.* It is possible to do this part of the activity without stripping!)
    (10 minutes.)

8. Before asking participants to turn around again, remind them that they may not tell their partners about changes they were unable to guess. Have them turn around.

9. After partners have had time to guess the others' changes, tell them they can now reveal any change their partners were unable to identify. Thank them for their cooperation and ask them to return to their seats. People will automatically begin to put themselves back together. Rarely will they ask permission to do so; few participants will "keep" something they changed.

10. After everyone is settled, ask these questions:

    *   How did it feel to look so closely at another person for 60 seconds? (Elicit several responses. Most will say awkward, uncomfortable, embarrassed, intrusive, etc. After they have identified these feelings, point out that when changes are made, often it is very uncomfortable for us, or for higher management, to look closely at what we have before a change is made.)

    *   Was it easier for you to make five changes or ten changes? Why was this? (Allow people who choose each option to express a rationale. Usually if they say that five changes are easier to make it's because there are fewer changes to make. When it comes to making ten, many people are asked to go beyond their level of comfort with risk. I have had participants refuse to make the ten changes and withdraw from the activity at this point. Those who say that ten changes were easier to make, it is usually because they were less resistant to making any change the second time. After the first experience, and they have seen others make similar or minor changes, it becomes easier for them to make changes. For some it is a challenge, and they enjoy trying to hide minute changes from their partners.)

    *   How did you feel when your partner guessed or did not guess your changes? (Often we are disappointed if no one notices a change that we have struggled to accomplish. That's also true at work. If you were

disappointed that your partner was successful at identifying all the changes you made, rather than glad for his or her success, there's a message for you in that reaction.)

- How did it feel after you had made your ten changes and then turned around? (Most of us feel pretty foolish and awkward. We are often laughing at our appearance and that of others as a way of covering up the embarrassment.)

- What did you do at the end of the activity while you were sitting down? Did you put yourself back together? Didn't it feel much more comfortable than when you had just made all of those ten changes? (When we are asked to make changes, often we feel awkward about doing something that is unfamiliar. We even sometimes deliberately do something the wrong way, go back to the old way, and refuse to do it the new way. We do so because we were comfortable with the status quo.)

(15 minutes.)

11. You may want to record the answers to the following questions on a flip chart as a takeaway.

- What did you learn about why individuals resist change?

- What can be done to reduce resistance to change?

- Based on this activity, identify what can be done to help make change take place successfully.

- What is the difference between successful and effective change? (Effective change takes place, but often with resistance and whining. Successful change takes place willingly.)

- How will you use or apply what you have learned about why individuals resist change?

- If you are being asked to make a change in your organization, we [the trainers] recognize your discomfort [anger] at being forced to go through this change. We realize that you would be much more comfortable the way things used to be. However, the change is real, the change is here, and it's not going to be the old way any longer. Our role as trainers is to try to help you feel more comfortable with the new way of doing things.

- If you are a manager asking others to make a change, realize that your employees will feel uncomfortable with change and want to go back to the old way (just like you put yourself back together after the ten changes). It is up to *you* to help your employees reach a new comfort level to reduce their resistance to the change. Unless you make them feel comfortable, they'll go right back to the old way or try to defeat the new way.

(15 minutes.)

Trainer's Notes

- **CAUTION:** For some participants, this is not a low-risk activity. They may refuse to participate because they will not allow others to see them with an "undignified" appearance. Others may pass it off as just a game. I encourage you to help these people identify the cause of resistance in themselves.

- Often trainers are asked to implement changes in company policies and procedures. As a change agent, the trainer sometimes finds he or she is the target of hostile reactions. Trainers can help employees acknowledge and accept their level of discomfort and anxiety. This activity can help your workshop participants work through a "forced" change and identify their own level of resistance. Your trainees may allow you to train them regarding new policies with less resistance if you acknowledge the resistance. They may then see training as a means to help make a change go more smoothly for themselves.

- You can also help managers who will act as change agents by making them aware of their employees' anxiety. Managers can be taught to empathize with changes employees are forced to make.

Submitted by Jean Barbazette.

Jean Barbazette, MA, *founded The Training Clinic in 1977 as a training consulting firm that specializes in train-the-trainer, new employee orientation, and enhancing the quality of training and instruction for major national and international clients. Her books published by Pfeiffer include* Successful New Employee Orientation *(3rd ed.) (2007);* Instant Case Studies *(2003);* The Trainer's Journey to Competence *(2005);* Training Needs Assessment *(2006);* The Art of Great Training Delivery *(2006); and* Managing the Training Function *(2007).*

International Candies
Exploring Cultural Expectations

Activity Summary

An introductory activity that helps participants meet others and explore the meaning of intercultural competence.

Goals

- To ground participants in the business need for intercultural competence.
- To help participants meet others, become familiar with an interactive learning style, and explore intercultural competence.

Group Size

10 to 100.

Time Required

35 minutes.

Materials

- One International Candies Responsibilities Poster created in advance and posted on the wall.
- International candy or an artifact from another culture, one per participant.
- International Candies Sentences, cut in half and taped to the bottoms of pieces of candy or artifacts.
- Masking tape.
- Flip chart and felt-tipped markers.

Physical Setting

Any room configuration in which participants can move around freely.

Facilitating Risk Rating

Low.

Process

1. Before beginning, cut apart the sentences (being sure you use both halves of the sentences so that pairs can form), tape them to the candies or artifacts, and place one at each participant's seat. If there are more than 18 participants, make more than one set of sentence fragments. Also post an International Candies Responsibilities Poster on the wall.

2. Open the activity by stating that a high level of intercultural competence can help us become good corporate citizens and that the purpose of the activity is to explore how to improve on this dimension.

3. Introduce the Responsibilities Poster on the wall that shows the various areas of employee responsibility (to clients, colleagues, and the organization). Review these responsibilities briefly.

4. Explain the activity before beginning: Your small welcome gift for each participant is an international candy or artifact with half of a sentence attached to the bottom. The sentences correspond to possible employee responsibilities and also to the subject of the workshop, intercultural competence. Tell them that each of them needs to find the person with the other half of the sentence on his or her candy. (*Note:* If you have an odd number of participants, participate yourself.)

5. First, participants should read what is taped on their candies in order to figure out what is missing that would complete their sentences. Answer any questions and then give them time to read and think.
   (5 minutes.)

6. Call time and instruct them to begin milling around the room, comparing sentences, searching for whoever's sentence completes theirs. Once they find a match, they should introduce themselves, discuss the completed sentence, and generate at least one example of how this responsibility applies to them in real life.
   (5 minutes.)

7. Now tell pairs to discuss how intercultural competence affects their shared responsibility. Each pair should generate at least one example from this point of view. (Examples include: in one community employees might help in the schools, in another community they might fund a special event.)
   (10 minutes.)

8. Once all pairs have had time to discuss the two questions, call time and have partners tape their sentences to the space on the Responsibilities Poster in which they feel it belongs.

9. After they are finished, ask each pair of participants, in turn, to share their sentence and their examples.
   (1 minute per pair.)

10. Reinforce the need for intercultural competence if the organization is to be successful. Say that ongoing growth requires that each employee take responsibility to use intercultural competence in his or her role in the organization. Summarize the exercise with a discussion around the following questions, writing on the flip chart for better retention:

    • What kind of skills would it take for you to demonstrate intercultural competence? (Anticipate answers such as ability to listen, demonstrate respect, patience, flexibility, sensitivity, empathy, creativity, and enthusiasm.)

    • How does intercultural competence (or a lack of it) affect your own on-the-job performance?

    • How is intercultural competence a part of what you need to accomplish on the job?

    • How does intercultural competence affect what you do, how you do it, and how you are measured?

    • How can you expand on what we have discussed here today when you return to the workplace?

Variations

• The poster can be altered to reflect the responsibilities as seen by members of any organization.

• Sentence halves can be rewritten for other topics.

Submitted by Dianne Hofner Saphiere.

Dianne Hofner Saphiere *is the creator of Cultural Detective®, a series of global managerial effectiveness tools and materials used by over eighty-five international intercultural experts. She has worked in intercultural organization development, training, and consulting since 1989; her current emphasis is curriculum design. Ms. Saphiere also authored* Communication Highwire: Leveraging the Power of Diverse Communication Styles*;* Ecotonos: A Multicultural Problem-Solving Simulation*; and* Redundancia: A Foreign Language Simulation.

International Candies Sentences

The more we can understand the culture of the communities in which we operate, . . .	. . . the better our organization can contribute to development of those communities.
The better we understand the culture of the clients we are serving, . . .	. . . the better able we will be to understand and satisfy our customers' needs.
The better we understand the cultural backgrounds and imperatives of our colleagues, . . .	. . . the better able we will be to create a productive and respectful work environment that fosters work-place satisfaction.

Responsibility to our clients includes providing superior products and services , . . .

. . . and clients from different cultures often desire different products and services.

Responsibility to each other includes treating our teammates with respect, . . .

. . . yet teammates from different cultures often find different behaviors "respectful."

Responsibility to our franchise includes balancing long-term and short-term interests, . . .

. . . and such balancing requires the ability to understand short-term and long-term consequences across cultures and in multiple contexts.

Responsibility to our clients includes providing superior advice, . . .

. . . and clients from different cultures often prefer to receive advice in different ways.

Responsibility to each other includes helping our teammates to realize their potential, . . .

. . . yet teammates from different cultures often prefer to be helped in different ways.

Responsibility to our franchise includes taking an active role in the communities in which we work, . . .

. . . and different communities have different expectations of how our organization may act as a good corporate citizen.

International Candies Responsibilities Poster

Black Sheep
Dealing with Diversity

Activity Summary

A lesson in diversity presented as a fable.

Goals

- To create greater awareness about diversity in an organization.
- To highlight how painful prejudice can be in any situation or setting.
- To reinforce the fact that different isn't bad—it's just different.

Group Size

Any.

Time Required

60 minutes.

Materials

- One copy of the Black Sheep Family Story for each participant.
- Flip chart and felt-tipped markers.

Physical Setting

Any meeting or conference room in which participants can discuss the issues.

Facilitating Risk Rating

High.

Process

1. Introduce the activity as being a discussion about diversity, as exemplified by a fable.

2. Distribute copies of the Black Sheep Family Story to all participants or display the story for participants to see. Either read the story aloud as people follow along or ask participants to read the story silently to themselves. *(10 minutes.)*

3. Once everyone has had a chance to read or hear the story, begin a discussion. Use the following questions:

   - What analogies do you see between what happened in the barnyard and how people sometimes react to someone who is different from them or unlike the norm?

   - Why do people sometimes react in such a way?

   - How did the Sheep family feel when their unorthodox-looking child was born?

   - How well do you feel the Sheep family handled their situation?

   - What did they learn as a result of adversity?
   (30 minutes.)

4. Summarize by emphasizing these points on a flip chart, if they are not brought up by the group:

   - The other animals could be very unkind and even cruel for no reason except that the Sheep family had a child who looked different.

   - The Sheep family learned who their true friends were.

   - It is important for family to support one another, no matter what happens.

   - Social status in the barnyard didn't have any real value if it could be lost so easily.

   - In this story, the other animals spread vicious rumors about the sheep just because they no longer conformed to the norm.

- As was the case with the black sheep himself, adversity can help build character and insights that you might not gain otherwise.

- People may eventually learn to respect you for your character, principles, and heart if you give them a chance.

- Modeling positive behaviors can serve as a good example for others.

- It is important to understand other people's perspectives, especially if they are different from your own.

- Appreciating diversity can lead to a greater understanding and awareness of others.

- Diverse perspectives can help solve even the most difficult problems.

- Both organizations and people can grow as a result of learning and appreciating different perspectives.

- Understanding more about diversity can help people gain acceptance and respect.

- You must look beyond physical appearance and appreciate the true character of others.

  (10 minutes.)

5. Before ending this discussion reemphasize these final two points:

   - Different is not bad—it is just different.

   - Diversity is a good thing, even in a barnyard!

Variation

Instead of discussing the story with the entire group, break into discussion groups of three to five people and assign specific questions from Step 3 above to each group. Reconvene the entire group and have spokespersons from each group summarize their discussions.

Submitted by Peter R. Garber.

Peter R. Garber *is manager of employee relations for PPG Industries, Inc., Pittsburgh, Pennsylvania. He is the author of a number of management books, including* Turbulent Change: 10 Natural Forces for Business Success, Winning the Rat Race at Work, *and* 100 Ways to Get on the Wrong Side of Your Boss *and over forty other articles and training tools.*

Black Sheep Family Story

Life on the farm had been happy for the good Sheep family over the years. They were considered by the farmer to be excellent wool producers and were often the first picked to be sheared. They had a proud lineage and were always considered to be of strong fabric. The Sheep family had many lambs, each maintaining or enhancing the family's fine wool reputation. Life on the farm was good for the Sheep family.

However, one spring Mrs. Sheep had an unexpected birth. A black sheep was born. The entire pasture was in shock. Mr. and Mrs. Sheep were beside themselves. They never imagined that such a thing could happen to them. Many rumors went around the pasture. It was even said that Mrs. Sheep had a black sheep in her past. Their barnyard friends would wander over to get a look at the new arrival and just shake their heads. "Poor Sheep family, what are they going to do?" the horses and mules said, as they extended a hoof in support. Some of the other farm animals were very unkind. "What a disgrace," the pigs said, as they wallowed in the mud. Word quickly spread throughout the barnyard. Even neighboring farms heard about the black sheep in the family and spread nasty rumors about this good Sheep family.

Life became much harder than it was before for the Sheep family. They coped with the situation the best they could. They loved their baby lamb despite his unorthodox appearance, but were concerned about his future—and about theirs. They began to be ostracized by the rest of the sheep in the farm community. Mr. Sheep began to lose status in the flock as the elder sheep began to shun him. Mrs. Sheep was no longer invited to lunch in the better parts of the pasture. The other lambs picked on the black sheep constantly. "Baa-baa, black sheep—nobody will want your wool!" they would taunt him. He felt bad when they said these things to him. He asked his mother why the other sheep were so cruel to him, and she told him that it was just because he was different from the others. It broke her heart to see her child persecuted in such a way just because of the color of his wool. "Why is being different so baa-baa-bad?" he asked his mother throughout his childhood years. Unfortunately, she didn't have an adequate answer.

However, as the months passed, their different child began to add things to their lives in other ways. He began to show them the world in a whole new light. For one thing, they were taught who their true friends were. Only their closest and truest friends stood by them and offered help and support. The Sheep family realized that they needed to depend on one another. They learned the true meaning of friends and family.

As the black lamb grew into an adult sheep, he seemed to have qualities that others lacked. He grew to have a wisdom and character that other sheep learned to admire and respect. Perhaps it was from all the adversity he had to endure because of the color of his wool. Or maybe it was because he was different that he saw the world from a unique perspective. Everything wasn't black and white to him. He appreciated shades of gray—something the other animals were not capable of optically discerning. Other animals began to bring their problems to him and ask for his advice. He would listen carefully before replying and ask for clarification when not sure he fully understood a problem. This was a totally new level of communication for the entire farm. He soon became the leader of the sheep community and was even given certain barnyard responsibilities typically reserved for the animals of greater stature, such as the cows and bulls. This was unprecedented in the memory of any of the elder animals. (Unfortunately, the history of the barnyard had to be kept by memory, as the animals had not acquired the ability to keep written records.)

As a result of the respect and admiration the black sheep had earned, his family was viewed in a whole new way. No longer did the elite animals of the barnyard shun them.

They were invited to the most prestigious events in the barnyard. They were even invited to drink from the same water trough again. However, the Sheep family didn't seem to be very interested in the politics or high society of the farm. Although they followed the advice of their dark-wooled son and didn't hold a grudge against the other animals, their values seemed to have changed. The other animals took notice of this change and began to adopt the same ideals. They stopped judging the other animals by their appearance and began to pay attention to such things as character, principle, and heart. Even the farmer began to value the wool that he clipped from the black sheep and found new markets for this unique and highly valued product.

The point is that different is not bad; it is just different. This is one of the most important lessons that the black sheep taught the others on the farm. They learned that it is important to understand other perspectives, even if they are different from yours. Diversity can lead to greater understanding and awareness of others. Those with diverse perspectives can help solve even the most difficult problems when working together. Looking at the world in different ways is important to the growth and development of any individual or organization. Being different is not something to be feared, despite other people's initial reactions. Learning more about differences can change people's prejudice into acceptance and respect. Diversity can be a good thing, even in a barnyard!

Changing Places, Facing Changes
Understanding Feelings Evoked by Change

Activity Summary

A highly kinesthetic shifting role-play activity that allows participants to recognize and articulate the different feelings evoked by change so that they can better introduce and manage change in their organizations.

Goals

- To recognize and articulate the reasons behind the feelings that change evokes in those affected by it.

- To gain a better appreciation of different emotional responses to change.

- To plan how to apply this new understanding when introducing and/or managing change.

Group Size

Subgroups of 4 participants from an organization undergoing a change initiative.

Time Required

2 hours.

Materials

- One copy of the Changing Places, Facing Changes Worksheet for each participant.

- Small stickers for the groups.

- Four 8½ by 11-inch sheets of paper for each group of four participants.

- Four different colored markers for each group of four.

- Masking tape.

- A flip chart and felt-tipped markers.

Physical Setting

A room with tables that is also large enough for the groups of four to stand around 3-foot-by-3-foot square formations and to work without disturbing one another.

Facilitating Risk Rating

Moderate.

Process

1. Place four sheets of paper, four markers, and some small stickers at each table. Seat the participants randomly in groups of four.

2. Introduce the session by explaining that change can affect individuals in a variety of ways and that this activity is intended to help the participants recognize, articulate, and better handle emotional responses from others when introducing or managing change.

3. Ask participants to identify the various emotional responses that change seems to evoke in those affected by it. Post their responses on a flip chart in front of the group.
    (10 minutes.)

4. Have the groups pare down the number of emotional responses listed on the flip chart by voting for the three emotional responses they consider to be most typical in their organization. Have participants vote by pasting one of their stickers next to each of the three emotional responses they choose. Name the four emotional responses that received the greatest number of stickers. If there are more than four, combine some or vote a second time so that the final list has only four.
    (10 minutes.)

5. Have each group of four use markers to write the four emotional responses from the flip chart on their sheets of paper, with one emotion on each sheet. For example, FEAR on one sheet and EXCITEMENT on another.
    (5 minutes.)

6. Demonstrate how to place the four sheets at the north, south, east, and west sides of a 3-foot-by-3-foot square on the floor and tape them down with masking tape. The sheets should be facing away from the center of the square, so that they can easily be read by a participant standing at that side of the square. You may wish to post the following diagram on the flip chart.
    (5 minutes.)

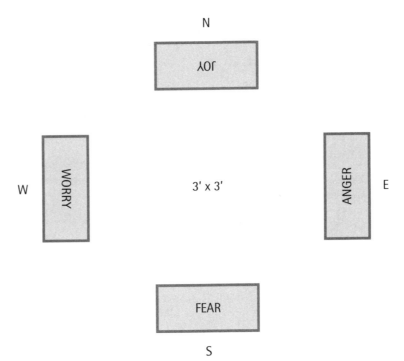

7. Once all groups have taped down their sheets, ask the four members of each group to stand in front of the four sheets of paper, one each on the north, south, west, and east sides. Explain that they are to think about the specific change they are currently experiencing in the organization and take turns expressing and acting out the emotional responses listed on the sheets of paper in front of them, explaining why they feel that way. (This may require the participants to role play the change situation from a different perspective than they actually have experienced.) Tell participants that they will each have 2 minutes to express the emotions on their papers.
    (10 minutes.)

8. Tell participants to begin with the person in the "North" position. Once "North" has completed acting out that emotion and has stated why he or she feels that way, go around the group until all three have had a turn. *(10 minutes.)*

9. After each participant has had a turn to act out and discuss the emotional response on the sheet in front of him or her, have all four participants in each group move clockwise around the square to the next sheet. Repeat Step 8 until all four members of the group have had an opportunity to express and experience all four of the emotional responses to change that they thought were most prevalent in their organization. *(20 minutes.)*

10. Once all of the groups have completed the exercise, have two groups of four create a group of eight. Give each person a copy of the Changing Places, Facing Changes Worksheet. Have them list the four emotions in Column 1.

11. Work through the first emotional response with the entire group so that they have a model of what they will do for the remaining three emotional responses. First, lead a discussion about the reason this particular emotion occurs and post their ideas. Also lead a discussion about how to introduce and manage the change in light of this emotion. Draw answers from the group and post them on the flip chart. *(10 minutes.)*

12. Have the eight participants in each combined group work together to complete the Changing Places, Facing Changes Worksheet for the remaining three emotional responses. *(15 minutes.)*

13. Once the groups have completed their task, work through each emotion. Use a round-robin process to identify all the ideas from each group and post them on the flip chart. *(15 minutes.)*

14. Conclude by asking participants to pop up out of their chairs in turn to identify one key takeaway from the exercise that will help them better introduce or manage change, now that they have experienced other people's emotional responses to change. *(5 minutes.)*

Submitted by Deborah Spring Laurel.

Deborah Spring Laurel has been a trainer and a consultant in workplace learning and performance improvement for over thirty years. She was adjunct faculty at the University of Wisconsin-Madison for thirty years. The principal of Laurel and Associates, Ltd., Ms. Laurel has her master's degree from the University of Wisconsin-Madison. She is a past president of the South Central Wisconsin Chapter of ASTD and facilitates the three-day ASTD Training Certificate Program.

Changing Places, Facing Changes Worksheet

Instructions: Working with your new combined group, complete the form below and be prepared to report out your conclusions about how to best introduce and manage change when dealing with individuals who have one of the four emotional responses you have identified.

Emotional Response	Underlying Rationale	How to Introduce and Manage Change When Someone Feels This Way
1.		
2.		
3.		
4.		

Creativity
Producing Change Through Chaos

Activity Summary

A series of exercises planned to help people capitalize on becoming more creative and learning to deal with the resulting changes.

Goals

- To develop creative thinking skills.

- To experience expanded creative thinking.

- To explore how to capitalize on the chaos that creative thinking can generate.

Group Size

Any number in groups of 4 to 5, preferably 5.

Time Required

75 to 90 minutes.

Materials

- A collection of unusual props or toys.

- Blank paper and a pencil for each participant.

- A flip chart and felt-tipped markers.

- Masking tape.

- One copy of Creativity Notes for the facilitator.

Physical Setting

A room large enough for the groups to work without disturbing one another. Writing surfaces should be provided. Wall space is recommended for posting flip-chart sheets.

Facilitating Risk Rating

Moderate.

Process

1. Begin the session by introducing the main point that creativity often yields chaos, and chaos generally produces the types of change that people resist. Also state that business journals around the globe report that successful companies have to become more creative in order to keep up with their competition, let alone succeed and climb to the top in their fields.

2. Lead a discussion of changes that have occurred that have created frustration for people in general recently.
    (10 minutes.)

3. Divide people randomly into groups of four or five and assign them to tables. You may wish to divide the group into small mixed groups using some demographic of the group: region, location, departments within company, years on the job, years with company, age, height, hair color, etc. The primary goal is to create a change through separating people from the groups they naturally formed when they walked into the room.

4. Give each group an assignment to discuss different types or sources of change: environmental, economic, social change, time, technology, etc. Ask them to discuss the various changes they are aware of in their particular subject areas and to identify the chaos that has been produced. Ask them to also identify the creative results, that is, positive, negative, or neutral.
    (10 minutes.)

5. Take time to gather input from the groups. Depending on how much time you have, you may wish to go into some depth on what they say.
    (10 minutes.)

6. Hand out unusual objects to each table, preferably objects they will not recognize. Look for things from totally unrelated industries or businesses or other cultures or from the past.

7. Assign them the following task: Treat the products I have given you as though they are new products for your organization. Your challenge is to generate twelve or more ideas for what your product could be used for or sold as.
    (15 minutes.)

8. Introduce a creative idea-generating technique that the group does not know: Forced Relationships, Attribute Listing, Morphological Listing, White Paint, What If-ing? etc. See the Creativity Notes for several possibilities.
    (10 minutes.)

9. Assign groups the task of generating twenty-four or more totally bizarre ideas for what their products could be sold as by modifying them any way they choose.
    (15 minutes.)

10. Tell them to discuss the difference between what they came up with using a basic idea-generating approach and what they produced when using the specific idea-generating technique you assigned. Lead a discussion using the following questions:

    - How did the two different approaches to idea generation differ? How did they feel different to use?

    - How were the ideas you generated different?

    - Which approach produced the more creative, although perhaps strange or potentially chaos-producing, result?

    - Which ideas would probably produce the most changes in your company?

    - How might you as a team deal with the changes in order to produce success if your CEO said, "You *will* introduce the new product or service"?

    - What might you do in the future to be better prepared for the cycle of creativity-yielding-chaos as change came about so that you could experience success?

    (15 minutes.)

Submitted by Robert Alan Black.

Robert Alan Black *is the founder of Cre8ng People, Places & Possibilities, an international creative thinking consulting company with colleagues and continents around the world. CP3 works with business, industrial, governmental, and education clients in helping them to S.P.R.E.A.D. creative thinking throughout their entire organizations in all their employees. Mr. Black is based in Athens, Georgia, when he is not traveling the world. He has had over 350 articles published in the United States and around the globe in newspapers, magazines, trade journals, newsletters, ezines, and websites on creative thinking, leading, communicating, and teaming since 1976. He has also authored or co-authored over twenty books. One of his books,* Broken Crayons, *has been translated and published in Turkey, Slovakia, South Africa, and Japan. Several of the books he has authored or co-authored are focused on training exercises, including several in the* Pfeiffer Annuals *and two with Arthur VanGundy on creative training techniques.*

Creativity Notes

Forced Relationships

This creative thinking tool/technique, one of the oldest, is about ninety years old. When using this technique, you take two unrelated things, such as designing a chair (problem) and a canary. Step 1 is to list everything that is known about a canary. Step 2 is to list everything that is known about the problem, designing a chair. Step 3 is to take one trait, characteristic, or aspect of a canary and apply it to some trait, characteristic, or aspect of a chair. Example: A canary is yellow. Chairs are painted or finished; therefore you could paint them yellow. This is done using many traits from the *forced* thing and applying them to some aspect of the problem.

Attribute Listing

This tool/technique is also about ninety years old. First, list every part, detail, step (if a process), and every process used in making something. Second, examine each part, detail, and step and improve each one in as many ways as you can. Third, combine the best of the improvements of each part into a whole new solution.

Morphological Listing

Again, this technique is about ninety years old. First, generate a list of the parts of a problem, for example: Meal: main course, vegetable, starch, salad, dressing, bread, dessert.

Second, draw a grid or chart using the parts of the problem/meal as the columns of the grid/chart.

Third, generate ten to twelve different versions of each, for example: Main course: roast beef, pork, chicken, veal, fish (list several fish), lamb, ground meat, ham, etc.

Fourth, randomly choose one from each column to create a meal or total solution.

If you have six columns/parts/categories and you generate ten possible variances for each, you have created potentially 1,000,000 (6 to the 10th power) possible variances. Some will work. Some will be losers or even disgusting.

White Paint®

This tool is similar to the morphological grid. First, examine the name of your problem, focusing on the key adjectives, adverbs, and nouns, for example, white paint. Imagine your problem is to invent a new kind of white paint.

Next, generate a list of words sparked by or related to "white": snow, milk, paper, ice cream, whipped cream, clouds, etc.

Third, generate a list of works sparked by or related to "paint": covering, protective surface, latex, enamel, watercolor, etc.

Fourth, study the individual list for groups or clusters of common terms. You are looking for clues from the information in order to make breakthroughs. For example, often when people do this warm-up version they discover that many of the things they listed as "white" really are not white: snow, ice, diamonds, etc.

Fifth, ask questions. Why do they look white? What causes them to appear white?

Sixth, examine the "Paint" column for things or groupings in the list that can be related or connected to the concept of "white without really being white."

This technique is based on an actual Pittsburgh Paint research project. The solution was an acrylic clear paint that, when wiped down with another chemical, became white-looking because the added chemical that was wiped on turned the surface of the paint into a crystalline surface, much like diamonds, snow, clouds, etc.

The principle behind this idea-generating technique is to explore and discover answers *within* the information.

What If-ing

Using the tool called What If-ing consists of continuously asking "What If?" questions to explore for potential solutions.

- What if we painted it?

- What if we didn't paint it?

- What if we made it smaller, larger, wider?

- What if we can't make the deadline? What else might we do?

"What else?" often is the second step. What Else-ing is another tool that can be used on its own without "What If?"

Who Am I?
Challenging the Team

Activity Summary

A brief exercise to explore ways a team could be more successful by changing how it envisions a task.

Goals

- To provide an opportunity for participants to get to know each other better.

- To begin to generate team spirit.

- To help establish a comfortable and supportive environment.

Group Size

Any size in groups of 5.

Time Required

30 minutes.

Materials

- One Who Am I? handout for each group of 5 or another list of questions that you have prepared.

- Who Am I? Answer Key for the facilitator.

- A watch or way to track time.

- Prizes for the winning group members if you want to introduce an element of competition.

- Flip chart and markers.

- (Optional) Paper and pencils or pens for participants.

Physical Setting

Room arranged with tables for 5.

Facilitating Risk Rating

Low.

Process

1. Briefly explain the goals of the session. Then ask for volunteers from each table group to come to the front of the room or specify an approach for selecting the volunteer, for example, wearing the most blue, has the most unique hobby, or whose last name is first in the alphabet.

2. Give one Who Am I? handout to the volunteer from each table.

3. Briefly explain that everyone is to work together in their groups to try to determine who the famous people are on the handout. (If you want to create a competitive environment, announce that there will be a prize for the group with the most correct answers.) Tell them they have 7 minutes.
   (10 minutes.)

4. Give a 1-minute warning. When the time is up, call on groups for the answers and check them against the Who Am I? Answer Key.

5. Debrief the exercise with these questions, summarizing points on the flip chart:

   - How did you feel as time was drawing to a close?

   - Did your team have all the correct answers?

   - What would have made you more successful?

   - What might have happened if all the groups had collaborated?

   - What would have to change for that to happen?

   - What led to the assumption that you were *not* to work together?
   (10 minutes.)

6. Summarize by referring to the various points made by the team members. State that we only improve if we are willing to change and that we must consider all possibilities when attempting to complete a task successfully.

Submitted by Robert Alan Black.

Robert Alan Black, Ph.D., CSP, *is founder and president of Cre8ng People, Places & Possibilities, a creative thinking consultant, and award-winning professional speaker who specializes in the S.P.R.E.A.D.ng™ of Cre8ng™ and Creative Thinking throughout workplaces around the world. Each year he speaks at many executive development institutes, conferences, and conventions in the United States, Canada, Turkey, and South Africa. He has written eleven books, including* Broken Crayons: Break Your Crayons and Draw Outside the Lines *and over 250 articles that have been published in the United States, Canada, Malaysia, Thailand, Turkey, and South Africa.*

Who Am I?

With your teammates, determine who the following famous people were/are.

Gave a short speech to dedicate a cemetery.

Born Ted Geisel.

Was the last person many Americans saw each night for thirty years.

Started as a nightclub singer and actress in Harlem and became famous reading a poem for a presidential inauguration.

Scored 100 points in a single professional basketball game.

Many fantasies became scientific breakthroughs later, including air conditioning and television and trips to the moon.

Went blind at three and later took a military writing technique and turned it into a way for the blind to read.

Was first African-American woman elected to Congress.

Shared a Nobel Peace Prize with a previous arch enemy and was assassinated three years later.

Korean War pilot, first civilian to join NASA astronaut program; was the command pilot of the first docking of two spacecraft in space.

Known as "strange one" among his people, joined Sitting Bull at Little Big Horn to defeat General Custer.

Worked in a defense plant in WWII. Married to both a famous baseball player and a famous playwright and sang "Happy Birthday" for a president.

Italy's first female doctor; worked with retarded children and learned to let children learn at their own pace.

Who Am I? Answer Key

Abe Lincoln

Dr. Seuss

Johnny Carson

Maya Angelou

Wilt Chamberlain

Jules Verne

Louis Braille

Shirley Chisholm

Anwar Sadat

Neil Armstrong

Crazy Horse

Marilyn Monroe

Maria Montessori

Collaborative Tales
Using Reflective Analysis

Activity Summary

A group activity that allows participants to explore the significance of collaboration.

Goals

- To analyze collaborative experiences using reflective analysis.

- To reflect on the possibility of change by enhancing collaborative experiences.

Group Size

8 to 36.

Time Required

Approximately 60 minutes.

Materials

- One copy of the Collaborative Tales Lecturette for the facilitator/trainer.

- Two copies of the Collaborative Tales Octagon Analysis (Personal) for each participant.

- Two copies of the Collaborative Tales Octagon Analysis (Organizational) for each participant.

- One copy of the Collaborative Tales Suggested Readings for each participant.

- Blank paper and pens or pencils for each participant.

- A flip chart and felt-tipped markers.

Physical Setting

A room large enough for concentrated group work, with groups varying in size from 4 to 6.

Facilitating Risk Rating

Moderate.

Process

1. Form groups of four to six persons each. Ask the participants in each group to introduce themselves to one another while you hand out blank paper and pens or pencils.
   (5 minutes.)

2. Explain a little about the goals of the workshop and then announce the following to the participants:

   - Each group is to create and will then share with the large group one story about a collaborative experience in the workplace.

   - The presentation should be approximately 3 minutes in length.

   - The story should be based on real-life experiences, past or present, of at least one of the group members.

   - The experience must be related to the workplace, for example, writing a paper for journal publication, research on a specific issue, inter-departmental collaboration, inter-organizational collaboration, and so forth.

   - The story must contain information on how the collaboration started and the journey thereafter.

   - Each group must identify what they want their audience to know, what they want their audience to remember, and any changes that could have enhanced the collaborative experience.

3. Tell the groups to work independently for 12 to 15 minutes to construct their collaborative tales and plan their presentations. Respond to any ques-

tions from the participants and be available should any groups seek clarification while they construct their tales.
(15 minutes.)

4. Give the participants a 5-minute reminder before calling time. Have each group present its collaborative tale.
    (3 minutes per group.)

5. After each group presents its story, ask for 2 minutes of silence so that the participants can jot down their impressions and learnings from the collaborative tale sharing.
    (2 minutes per group.)

6. Lead a discussion about the significant learnings from the shared collaborative experiences and the need for carefully exploring future collaborations, using the following discussion starters:

    *   What did you learn from this activity?

    *   How can you use this information back on the job?

    (10 minutes.)

7. Using the flip chart and making a rough sketch of the Collaborative Tales Octagon Analysis, demonstrate how to do an analysis, explaining the terminology by giving the Collaborative Tales Lecturette. Use examples from their stories to illustrate the points as you make them, being sure that participants are clear on the principles involved before continuing.
    (10 minutes.)

8. Give each participant a copy of the Collaborative Tales Octagon Analysis (Personal) and a copy of the Collaborative Tales Octagon Analysis (Organizational) and explain that they should now do a reflective analysis of their own collaborative experiences. They can choose to do this solo or in dyads, either personal or organizational.
    (5 minutes.)

9. Tell participants that they can use the Collaborative Tales Octagon Analysis they did to understand the need for current collaborations or any that come up in the workplace in the future. Give each participant extra copies of each of the Octagon Analyses and a copy of the Collaborative Tales Suggested Readings.
    (2 minutes.)

10. Thank participants for sharing their collaborative stories. Wish them luck and enduring success for current and future collaborations.

Trainer's Notes

- Keep the structure in terms of instructions and clarifications on the collaborative tales fairly loose to give space for the participants' perceptions and experiences to emerge. However, the tales must be work-related.

- Encourage participants to focus on recent experiences, as well as changes that may enhance their collaborative experiences.

- Focus on the word "collaboration" and the layers of meaning that are possible when doing the discussion on collaboration. This will facilitate their Collaborative Tales Octagon Analyses.

- If the group is small, ask each small group to construct two collaborative tales, or alternatively spend more time on the changes that collaborative experiences may require.

Submitted by Edwina Pio.

Dr. Edwina Pio (Ph.D., MA, B.Ed., BA, MNZAC) *is senior faculty at the Business School of AUT University, Auckland, New Zealand, and visiting professor at Boston College, with research interests at the intersection of management, psychology, and spirituality. She travels extensively for research and dissemination of her work. Her accolades include the Duke of Edinburgh Fellowship, Research Fellowships at Boston College and at Jonkoping International Business School, Sweden; and she is the winner of the outstanding field report paper at the Academy of Management (2006). She is on the Board of Studies and Exam Board of the MBA at AUT University and on the editorial board of the* Journal of Enterprising Communities: People and Places in the Global Economy, *the* Journal of Immigrant and Refugee Studies, *and the* International Journal of Entrepreneurship and Small Business. *She also works with women and children of domestic violence on a voluntary basis and is registered with the New Zealand Association of Counselors. She is a regular contributor to the Pfeiffer Annuals.*

Collaborative Tales Lecturette

Collaboration consists of a broad spectrum of possibilities and can involve inter-institutional, international, and/or interpersonal aspects. It can be seen as a loosely or tightly coupled community of practice or as "significant others" whose complementary assets and knowledge are brought together to achieve a common goal.

The reasons for collaborating are varied, including the need to clarify answers to questions, sharpen arguments, or influence practice, or collaborating with someone could be useful when the other person has special competence, data, or equipment. Other collaborative partnerships could the supervisor/student relationship or past friendships. The reason for choosing someone with whom to collaborate could be financial, interdisciplinary specializations, physical proximity, or political factors. Interpersonal aspects could include perceived trustworthiness and compatible working styles.

Success might be more likely with a common language, agreed-on cultural norms, similar organizational structure, agreement on how decisions should be made, similar recognition and reward systems, when the results build capacity or utilize resources, when the participants have equal status and share authorship, and when both are responsible to the same local authority.

As you can see, there is a lot of complexity involved in collaboration. You may need to build research networks, consider ethical aspects, discipline, and controls, as well as serve as gatekeepers of some organizational research.

The outcomes of collaboration could be increased knowledge, new ideas, networks, publications, or continued support for research and development work.

Enablers for collaboration are often factors such as accountability, cross-fertilization of ideas, disclosure, flexibility, humor, intellectual companionship, intellectual space, knowledge that cannot be created by the same person in solo work, networking, risk taking, sharing, and transfer of knowledge/skills/techniques, transparency, trust, and visibility.

There are some constraints, however, in that not every partnership is desirable. Interaction by itself does not lead to and is not necessarily collaboration; shared and equitable benefits do not simply "happen." Collaboration has many layers. Personal and organizational stakes have to be discussed, and people must tolerate each other's methods and beliefs. Because of its great potential, there is always room for enhancing and enriching collaborative experiences.

Collaborative Tales Octagon Analysis (Personal)

Instructions: Note that your analysis will vary depending on the specific collaboration that you are analyzing. The inner octagon indicates low importance, the middle octagon indicates moderate importance, and the larger outer octagon indicates high importance. Shade the octagon in response to the following questions about a personal collaborative relationship you have. Use different colors for yourself and your collaborative partner if you perceive a difference.

- How important is each of the aspects to you in this relationship?

- How important is each of these aspects to your collaborator?

- Changes in which areas could enhance your collaboration?

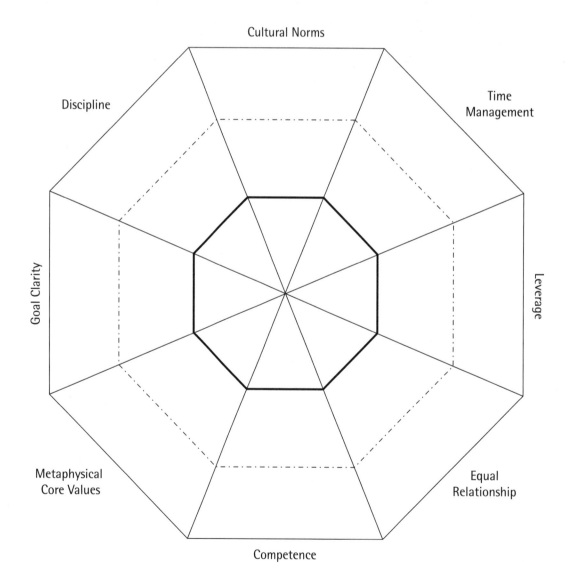

Collaborative Tales Octagon Analysis (Organizational)

Instructions: Note that your analysis will vary depending on the specific collaboration that you are analyzing. The inner octagon indicates low importance, the middle octagon indicates moderate importance, and the larger outer octagon indicates high importance. Shade the octagon in response to the following questions about an organizational collaborative relationship you have. Use different colors for yourself and your collaborative partner(s) if you perceive a difference.

- How much is the organization willing to invest in the areas shown?

- What suggestions do you have for change, based on your organizational octagon analysis?

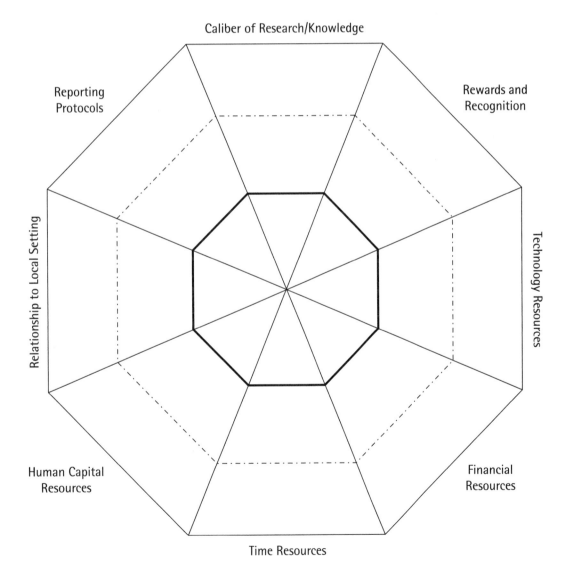

The 2008 Pfeiffer Annual: Training

Collaborative Tales Suggested Readings

Austin, J.E., & The Peter Drucker Foundation. (2000). *The collaborative challenge.* Hoboken, NJ: John Wiley & Sons.

Coffin, B. (2005). Building ethical capacity for collaborative research. *Nonprofit and Voluntary Sector Quarterly, 34*(4), 531–539.

Forman, J., & Markus, M.L. (2005). Research on collaboration, business communication, and technology. *Journal of Business Communication, 42*(1), 78–102.

Jentsch, B., & Pilley, C. (2003). Research relationships between the south and the north: Cinderella and the ugly sisters? *Social Science & Medicine, 57,* 1957–1967.

Rigby, J., & Edler, J. (2005). Peering inside research networks: Some observations of the effect of intensity of collaboration on the variability of research quality. *Research Policy, 34,* 784–794.

Straus, D., & Layton, T. (2002). *How to make collaboration work: Powerful ways to build consensus, solve problems, and make decisions.* San Francisco, CA: Berrett-Koehler.

Solomon, N., Boud, D., Leontios, M., & Staron, M. (2001). Researchers are learners too: Collaboration in research on workplace learning. *Journal of Workplace Learning, 13*(7/8), 274–281.

Tamm, J.W., & Luyet, R.J. (2004). *Radical collaboration: Five essential skills to overcome defensiveness and build successful relationships.* New York: HarperCollins.

Tools for Change
Identifying Your Role on the Change Team

Activity Summary

An interactive kinesthetic group exercise that allows participants to discover the roles they play in the execution of a successful organizational change and ways to improve their effectiveness.

Goals

- To understand that organizational change is a team effort.

- To help individual team members uncover their roles and strengths in implementing change.

- To determine ways an organization can better support individuals and managers during the change process.

Group Size

Teams of 7 to 10 from an organization undergoing a change initiative.

Time Required

40 to 50 minutes.

Materials

A tool box with various toy or real tools such as hammers, screwdrivers, pliers, wrenches, tape measures, saws, clamps, T-squares, levels, trowels, paintbrushes, etc. (Toy miniature replicas of tools are often available in toy stores or Dollar stores.)

Physical Setting

A circular table with seating around the table or room.

Facilitating Risk Taking

Low.

Process

1. Display tools in the middle of the table so that they can be easily seen by all participants.

2. Introduce the activity using the metaphor of building a house. State that, in order to build a house or make any change successfully, many different skills and tools are required. Ask: What if you had only one or two tools to build a house or to implement a change? Abraham Maslow is supposed to have said, "If the only tool I have is a hammer, then I will treat every person or situation as a nail."

3. Instruct participants to choose the tool or implement that most closely represents their respective roles in the organizational change process. For example, a person who likes to cut through obstacles and red tape might choose a saw or cutting implement.

   (5 minutes.)

4. After everyone has selected a tool, have all participants take turns to describe how the tools chosen are metaphors for their roles in organizational change initiatives. For example, a person choosing a paintbrush might hold it up and say, "I paint a picture for my staff of our desired outcomes, and the clearer the better!"

   (20 minutes.)

5. Wrap up with a discussion of the skills and tools that are prevalent in their organization and which ones may be weak or missing altogether. Make the point that, if you are missing a skill or tool, it is tempting to use the wrong one (for example, attempting to open a bottle with your teeth). Obviously, it would be difficult to implement a successful change without a full array or skills and tools used properly.

   (15 minutes.)

Variation

For a more challenging activity, up to ten individuals could be charged with choosing tools that most personify or describe other members of their group and those people's roles in the change process. In this variation, consensus must be achieved regarding the metaphor for each person before proceeding to the next person. Be sure to keep the discussion positive and give opportunities for each team member to respond to the group's choice of change tools for him or her.

Submitted by Donna Goldstein and Dennis Collins.

Donna Goldstein, Ed.D., *is the managing director of Development Associates International, a human resource consulting and training group that helps organizations succeed by creating more productive workplaces and higher performing teams and staff. Dr. Goldstein holds a doctorate in human resource development and a master's degree in psychology and has taught over 100,000 people in three hundred organizations worldwide. She has an active executive coaching practice, has contributed to twenty-six books, including the 2004 and 2005 Pfeiffer Annuals, and the new* 101 Great Ways to Improve Your Life *(Volume II). She has published dozens of articles on innovative approaches to team building, change management, customer service, sales, and diversity.*

Dennis Collins *is one of the nation's most successful radio executives. He is currently the senior vice president and general manager of the Lincoln Financial Media group of stations in Miami: LITE-FM-101.5, MAJIC-FM-102.7, and WAXY-AM-790. With a thirty-year career in advertising, communications, and marketing, Mr. Collins has had the opportunity to assist hundreds of businesses, both large and small, in nearly every industry. He has trained thousands of record-breaking, unstoppable salespeople. In 2001, he received the highest honor in the radio industry, the A.I.R. Excellence in Radio Award.*

Corporate Box
Learning to Listen

Activity Summary

An initiative focused on helping people become aware of their assumptions and problem-solving capacity during a seemingly impossible task.

Goals

- To allow a group an opportunity to problem solve together.

- To highlight the need for participants to see beyond the obvious.

Group Size

12 to 50 or more who work together on a daily basis.

Time Required

60 to 90 minutes.

Materials

- 80-foot to 100-foot lengths of rope.

- Eight to fifteen 12-inch squares, made of cloth, carpeting, or foam shelf liner.

- Two to four Hula Hoops®.

Physical Setting

Any setting inside or outside large enough to lay the rope on the ground in a rectangle and have the entire group stand around the outside of the rectangle.

Facilitating Risk Rating

Low to Moderate.

Preparation

1. Use the rope to create a rectangle on the floor or ground approximately 15 feet by 25 feet. For groups larger than thirty, make this box larger. Place two Hula Hoops in the center of the rectangle. The box must be large enough so that participants cannot just step into the Hula Hoops in the middle.

2. Have eight to fifteen squares sized 12 inches by 12 inches available. These can be made of carpet, foam shelf paper, or cloth. Be sure that the material of the squares does not pose a risk of slipping on the floor.

Process

1. Ask participants to stand in the vicinity of the box you have created. Say:

   "In the fast-paced corporate world that we find ourselves in, innovation, a willingness to take calculated risks, and openness to new ideas are valuable assets. A phrase that is often used to describe this kind of creative thinking is 'out of the box.' As we begin today, our first project will be a living metaphor for what it means to move out of the box. Everyone take a position on one of the four sides of our box. As we begin to move out of our self-perceived limits, we do not move in just any direction. There is a purpose to our movement. For each of you, this movement will be represented in your attempt to *move across the box to the opposite side* from where you are standing now. You will have all the resources necessary to make this move successfully and safely. Please listen to the instructions I am going to give."

2. Provide the following instructions verbally:

   - "To move, you must enter the box from the side where you are now standing."

   - "Once a resource is put in use, it must be used (touched) at all times."

   - "If you do not utilize a resource or you misuse a resource, you will lose that resource."* (ONLY IF SOMEONE ASKS FOR CLARIFICATION, say that this rule means that, if someone lets go of a resource, whether by

---

*Do not explain this rule unless someone asks. There are typically so many guidelines in an activity that people stop listening half-way through. I have never had a group that has not lost at least one resource, most likely from not listening or from not seeking to understand the rules. This behavior most likely also relates to their on-the-job behavior, which is a good teaching point. If groups do ask about this rule and ask me to explain what I mean by "not utilizing a resource," I tell them. I want to reward the behavior of asking for more information so that they will, hopefully, do it again.

dropping it on the ground to step on it or throwing it to another side of the box, he or she will lose it. Any time someone comes out of contact with a resource, whether with a hand, shoe, or foot, he or she loses it.)

- "No one may touch the floor inside the rectangle. The consequence for this infraction is that everyone must begin again from his or her original position if one person touches the floor."

- "A maximum of two feet can be on a square at any time."

- "If you choose to use the safe zones (the Hula Hoops), a minimum of two feet must be inside a hoop or you lose the safe zones (Hula Hoops)."

(10 minutes.)

3. Tell the group to begin. It typically takes groups 15 to 25 minutes to make the first successful attempt across the rectangle. After the group has successfully crossed the rectangle, offer the following seemingly impossible challenge:

> "The group must now make the crossing in less than 15 seconds" [or give up to 60 seconds, depending on the size of the group]. (Note that 12 to 25 people can do it in under 15 seconds, 26 to 50 people can do it in 25 seconds, more than 50 people can do it in 45 seconds. Allow more time if participants have physical limitations.)

On the surface, it seems impossible, and participants will need to fail a time or two to bring out the power of the exercise.

(30 minutes.)

4. To wrap up, ask participants to reflect on what occurred:

- "What did you notice happening during this activity?"

- "What helped you be successful?"

- "What were some barriers to your success?"

- "What does that suggest about how this team works in general?"

- "What surprised you about this activity?"

- "What was frustrating or difficult about this activity?"

- "How could you repeat your success?"

- "What would you do differently if you did this activity again?"

- "How does this relate to how this group works on a daily basis?"

- "What lessons are you taking back to the workplace?"

(15 minutes.)

Trainer's Notes

- It is important to give the group all the information, but do not over-engineer the activity. Most groups listen to about half of the instructions and have to learn through experience that not listening can be costly. This is a very important learning that should be discovered and not supplied by you.

- Many groups will initially work in isolation on their respective sides of the box. Again, observe but do not over-control the activity. Let the group discover the limitations of not working together.

- Expect a good deal of chaos at first. Everyone talks at once, with many people subgrouping. This is normal and should be tolerated for a time because, again, it is an important learning moment for the group.

- Anticipate the first time a participant lays down a square and loses contact with it. If the square is not being touched, it is not being utilized and should be taken away at once. Because they did not listen or check their understanding of what that instruction means, this is often the group's first mistake. It is also the first time that they might stop and consider their process. It will be important to act quickly to remove the square, but not in a way that antagonizes the group. You are not out to take the resources. You are just enforcing the guidelines. Be prepared for shock, complaining, and confusion from the group.

- When the challenge is given, the group will usually just try to do what they have already done, but faster. It may take them a few iterations to realize that what helped them be successful before will not work now. They must challenge their assumptions because they have a working paradigm in place from their previous tries.

- The easiest answer is, of course, to build paths across the squares, ensuring that one person is always touching a square and that one person remains inside each Hula Hoop as the parade passes by from one side to the other. The most effective solution we have seen (see diagram) is, when the time starts, to lay four resources in the four corners of the rectangle. Have one person keep a foot or hand on each resource and then have the rest of the group step into the box from the side they are now in and then out diagonally on the next side. They have now satisfied the guideline about entering the box. Now people can walk around the outside of the box to get to their goal sides. The Hula Hoops are just distractions and really don't need to be used. This type of solution fits and drives home the point (albeit tired and overused) of the introduction about people thinking "outside of the box" literally.

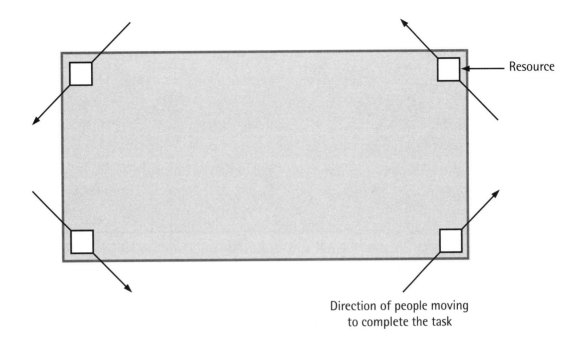

Direction of people moving
to complete the task

- Another point can be made about the Hula Hoops. Most groups struggle with trying to use the Hula Hoops, and they really just slow the group down. But most groups will still try to use them because they are there.

Submitted by Mark Rose and Greg Robinson.

Mark Rose *is the business development leader at Challenge Quest. His main focus is equipping teams with skills and tools to become more effective. He is co-author of* A Leadership Paradox: Influencing Others by Defining Yourself, *which provides a model for differentiated leadership based on two years of research inside a Fortune 500 company.*

Greg Robinson *is currently president of Challenge Quest in Pryor, Oklahoma. He has a Ph.D. in organizational behavior and leadership from The Union Institute and University in Cincinnati. Dr. Robinson's professional career has concentrated in the areas of team development, leadership development, facilitation, and consulting with organizational change efforts. He is the author of* Teams for a New Generation: An Introduction to Collective Learning *and* A Leadership Paradox: Influencing Others by Defining Yourself.

Alphabet Soup
Building Skills to Deal with Change

Activity Summary

Simple but powerful group activity to build the skills needed to handle change: adaptability, flexibility, and resiliency.

Goals

- To build adaptability, flexibility, and resiliency.

- To build teamwork and communication skills.

- To enhance camaraderie and team spirit.

Group Size

Unlimited.

Time Required

30 to 60 minutes.

Materials

- (Optional) Alphabet Soup Checkoff List.

- Flip chart and felt-tipped markers.

Physical Setting

A room large enough for small groups to talk together without disturbing one another.

Facilitating Risk Rating

Low.

Process

1. Introduce the activity by explaining that we live in a constantly changing world. In order to remain functional and resilient, it is important to develop our ability to be flexible and responsive to the changing environment.

2. Explain that one of the keys to dealing with change is the ability to think on your feet and to maintain a sense of humor! Say that this activity will help them learn to do both of these things.

3. Invite everyone to find partners. (If you have a very large group, ask anyone who still needs a partner to raise his or her hand; then have those people seek each other out to ensure everyone is matched up. If there is an odd number, you can be a partner or create a group of three.)
   (10 minutes.)

4. Explain the process: In pairs, participants are to have conversations. The rules are as follows (post these on a flip chart):

   - The conversation is created one sentence at a time, with sentences alternating between people.

   - Each sentence must begin with the next sequential letter of the alphabet. (Example: **A**re you feeling okay? **B**etter than I did yesterday. **C**ome on, what happened yesterday? **D**idn't you hear?)

   - Start with any letter, then continue sequentially until someone misses!

   - When someone either uses the wrong letter or cannot think of a sentence for the letter, that round ends. The pair picks a new topic and starts again.

5. Distribute the Alphabet Soup Checkoff List (or show it on a slide). This makes it easier for people to remember what their next letter is, so they can concentrate more on creating a plausible conversation.

6. Circulate throughout this activity, offering guidance or ideas when the pairs get stuck.
   (10 minutes.)

7. After about 10 minutes, invite people to join pairs (creating groups of four). Then do another round, this time with a goal of creating a conversation among the four individuals.

   (10 minutes.)

8. To take this to a deeper level, follow up by suggesting specific topics for the groups to discuss, still using the Alphabet Soup rules. Topics could include issues you want to explore, such as "Dealing with Change," "Living Our Vision," or "Customer Service."

9. To debrief and use this activity for a more intense discussion, use the following discussion questions:

   - What kinds of things happened as you went through this activity?

   - What happened as you continued with the activity? Did it become harder or easier? Why was that true?

   - What surprised you as you went through the activity?

   - How did you use the skills of adaptability, flexibility, and resiliency during this activity?

   - How can we translate what happened during this activity to how you deal with the changes we are experiencing? (For example, you had to focus on both the alphabet and the flow of the conversation. As we deal with change, we need to be able to focus on both the impact of the change as well as the issues we are working on in terms of maintaining quality and productivity.)

   - How did you use teamwork to create a viable conversation? What does that mean to us as we work with each other in our work setting?

   - How can we use what we have learned to help us deal with the changes we are facing?

   (20 minutes.)

Variations

- Instead of a conversation, have teams create a story that flows, with each sentence of the story beginning with the next sequential letter.

- Do this same activity in teams rather than pairs. It is most effective in teams of no more than five people. Have a basket filled with slips of paper, each paper containing a topic or issue for discussion. Teams draw a topic, then create a conversation around that topic using the Alphabet Soup rules. They can either rotate sequentially among team members or just use a free-flow process, which allows any team member to offer a sentence.

- Create triads and select an observer/judge for each group. This person ensures the rules are followed, makes determinations when there are questions, and provides feedback to the group about how they completed the activity. This role can rotate among team members.

———————

Submitted by Cher Holton.

Cher Holton, Ph.D., *president of The Holton Consulting Group, Inc., is an impact consultant focusing on bringing harmony to life with customers, among team members, and in life. In addition to being one of a handful of professionals world-wide who have earned both the Certified Speaking Professional and Certified Management Consultant designations, she has authored several books, including* The Manager's Short Course to a Long Career, Living at the Speed of Life: Staying in Control in a World Gone Bonkers!, *and* Crackerjack Choices: 200 of the Best Choices You Will Ever Make.

Alphabet Soup Checkoff List

Instructions: Have a conversation, one sentence at a time, alternating sentences between you. Each sentence must begin with the next sequential letter of the alphabet. (Example: Are you feeling okay? Better than I did yesterday. Come on, what happened yesterday? Didn't you hear?)

Start with any letter, then continue sequentially till someone misses! When someone either uses the wrong letter or cannot think of a sentence for the letter, that round ends. Pick a new topic and start again.

A	J	S
B	K	T
C	L	U
D	M	V
E	N	W
F	O	X
G	P	Y
H	Q	Z
I	R	

Tic Tac
Deciding What to Do

Activity Summary

A simple game of chance that challenges participants to appropriately apply suggested behavioral principles to scenarios found in the everyday workplace.

Goals

- To decide whether situations adhere to an organization's ethical standards.

- To differentiate between actions that violate organizational standards and those that comply with the organization's guidelines.

Group Size

3 to 15.

Time Required

90 minutes.

Materials

- One Tic Tac Sample Code of Conduct for each participant.

- One Tic Tac Game Board for each participant.

- A pencil or pen for each participant.

- One Agree/Disagree sign for each participant, prepared by printing the word Agree in green on one side of a sheet of card stock and the word Disagree in red on the other side.

- The nine Tic Tac Scenarios, each printed on a single sheet of paper.

- (Optional) Assorted prizes for participants.

Physical Setting

A room with appropriate lighting that provides a writing space for each participant and that is arranged so that the facilitator can see all participants.

Facilitating Risk Rating

Moderate.

Preparation

1. Cut apart and make copies of the nine Tic Tac Scenarios on separate sheets of paper. Make them into a deck in random order.

2. Create Agree/Disagree signs by printing "Agree" with a green marker on one side and "Disagree" with a red marker on the other side of pieces of card stock, one sign for each participant.

Process

1. Introduce the activity by discussing the value of having an organizational code of conduct and the important role that one plays in the success of any organization. Some points to make include:

   - A code of conduct sets the ethical standard for all employee behavior.

   - A code of conduct defines the organization's culture and moral and ethical expectations.

   - A code of conduct ensures compliance with regulators and legislative statutes.

2. Distribute the Tic Tac Sample Code of Conduct, the Tic Tac Game Board, a pencil or pen, and the agree/disagree signs to all participants.

3. Instruct the participants to review the Sample Code of Conduct. Allow 3 to 5 minutes.
   (5 minutes.)

4. Have the participants follow along as you read the instructions on the Tic Tac Game Board. Allow the participants 2 minutes to write the numbers 1 through 9 on their game boards in any order they wish.
    (2 minutes.)

5. Randomly select a scenario from those you have created. State the number of the scenario and read it aloud. Have participants consider the question, determine individually whether they agree or disagree that the scenario supports the Sample Code of Conduct, and then hold up either an agree or disagree sign to signal their positions.
    (3 minutes.)

6. Question random participants and ask them to explain their responses. If a response is different from the one on the Sample Code of Conduct, lead a discussion so that participants recognize and understand the rationale for the correct answer.
    (5 minutes.)

7. Instruct participants who were correct to circle the number of that scenario on their Game Boards. If a participant responded incorrectly, have him or her place an "X" over the appropriate number.

8. Repeat Steps 5 through 7, using a different scenario each time, until a participant wins by having three circles in a row. Award the winner a prize, if desired.

9. Continue with the game until you have read all nine scenarios. Wrap up with a discussion of organizational ethics and what has been learned. As much as possible, apply the points to the participants' organizations and own behavior.
    (25 minutes.)

Variations

-   To shorten the length of time required for the game, only present scenarios until one or two participants have won.

-   If all participants are from the same organization, you may wish to create scenarios specific to their organization and use their actual code of conduct.

Submitted by Kathleen Finch.

Kathleen Finch *is an organization development consultant focusing on organization culture and vision and their impact on employee performance. She has an extensive background in human resources and is experienced in constructing behavioral competency-based appraisal systems and employee performance improvement models. Ms. Finch has her M.A. in human resource administration and is a certified employee benefit specialist. She has been certified in several training courses and currently develops and conducts behavioral-based performance improvement training courses.*

Tic Tac Sample Code of Conduct

This Code of Conduct outlines the principles and standards that govern the day-to-day activities of our employees. All employees are required to read and follow the Code of Conduct. The Code of Conduct offers guidance under thirteen main headings.

Confidential Information

- Employees shall safeguard and protect any and all client confidential information and internal confidential information from disclosure to unauthorized third parties.

- Employees are prohibited from reviewing or accessing client information unless the employee has a job-related reason to know such information.

Conflicts of Interest

- Employees must avoid any actual or potential conflicts of interest.

- Employees may only give or accept gifts, favors, and business entertainment that is of reasonable value or which gift, favor, or business entertainment would be properly paid for by the organization as a reasonable business expense.

- The hiring of relatives is prohibited if such hiring would result in a direct or indirect supervisory relationship or if an actual or potential conflict of interest would exist.

Use of Organization Property

- All organization property shall be handled with due care and used primarily for business-related purposes.

- Employees' personal use of voice mail, electronic mail, Internet access, and other electronic communication services should be kept to a minimum.

Outside Activities

- Employees are not to have outside interests that will materially interfere with the time or attention that should be devoted to their organizational duties.

- Employees must seek approval from the human resources department before engaging in outside employment that will interfere with their regular job duties, create any conflict of interest or the appearance of such, or necessitate such time as to affect the employee's performance for the organization.

Managing Personal Affairs

- All employees must conduct their personal business, personal banking transactions, and organization business in a responsible manner.

- Employees must process all personal financial transactions with the organization following the same procedures that are used by customers.

Discrimination and Harassment

- The organization supports a culturally diverse community and an environment that fosters respect among all persons associated with the organization. Harassment and discrimination for any reason will not be tolerated.

- It is important to remember that the perception of the victim—not the intention of the person accused—is the critical factor in determining whether a hostile work environment exists.

Reporting Unethical Behavior and Non-Retaliation

- Employees who become aware of any unethical, inappropriate, or illegal activities within the organization have an affirmative responsibility to promptly report such activities, and the organization will not tolerate retaliation against good faith reports.

- Employees who become aware of any unethical, inappropriate, or illegal activities within the organization have an affirmative responsibility to promptly report such activities to the director of human resources, the general auditor, or the general counsel.

General Conduct

- An employee's actions and conduct must always reflect favorably on the organization.

Tic Tac Game Board

Instructions

- Randomly number the squares from 1 to 9. Use each number only once.

- After each statement the facilitator reads, answer *Agree* or *Disagree.* If you are correct, place a circle around the number in the box that corresponds to that statement. (The facilitator will inform you of the number.) If you are incorrect, place an **X** over the corresponding number.

- When you have three **O**'s in a row, shout out: "I've got it!" You're a winner!

Tic Tac Scenarios

Scenario 1

Because you will be bonded by an insurance company when you work for this organization, you should have access to all client information. Do you agree?

Scenario 2

Melody, a personal banker, received a fruit basket from a client as a thank you gift. She appreciated the gift and thought it was appropriate to accept it. Do you agree with Melody?

Scenario 3

George, a facilities worker, referred his sister-in-law to the bank for a teller position. He was confident that her working at the bank would not be a conflict of interest. Do you agree with George?

Scenario 4

Phillip made a quick call to the local hospital four times last week to check on his father's condition. He thought that was OK and didn't break the rules. Do you agree with Phillip?

Scenario 5

Jill, a teller, is working part-time on weekends at the local movie theater selling tickets. Although she did let her supervisor know, she didn't think she needed to tell anyone in human resources. Do you agree with Jill?

Scenario 6

When Roberta, a teller, told Sally, her supervisor, that a commercial customer made her uncomfortable with his comments, Sally told her not to worry about it because he was harmless. Sally thinks everything's OK. Do you agree with Sally?

Scenario 7

Jody, a teller, is worried that her friend is having money problems and may be doing some minor things with her money drawer to cover herself. She decides not to say anything because she's not absolutely sure, and besides it is her friend and it's not really Jody's job to be the police. Do you agree with Jody?

Scenario 8

Dave was at a barbeque last Saturday and boasted to his friends about the incentive money he was going to receive for closing a loan for "Hammers and More," the local hardware store. Since other people could see the owners come into the bank, he felt it was no big secret that they were bank clients. Do you agree with Dave?

Scenario 9

Larry, a financial analyst, is running for the local school board. He copied some of his campaign fliers on the department's copy machine during his lunch hour so that he could hand them out right after work. He figured it was only 250 copies, and it was on his own time so it was OK. Do you agree with Larry?

Clouded Visions
Avoiding the Perils of Prediction

Activity Summary

A thought-provoking activity that encourages participants to examine their own ideas about what is possible for the future of their organization.

Goals

- To focus on our rapidly changing world.

- To highlight the difficulties inherent in predicting the nature of change.

- To provide an opportunity to surface expectations of the future.

Group Size

10 to 50 from the same organization.

Time Required

60 to 90 minutes.

Materials

- One Clouded Visions Instruction Sheet for each participant.

- A pen or pencil for each participant.

- Separate overhead transparencies or PowerPoint slides of the Clouded Visions.

- A flip chart for each subgroup.

- Felt-tipped markers for each subgroup.

- Masking tape.

- An overhead projector or computer and screen.

Physical Setting

A room with tables and flip charts for each group.

Facilitating Risk Rating

Low.

Preparation

1. Copy each of the Clouded Visions separately onto overhead transparencies or into a PowerPoint format so that one Clouded Vision can be exposed at a time.

2. Copy enough Clouded Visions Instruction Sheets for all participants.

Process

1. Introduce the session by explaining that we all have notions of what the future will involve and that these visions impact how we behave in the present, especially in how we plan for the future of the organization.

2. Divide the group into subgroups of four to six and have each choose a recorder to record the subgroup's output on a flip chart.

3. Ask the participants for the next 4 minutes to silently and independently consider how they think that the world will be different in the next twenty years, that is, what important changes they believe will occur and how it will impact their organization.

4. Ask the participants to write two or three of the most important things they have identified on their Clouded Visions Instruction Sheets.
   (10 minutes.)

5. Tell the subgroups that they have 7 minutes to share their visions of the future among themselves, to identify the four or five that they consider the most realistic, and to post them on their flip charts.
   (10 minutes.)

6. Allow the subgroups to view each other's flip charts. Lead a discussion about the impact that any of their ideas will have on the organization. *(10 minutes.)*

7. Explain that there have been many attempts to predict aspects of the future and that there is a great deal of risk in making such predictions because much of the future is unknowable. Explain that, despite such risks, people continue to make predictions and that it is interesting to examine some of the predictions from the past.

8. Present each of the Clouded Visions and allow comments. *(15 minutes.)*

9. Question the group as to whether reviewing these clouded predictions has impacted their confidence in their own predictions for their organization. Ask how confident they are in their own predictions for the organization. *(10 minutes.)*

10. Lead a concluding discussion of how the "perils of prediction" impact any organizational planning process, especially focusing on how their organization can avoid these perils. *(15 minutes.)*

Variation

Simply show each of the Clouded Vision statements and then lead an open discussion about the "perils of prediction." This is especially useful as an early activity in any strategic or long-term planning process.

Submitted by Leonard D. Goodstein.

Leonard D. Goodstein, Ph.D., *is a consulting psychologist based in Washington, D.C., as well as a principal with Psichometrics International, LLC, an Atlanta-based test development and distribution company. He formerly was CEO and executive vice president of the American Psychological Association and CEO of University Associates (now Pfeiffer). He also has held a variety of academic positions, including professorships at the Universities of Iowa, Cincinnati, and Arizona State, where he also served as department chair. He is a frequent contributor to the professional literature and is one of the co-authors of* Applied Strategic Planning: How to Develop Plans That Really Work. *His most recent book, co-authored with Erich P. Prien,* Individual Assessment in the Workplace: A Practical Guide for HR Professionals, Trainers, and Managers, *was published by Pfeiffer in 2006.*

Clouded Visions Instruction Sheet

We all have visions of the future, of how things will change over time. These notions about the future are important on both the personal and organizational levels, as they impact our present behavior. That is, our view of how things will change has implications for how we think about and prepare for a somewhat uncertain future. For example, if you believe that the Social Security program is bankrupt and that you will receive no benefits from it when you retire, then this belief about the future should affect your financial planning for retirement. Or if you believe that gasoline prices will continue to escalate, that will or should impact your next automobile purchase. While our two examples are financial ones, we have notions about many different aspects of the future—technological, political, environmental, and so on.

Take the next few minutes to consider your own notions about the future. How do you think things will be different in the next twenty years? Develop a list of the changes that you think are likely to happen and then select from your list the two that you think are the most likely to happen and be prepared to share these in your subgroup. Feel free to continue on the back of this page.

Clouded Visions

"This 'telephone' has too many shortcomings to be seriously considered as a means of communication. The device is inherently of no use to us."

Western Union internal memo, 1876

"Heavier-than-air flying machines are impossible."

Lord Kelvin, Royal Society, 1895

"Everything that can be invented has been invented."

Charles H. Duell, U.S. Patent Commissioner, 1899

"Airplanes are interesting toys but are of no military value."

French Field Marshall Ferdinand Foch, 1914

"The wireless music box has no imaginable commercial value. Who would pay for a message sent to nobody in particular?"

Staff memo to David Sarnoff, RCA CEO, 1920

"Fifty years hence automobile traffic will have completely disappeared from the surface of New York City and people will be shot through tubes like merchandise."

Harvey W. Corbett, American Institute of Architects, 1925

"Who the hell would want to hear an actor talk?"

Harry M. Warner, CEO Warner Brothers, 1927

"The well-dressed man of 2020 will wear shorts for every occasion except for formal events."

New York haberdasher John David, 1929

"It is not difficult to imagine that in the future, the entire aerial transportation will be unaffected by fog and weather conditions in general."

Charles F. Kettering, Vice President, General Motors, 1934

"I think there is a world market for maybe five computers."

Thomas Watson, CEO, IBM, 1943

"There is no reason for any individual to have a computer in their home."

Kenneth Olsen, CEO, Digital Equipment Corporation, 1977

Forty-Five
Reacting to Workplace Change

Activity Summary

A change activity designed to be different from typical experiential activities in that the first portion is facilitated by an audio recording.

Goals

- To exchange best practices related to reacting to change in the workplace.

- To experience feelings and emotions elicited by new procedures that are different from expectations.

Group Size

Any number between 10 and 100, but best between 15 and 30.

Time Required

30 to 50 minutes.

Materials

- Forty-Five Script for the facilitator.

- Prerecorded audiotape of the script.

- Cassette player (with additional speakers if needed).

- Flip chart and markers.

- Four or five index cards per participant.

- Pens or pencils for participants.

Physical Setting

A large room with a table in front and enough space for participants to walk around.

Facilitating Risk Rating

Moderate to High.

Preparation

1. Review the Forty-Five Script and familiarize yourself with the steps of the activity. Prepare (and test) the audio recording.

2. Because participants are supposed to follow instructions from your audio-tape recording in your absence, you will need one or two volunteers to turn the audio recording on and off at appropriate times. The day before the training session, recruit one or two confederates and explain the procedure to them. Walk them through the activity, playing the audio recording. During the actual session, if no participants volunteer to take charge of the audio player, ask your confederates to encourage someone to volunteer or to volunteer themselves.

3. Long before the session, place the audio player and piles of index cards and pens or pencils on the table. Place a flip chart nearby with this instruction: *Please turn this audio player on at 5 minutes after the scheduled start time of the session.*

Process

1. Stay away from the room until all participants are safely inside. Then, lurk outside the room, listening in on what is happening inside.
   (15 to 20 minutes.)

2. Near the end of the session, when the audio recording announces that it is going to hand over the session to the local facilitator, enter the room. Without any unnecessary explanation, conduct the final part of the activity and the debriefing discussion (as explained below).

3. Explain that the maximum possible total score for any guideline is 45. Announce that you are going to count down from 45. When a participant hears his or her total from a card, he or she should stand up and read the guideline from the card.

4. Begin counting down from 45. When one or more participants stand up, invite them to take turns to read the guidelines on their cards. Applaud each guideline and briefly comment on it. Invite other participants to make their comments. Continue the countdown process until you have identified the top five or ten guidelines.

5. Debrief the activity using these questions:

   - Think back to your experience during the activity. What was your initial reaction to the unusual way the session was conducted?

   - How was this activity related to change?

   - How do your reactions relate to some of the guidelines that were offered by the group?

   - What have you learned about your response to change?

   - What are you taking away from this activity?
   (10 minutes.)

Variation

If you are conducting a public workshop and participants do not know what you look like, mingle with the participants at the beginning of the session without identifying yourself. Play the role that you would have assigned to your confederates. Identify yourself and take over the session during the final countdown.

_____

Submitted by Sivasailam "Thiagi" Thiagarajan.

Thiagi *is currently the "resident mad scientist" at The Thiagi Group, an organization dedicated to improving human performance effectively and enjoyably. Thiagi's younger co-workers keep him supplied with food, books, and mortgage money and let him design training games every day.*

Forty-Five Script

Suggestion for Recording

Have a count-down timer and a bell (or buzzer) handy. Ring the bell (or sound the buzzer) whenever the script says "tone."

Greetings!

Thank you for turning the audio player on. I was getting claustrophobic waiting to talk to you.

This training session is about change in the workplace. I am sure that all of you have experienced big and small changes in your workplaces. This makes you something like experts on the topic of change in your workplace. So instead of hiring an expensive consultant to train you, we decided to let all of you train yourselves. Take a few index cards and a pen or pencil from the table now.

I will be giving you recorded instructions on how to take part in an experiential activity called Forty-Five. To ensure that everything works smoothly, I need one or two volunteer "game wardens." Your primary task is to put the recording on pause whenever I ask you to do so. You may also rewind and replay the audio recording if necessary. May I have a couple of volunteers for the game warden job please?

While we wait for the brave volunteers, somebody put the audio recording on pause. Turn the recording back on when the game wardens have been appointed.

(Tone)

We are now going to participate in an activity that shifts the focus away from the managers of an organization to individual employees.

If you are directly impacted by a change, whether in the work process, equipment, or co-workers, what is the best way to handle the situation? Reflect on this question and write a practical guideline for effectively handling workplace change on one or your index cards. Keep your guideline brief, specific, clear, and legible. Do not write your name on the card.

Your guideline does not have to be one of earth-shaking significance. Quickly write down whatever idea comes to mind.

For example, when we conducted this activity once before, one of the participants wrote, "Invest some time and effort to learn the new skills that are required by the change."

Another participant wrote, "Remember that, whenever one door closes, another door opens. So look for the opportunities that accompany the change."

You have 2 minutes to complete the task. Game Warden, please put the audio player on pause. Then you too should write a change guideline on a card. When you think everyone has completed this task, begin playing the audio recording again.

(Tone)

If you have not yet finished writing your guideline, do so in the next 5 seconds. If you have already finished, please read your guideline silently and gloat to yourself about how brilliant it is. In a little while, we are going to send out your guideline on a paired-comparison evaluation adventure. The best guidelines will rise to the top, and the not-too-good guidelines will sink to the bottom. To prevent any damage to your self-esteem, please emotionally detach yourself from your guideline and get ready to launch it into the evaluation adventure.

Please stand up with your guideline card and a pen or pencil in your hand. Hold the card with the written side down. Walk around the room and exchange your cards with each other. Keep doing this without reading the guidelines on the cards you receive.

(Pause for about 20 seconds.)

(Tone)

Freeze! Please stop the card exchange process. Quickly pair up with another participant near you.

(Pause for 10 seconds.)

(Tone)

You and your partner have two cards. You do not know who wrote on the cards. Even if you see your own card, pretend not to recognize it. Review the ideas on the two cards you have.

Listen carefully as I explain how to score the guidelines. Distribute 9 points between these two guidelines to reflect their relative usefulness. If one guideline receives 9 points (because it is so brilliant), the other guideline receives 0 points. You can distribute the score points 9 and 0, 8 and 1, 7 and 2, 6 and 3, 5 and 4, and so on. Make sure that the two numbers add up to 9.

Two other major constraints: No fractions, please. You cannot give 4.5 points to each guideline. And no negative numbers either!

When you have decided how to distribute the 9 points, please write the numbers on the backs of the cards.

Game Warden, please put the audio recorder on pause. Turn it back on when participants have completed the distribution of their score points.

(Tone)

Thank you. We are going to repeat this comparative evaluation adventure a total of five times.

Please turn the card you have in your hand written-side down, walk around, and exchange the cards as before. Continue doing this until you hear the tone.

(Pause 15 seconds.)

(Tone)

Find a new partner, compare the two guidelines on your cards, and distribute 9 points as before. Write the new score points on the backs of the cards, below the previous numbers.

Game Warden, please put the audio recorder on pause. Turn it back on when participants have completed distributing the score points.

(Tone)

We have finished two rounds. Now for Round 3 of comparative evaluation. Please walk around and exchange the cards as before. Continue doing this until you hear the tone.

(Pause 15 seconds.)

(Tone)

Find a new partner, compare the two guidelines on your cards, and distribute 9 points. Write the new score points on the backs of the cards, below the previous numbers.

Game Warden, please put the audio recorder on pause. Turn it back on when participants have completed distributing the score points.

(Tone)

Onward to the fourth round. Please walk around and exchange the cards as before. Continue doing this until you hear the tone.

(Pause 15 seconds.)

(Tone)

Find a new partner, compare the two guidelines on your cards, and distribute 9 points. Write the new score points on the backs of the cards, below the previous numbers.

Game Warden, please put the audio recorder on pause. Turn it back on when participants have completed distributing the score points.

(Tone)

Now for the final round.

Please walk around and exchange the cards as before. Continue doing this until you hear the tone.

(Pause 15 seconds.)

(Tone)

Find a new partner, compare the two guidelines on your cards, and distribute 9 points. Write the new score points on the backs of the cards, below the previous numbers.

Game Warden, please put the audio recorder on pause. Turn it back on when participants have completed distributing the score points.

(Tone)

Thank you for your patient and enthusiastic participation. Please return to your seats with the cards you currently have in your hands. Sit down and add the five score points together. Write the total on the card.

(Pause for about 40 seconds.)

(Tone)

My job is done.

I want to thank those who were in charge of the audio recording. May we have a round of applause for these folks, please.

There are a couple more steps, but since they are fairly simple, I am going to hand you over to a local facilitator.

Thank you and good-bye.

(Tone)

Introduction
to the Editor's Choice Section

Unfortunately, in the past we have had to reject exceptional ideas that did not meet the criteria of one of the sections or did not fit into one of our categories. So we created an Editor's Choice Section that allows us to publish unique items that are useful to the profession rather than turn them down. This collection of contributions simply does not fit in one of the other three sections: Experiential Learning Activities; Inventories, Questionnaires, and Surveys; or Articles and Discussion Resources.

Based on the reason for creating this section, it is difficult to predict what you may find. You may anticipate a potpourri of topics, a variety of formats, and an assortment of categories. Some may be directly related to the training and consulting fields, and others may be related tangentially. Some may be obvious additions, and others may not. What you are sure to find is something you may not have expected but that will contribute to your growth and stretch your thinking. Suffice it to say that this section will provide you with a variety of useful ideas, practical strategies, and creative ways to look at the world. The material will add innovation to your training and consulting knowledge and skills. The contributions will challenge you to think differently, consider new perspectives, and add information you may not have considered before. The section will stretch your view of training and consulting topics.

The 2008 Pfeiffer Annual: Training includes one editor's choice item. Keep in mind the purpose for this section—good ideas that don't fit in the other sections. We are honored to have a submission from Vince Miller. He was the president of the National ASTD in 1974. He is truly the profession's historian. We are delighted to present here his recollection of the history of ASTD and the profession known as training and development. Enjoy Vince's collection of memories and thoughts about how the industry has changed.

Article

**Training and ASTD: An Historical Review, by Vincent A. Miller

---

**Topic is change focused

Training and ASTD
An Historical Review
Vincent A. Miller

Summary

As a long-time trainer and ASTD member, I wrote this article to provide readers with an inside look at the history of the training profession and of ASTD and how these two came to intersect. I accepted the opportunity to write this article because I have many memories that I think need to be told.

Could Training Be the Oldest Profession?

Most scholarly dissertations on the history of communication begin with the early cave wall drawings, which served as a documentary record and a textbook of the time. Isn't it conceivable that the etchings and paintings were used as effective instructional illustrations, orienting primeval youngsters and others to such skills as fishing or hunting or how to protect themselves from large mammoths that were roaming the countryside?

As archaeological excavations unearth information about the lives of people six thousand or more years ago, the place of training in the skyrocketing development of knowledge has become dramatically more evident. The Sumerian place of Kish, built in 3500 BC, is an example of the ancient use of brick. The work could not have been accomplished without the transfer of knowledge from one person to another, or from one person to many people.

Thus was developed an apprenticeship system whereby an experienced person passes along knowledge and skills to another person, who after a period of apprenticeship becomes a journeyman or yeoman. The apprenticeship was not restricted to artisans. The ancient temples taught religion and art. The armies took the responsibility for training soldiers, and apprenticeship was the vehicle of instruction in medicine, law, and many other occupations.

Provisions for governing apprenticeships were instituted as early as 1800 BC, when such rules were included in the code of Hammurabi, who placed a code of laws in the temple of Shamash (God of Justice) in Babylon.

Guilds were formed in England before the Norman invasion, which occurred in 1066. The basic purpose of guilds was mutual protection, assistance, and advantage. Guilds, in essence, created a private franchise, and at the same time established quality standards for products by setting quality standards for workmanship. During the peak of the guild system, between the 12th and 15th Centuries, the privileges of the members were protected by strict regulation of the hours, tools, prices, wages, and the strict training given to apprentices. In craft unions today, we find controls similar to those used by the guilds.

Training and the Industrial Revolution

The 19th Century was an era of social legislation that changed the concept of workers' organizations. Throughout all of the changes that were made, there developed an emphasis on the quality of training received by workers. This has culminated in the staunch support of the unions for any legislation that provides a wide range of vocational legislations.

The Industrial Revolution began in England about 1750, spread to France and Belgium, and then to Germany and the Untied States. After the Revolutionary War, the Americans turned their energy toward the pursuit of prosperity. They established an industrial economy through the use of power-driven machines and steam engines.

Industrialization meant two changes in work preparation: (1) specific training was now required before specific tasks could be performed and (2) work activity was now focused away from the individual, family, or small group and toward a large organization within a large, impersonal urban community. The Industrial Revolution required training for specific tasks. A worker did not have to be trained to perform every task necessary for producing a finished product. The worker performed one task over and over.

The history of the growth of training that accompanied the Industrial Revolution is fascinating. As early as 1809, the Masonic Grand Lodge of New York established vocational training facilities. However, most of the manual training schools that started shortly after 1825 were really places of incarceration for "bad boys." The so-called state industrial schools were more disciplinary than vocational schools. Nevertheless, the basic concept was correct.

The concept of applying higher learning to practical job training has flourished since 1824, when Rensselaer Polytechnic Institute became the first college of engineering. The college provided courses in engineering, agriculture, business administration, accounting, journalism, and a variety of other fields. Gradually, there was acceptance that there is a bona fide link between education and training.

In 1830 the trustees of Columbia University voted to provide a curriculum in which no Latin or Greek was required, and to make the courses available to young men in business and mercantile establishments. However, most companies did not use the educational systems to train their workers. They trained their own people. In fact, industry became the employer, guardian, and patron of body and soul. The new system of manufacture meant that the machines were skilled. The operators of the machines were not necessarily skilled. As viewed by the industrialists, craftsmanship belonged in the past. Industrial education was the future.

Other companies such as Western Electric, Goodyear, National Cash Register, and Ford soon installed factory training schools. By 1910, the Ford Motor Company had moved into a new plant at Highland Park and had established a production line concept. However, it was not until 1913 that the moving assembly line was first introduced by Ford Motor Company. This, of course, required special training for the entire workforce.

The Beginning of On-the-Job Training

The moving assembly line is hailed as the beginning of mass production. We should point out that, even before Ford perfected the moving assembly line, the company was mass-producing the low-priced Model T. In 1912, Ford had built 82,388 Model Ts.

What was this first moving assembly line like? Those who have seen the assembly lines in modern plants might visualize overhead lines carrying parts, and robot-like machines located on either side of a moving line with sparks flying as the machines performed weld after weld. It wasn't like that at all.

Ford didn't invent mass production or interchangeable parts. The moving assembly line was inspired, in part, by the moving disassembly lines of Chicago's slaughterhouses. Ford's first moving assembly line, in fact, consisted of a rope attached to a winch, which drew a Model T chassis across the plant floor. Yes, it was crude, but despite the enormous technological advances over the past ninety-five years, the manufacture of automobiles still relies heavily on production principles that Henry Ford put to work.

With a new plant and a new moving assembly line, the Ford Motor Company must have been faced with a monumental training task. We cannot find a record of how the workers were trained. Certainly, the training could not be accomplished by on-the-job training (OJT) because, in the beginning, there were no workers who had experience working on a moving production line. Thus began the need for special training of the production worker for a specific job, because each person on the assembly line had to be trained only in the tasks performed at that particular work station.

Our guess is that the training of workers for the new production line was started by assigning workers who had been working on the assembly of Model Ts before the moving assembly line was built. With a skeleton crew of workers in place, the production line could be started at a very slow pace, with most workers performing two or three tasks. Once the original workers were adept at performing their tasks, additional workers would be added to the line, and they would receive on-the-job training.

On-the-job training is still the most frequently used type of training because of its practicality and simplicity. The British have some words that describe OJT. They say that the person being trained is "sitting next to Nellie" or being trained by Nellie. This is a carryover expression from the early industrial era, when an employee was brought into the job and assigned to an experienced worker until the job was learned.

Unfortunately, in most cases, "Nellie" would start by saying, "This is what you do, and this is how you do it." The training would concentrate only on psychomotor skills. There was no attempt to supply sensory information, as an effective instructor would do. For example, an effective instructor would supply additional information such as, "Listen for this sound" or "Feel the tension on this belt."

Another method of training that could have been used is *vestibule training*. Vestibule training is designed to provide all of the benefits of on-the-job training with few of its shortcomings. In vestibule training, the production system itself is duplicated off-line. A separate area, which duplicates sections of the production line, is set up. In this "vestibule" area, the trainee experiences the on-line situation, but there are no time constraints. The trainee is not under great pressure to maintain a standard rate of production in the beginning and is not held accountable for a high reject rate in the first stages of the training.

Let's pause here and review which training materials were available for use by the training manager. The supply of training aids was very limited. There were no audio or video tapes, no slide or film projectors; there were no computers. About all that the instructor could use as visuals was the blackboard, a flip chart (usually with hand-drawn visuals), or a flannel board. (Flannel boards were popular until the 1950s.) Almost without exception, the instructors had to make their own visuals.

Training and World War I

Training has always grown best when there is an emergency and the need for a trained workforce is apparent. Even though the need for better-trained labor had been known to many managers, educators, and consultants for years, it was the crisis of an approaching war that finally caused training to be recognized as essential to the production of materials and equipment.

In 1914, World War I started in Europe. In 1915, German submarines set up a blockade of Great Britain, and one of the earliest casualties, the Lusitania, was torpedoed on its maiden voyage from England to New York. The casualty toll included at least 128 American citizens. Up to this time, President Wilson had maintained a strictly neutral position for the Untied States, but former president Theodore Roosevelt, who had long advocated intervention on the side of the allies, describes the vessel's sinking as an act of piracy and intentional murder.

Even before the United States entered the war on April 6, 1917, there was a vital need for a "bridge of ships" to Europe in order for America to do its part in "making the world safe for democracy." American shipyards had started to expand. The United States, despite its many declarations of neutrality, evolved as the principal source of food, raw materials, and ammunition that fed the allied war machine.

The Emergency Fleet Corporation of the United States Shipping Board found that sixty-one shipyards with fifty thousand workers had a need for ten times as many workers, but none were available. The only answer was to train new workers, so on September 12, 1917, the United States Shipping Board set up an educational training section.

Charles Allen, head of the program, had once been a vocational instructor and had been pleading for improvement in instruction. Until then, his pleas fell on deaf ears. This was his opportunity to demonstrate the practicality of his philosophy. He ordered that all training was to be done at the shipyards and that the instructors were to be the supervisors. Allen launched a four-step method of show, tell, do, and check for the job instruction training that helped to solve the World War I training problem.

As World War I progressed, and many manufacturing plants changed over from the manufacture of civilian goods to the manufacture of guns, tanks, ammunition, and other war materials, the need for training was apparent in those industries too, and they followed much the same pattern as had been established by Charles Allen for the shipyards.

The change-over from production of civilian materials to war materials was so drastic that thousands of workers needed to be trained for their new jobs. In many instances, the supervisor became the trainer, holding special classes. Some industries hired vocational instructors to do the training. The war, more than anything else, created a need for the training director and established the training director as an integral part of the working force.

From Allen's findings, and those of the army during the war, the following principles were developed for use in industrial training:

- Training should be done within industry.

- Training should be done by supervisors.

- Supervisors should be trained in how to instruct.

- The best group size for training is nine to eleven people.

- The preparation of a job breakdown is an important step before training.

- When given personal attention during training, the worker develops a feeling of loyalty.

Until World War I, the U.S. economy had been mostly agrarian. Most people walked to work, because there were few automobiles. Many people, even in the city, had chickens and cows and small gardens. Those who had telephones were on party lines, with four, eight, or sixteen people sharing the same line. Only those who lived in new homes had central heating systems.

The first electric washing machine was marketed in 1907. The first electric range had been produced in 1909. The first household electric refrigerator was introduced in 1918, and the first commercial radio station began weekly broadcasts on November 2, 1920. This was the state of technology in the United States between 1910 and 1920.

World War's I Effect on Training

After World War I, a series of factors combined to compel companies to provide a stable source of competent future management. Many colleges and universities responded to the industrial need for managerial-level personnel by offering business education courses.

The prosperity of the early 1920s tended to discourage the application of training to industrial situations. By this time, correspondence schools had gained recognition and acceptance and were serving the needs of the American wage earner. It was said that probably more men in American industry had gained their technical skills from correspondence schools than by any other means.

The loss of men in World War I and the inability of the economy in the late 1920s to support the surplus personnel required for managerial apprenticeship caused that program to die out. In fact, apprenticeship for the skilled trades faded away in the late 1920s and early 1930s, because there were not enough jobs for those who had already been trained.

Sales training seemed to receive some stimulus during the postwar period of the roaring 1920s. Local radio stations were just beginning their broadcasts, and families were buying their first radios. The ownership of an electric refrigerator, or an electric range, or a wringer washer was indeed a status symbol. Many salespeople were trained in door-to-door selling for these big-ticket items.

The Hawthorne Studies

The Hawthorne studies took place from 1924 to 1933. Those who seek the origin of the behavioral sciences in training consider the Hawthorne studies, conducted at the

Hawthorne works of Western Electric, as the watershed event. In cooperation with the National Research Council, the National Academy of Sciences embarked on an experiment to determine the relationship of the quality of physical and environmental influences to the efficiency of workers on the job.

The psychologists selected experimental groups of employees and manipulated workplace conditions such as temperature, light, humidity, and rest periods, and recorded the results to determine how much these factors affected the efficiency of the workers.

While they were able in some instances to determine cause-and-effect relationships between work conditions and environment, they also found that, almost regardless of what changes were made in the work environment, efficiency increased among the experimental groups of workers. This gave rise to what is called the Hawthorne effect, the theory that employees will perform more efficiently simply because they are given special attention.

More significant than the findings based on the original premise that physical conditions in the workplace will affect efficiency were the unexpected findings that were gleaned from the Hawthorne studies. The researchers found that there were influences that affected efficiency and productivity much more strongly than working conditions did.

The researchers found, for example, that employees were more productive when working in groups than when working in isolation. They found that wage incentives alone did not improve product output. They found that workers would sacrifice greater output for group acceptance.

The interviewing program demonstrated very clearly that complaints were often symptoms of underlying problems that employees could not recognize without help, or cannot state, except to a person whom they feel will understand what they are saying.

What can the supervisor do about this? He or she can try to understand and try to behave in such a way that employees will want to talk to him or her. The interviewing program brought out the significance of social relationships and the importance to the employee of the symbols of prestige and status connected with the job.

These experiments clearly demonstrated that an individual's response is usually determined by a complex system of related factors, which must be considered as a whole before predicting behavior.

The Depression Years

During the 1930s, as the economy plunged into the greatest depression in American history, more and more top management people decided that training was not necessary. The great number of workers whose jobs were terminated when businesses failed provided an adequate supply of skilled and experienced workers. Apprenticeship in the skilled trades was terminated in many industries.

On the other hand, a great influence to the furtherance of training was stimulated by this same set of depression-laden circumstances. Hundreds of thousands of unemployed people had nothing to do with their hands. State and Federal governments instituted training programs, and unemployed men and women occupied their time learning leather work, weaving, art and painting, jewelry making, and other such trades. The unemployed soon learned that they could occupy themselves making some useful things. In some cases, they could generate income by selling the things they had made. People became training conscious and also became conscious of their own learning potential.

I was privileged to see some of the first experiments with television in 1935, approximately ten years before it was released to the public. It was a great feat at that time to broadcast the television signal from one floor to another in the same building. Little did we dream, as we watched the broadcast of a style show, that this medium would be a great asset to trainers. These early broadcasts were very crude, and we knew as we watched that there had to be years of development work before television would be practical.

Training tools of the 1930s generally consisted of chalkboards, writing easels or chart pads, "magic lantern" slides, filmstrips, and, in later years of the decade, some commercially prepared 16-millimeter sound motion picture films. It was the development of the 16-mm movie projector that first brought audiovisual technology into practical prominence in the classroom. Of course, there were some enterprising trainers who were using "talking machines," both cylinder and disk, to give them some audio capabilities.

A Resurgence of Training

In the later 1930s, before Hitler sent his troops into Austria in March 1938, Britain and France began to build up their war arsenals. Both countries turned to the United States for defensive armaments. Likewise, the United States began to bolster its own defensive armaments. These "war" orders were eagerly accepted by American manufacturers and had much to do with improving the economy and reducing the size of the unemployment lines.

The need for training on a massive scale was recognized, as people who had been unemployed or under-employed for years again returned to skilled jobs, and people without skills were trained to do work that required skills. Training was needed, but who would do it? Most training departments within industry had been dismantled during the great depression.

Many vocational teachers had taken higher-paying jobs in industry, and in some cases those who were left in teaching positions were not familiar with the needs of the employers. In many industries, the burden of training was put in the hands of the foreman. After all, the typical foreman once had been a worker on the production line; therefore the foreman should know how to train a person who started to work on the production line. That was management's line of reasoning. Foremen generally accepted the responsibility for training their new employees. The National Association of Foremen considered training so essential that the organization held a national conference dedicated to training.

But that was not the solution to training the expanding workforce. Foremen had many other responsibilities and could not concentrate on the training job, and with so many foremen responsible for training their workers, there was no semblance of uniformity.

Of course, with the great need for training skilled workers, the apprentice programs were restored, but that was not the answer to training needs. Training became a necessity, and soon the title of "training manager" was common in the management hierarchy. As war approached, trainers suddenly needed to move vast numbers of people through orientation, attitude building, and technical training.

World War II Increased the Training Need

Registration for the draft in the United States occurred late in 1940, and some workers were drafted into the armed forces. People who had never worked in a manufacturing plant eagerly answered the call to replace those who had entered the armed forces.

It was obvious to all that the United States was on the brink of war, and our involvement was imminent, since we were supplying the Allies with ammunition, planes, guns, and tanks. By this time, many of our industries were involved in some way in the manufacture of war materials.

There was a shortage of males to work in the factories, and women started to apply for jobs that were once considered in the male domain. The new people needed to be trained to be welders, riveters, and machinists, and many of the new people were women.

At last, business and industry came face-to-face with the reality that they had too long ignored. They had neglected training during the depression years of the 1930s, and now they were in a bind. Suddenly, the training function of the supervisor became important. In fact, management found that supervisors without training skills were unable to produce adequately for the war effort. Supervisors with training skills established new production records using inexperienced, aged, handicapped, and female workers.

The actual training of supervisors to become job instructors was developed to classic simplicity by the Training Within Industry service (TWI), which was established in 1940 by the National Defense Advisory Commission. On April 8, 1942, by presidential order, TWI became a part of the War Manpowered Commission and operated under the Bureau of Training. By the time TWI ceased operations in 1945, it had been successful in training 23,000 persons as instructors and had awarded nearly two million certificates to supervisors who had gone through the TWI programs in more than sixteen thousand plants, services, and unions.

It was obvious that someone had to be in charge of these massive training efforts, and that person had to create some semblance of order and quality of training. The person in charge of these activities was typically called the "industrial training director," and the industrial trainers taught the skills.

ASTD: An Organization to Fill a Need

The industrial trainers at the time of World War II had a great need to communicate with each other. According to Tom Keaty, a member of the ASTD founding group, the National Training Society was first proposed on April 2, 1942. A number of trainers from the oil industry were meeting in New Orleans. Tom suggested the need for a National Training Society that would cut across all industries. The other men in the group enthusiastically endorsed the idea.

The years of 1942, 1943, and 1944 were formative years for ASTD. Tom Keaty had volunteered to develop a constitution. He was assisted by J.W. Bowling, Tom Hampton, Cliff White, Hall Terry, Earl Polick, Douglas Parkes, Don Freedlund, Dr. K.E. Loughmiller, and Dr. Nelson Hauer. These men also tested the first "chapter" concept, meeting regularly, and exchanging training information.

The first formal meeting, attended by fifteen men, was held in January 1943. By February 1944, the Society had one hundred members from sixteen states. Individual chapters were being organized. The first issue of *Industrial Training News* was published in June 1945, and the first National ASTD Conference, with almost two hundred people attending, was held in Chicago in September 1945.

Trainers wanted an organization that would allow them to meet together and exchange ideas with people in their own profession. They wanted the prestige that a true professional organization would give them. They wanted to better serve their employers, and at that time, they wanted to better serve their country.

Section 1 of ASTD's first constitution, as shown below, clearly states what the objectives of the Society were then, and I would not be in favor of changing any of them, except to remove the word "industrial."

> "Section 1: The objectives of this Society are to further the education and development of the profession of industrial training. In the furtherance of these objectives, the Society declares its proper activities to include the holding of regional and national meetings, for the presentation and discussion of industrial

training topics; the publication and distribution of the journal, papers, reports, and discussions; the development and maintenance of libraries devoted to training of industrial personnel, and the encouragement of their establishment by others; cooperation with other professional and engineering societies; co-operation with Federal, State, and Municipal education officials; groups from industries, colleges, and others interested in furthering its objectives; the furthering of research; making special studies; developing industrial training programs and procedures; and analyzing problems arising in their application."

Extending Its Reach

In the September-October 1947 issue of the *Journal of Industrial Training,* there was evidence that ASTD was reaching out to communicate with other trainers. There was a two-day seminar in Montreal, Quebec, Canada, attended by 350 trainers, on May 22 and 23, 1947. Trainers from all parts of Canada and the United States attended the conference. This first conference, presented by The Canadian Industrial Trainers' Association, had ten sessions. W.F. Mainguy, vice president of the Shaqwnigan Water and Power Company, spoke on "What Management Wants from the Training Director." Dr. Emile Bouvier, director of Montreal University's Industrial Relations Department, spoke on "The Absolute Necessity for Good Human Relations."

One of the early articles published in the *Journal of Industrial Training* was titled "We Are Making Progress—Why?" The response was: "Great Potentialities." As a group, training people were the first to recognize the fact that training skill is a job requisite of every leader in the organization. They accepted their duty to help everyone in a company who supervises the activities of others. In many ways, it is a vision that encompasses the significance of training to the most far-reaching problems of our day. These members were thinking of the great potentialities of the training function.

Some of the articles in these early journals included "Apprenticeship in England," "Management Training," "Training's Effect on Business," "Training Opportunities," "Developing Men Builds Profit," "Summary of Training Workshop on the Case Method," "Can Trainers Learn from Teachers?," "Wisconsin Seminars for Top Executives," and "Improving Staff Procedure in Training."

Personal History

I have been a trainer since 1948. I would have been one of the early members of ASTD if I had heard about ASTD. I was thirty-one years old when I was the field service representative for Servel gas refrigerators. After six months of training, my territory was Iowa, Nebraska, Minnesota, North Dakota, and South Dakota, and once each year I contacted gas utilities in Wyoming and Montana. I drove my automobile more than 50,000 miles each year and carried my training kits and flip chart in the trunk of my car.

I could set up my training kits and be ready for a training presentation in half an hour. Some training meetings were impromptu, but most were scheduled weeks in advance.

After more than a year, I returned to the factory, on special assignment to take care of service problems that were mostly located in Florida. During the next two years, I spent three to five weeks away from home on every training trip. In between trips, I would have one week in the Servel home office.

From 1953 to 1956, I was in the home office writing service manuals and presenting seminars to groups that were brought into the factory for training. In 1955, I had a different group of executives from Distributors and Utilities each week. They were brought into the company to be told about a special service problem. I was the instructor, except for two hours, the full week they were in town. Although I did not know it at the time, I was using the same primitive training equipment that prompted the organizers of ASTD to seek better ways of training.

When the scheduled meetings were finished, I decided to accept an offer from Whirlpool Corporation and started working there on April 1, 1956. I was offered an opportunity to establish the Service Training Department for Whirlpool Corporation in St. Joseph, Michigan, in June 1960. I had been a trainer for thirteen years, and I had never heard of ASTD. I was eating in a local restaurant shortly after I started working on my new job. The local ASTD chapter was holding its meeting in the same restaurant. I even knew some of the chapter's members from past training contacts. As I had just begun my new job, I needed all of the help I could get. I immediately became active in the local chapter of ASTD. I attended every National Conference from that time until I retired in January of 1983, and I have attended most of the National Conferences since I retired.

I have been an ASTD member for forty-seven years. I have been involved nationally and internationally. I attended the 2006 ASTD International Conference in Dallas. I will attend the International Federation of Training and Development Organizations (IFTDO) meeting in San Diego this September. I helped to organize IFTDO. It has been in existence for twenty-seven years. The effort to establish IFTDO has not hurt ASTD. In fact, about 30 percent of the attendees at the ASTD International Conference in recent years were from foreign countries.

International Training

ASTD's most concerted efforts in international training began in the early 1970s. Corporations began to expand their foreign operations. The Agency for International Development (AID), an arm of the U.S. State Department, asked ASTD to present some seminars in Mexico and Venezuela. AID was pleased with the seminars that ASTD presented and urged ASTD to attempt to organize a world federation of training and development organizations.

This was a difficult assignment, but the Agency for International Development would pay the cost, while ASTD did the planning and organizing. Subsequently, ASTD planned and presented a seminar in Geneva, Switzerland, in 1972. Training leaders from many countries were invited to participate in the discussions about forming a World Training Federation. Their reaction was favorable. Another conference was planned for Bath, England, September 27 through October 3, 1973. In the meantime, those interested would continue working on the structure of the new federation. It was tentatively decided that the name of the new organization would be the International Federation of Training and Development Organizations (IFTDO).

The first guidelines for the new organization were drafted in the ASTD office. After a review by interested parties, a second draft was prepared and reviewed at a meeting held during the ASTD National Conference in Miami. The second draft of the guidelines was mailed to all training principals who would be participating in the organization meeting at Bath, England.

On September 28, during the Bath Conference, a meeting was called to order for all interested delegates of training organizations. It was an open forum. Twenty-four persons attended, representing their organizations. Objectives of the Federation and the name were openly discussed. It was agreed that the first meeting of the International Federation of Training and Development Organizations (IFTDO) would be on October 1, and that an Executive Committee would be formed.

Tom Jaap of the Scottish Society for Training and Development was elected president. Vincent A. Miller of the American Society for Training and Development was elected secretary. Others elected to the Executive Committee were Gordon C. King of the Australian Institute for Training and Development, S.K. Parthasarathi of the India Society for Training and Development, Aharon Mitki of the Israel Society for Training and Development, Miguel Jusidman of the Association Capacitacion (Mexico), and Jon Ivarsonof the Norwegian Society for Training and Development. A total of twenty organizations officially signed the original IFTDO Charter. A second IFTDO Council meeting was held on October 2 to discuss the development of the IFTDO Constitution and Bylaws. ASTD, as secretariat of the Federation, and Vincent Miller, Secretary of IFTDO, were given the responsibility of preparing the Articles of Incorporation, the Constitution, and Bylaws to be approved at the next Council meeting. The next Council meeting was scheduled to be held during an IFTDO conference in Oslo, Norway, August 26 to August 31, 1974. ASTD would also prepare and distribute a quarterly newsletter to IFTDO members. IFTDO became a viable world federation.

Meeting the Challenges

In the 1970s, organization development was a popular form of training. Sensitivity training was popular, too, and programmed instruction was used extensively. The teaching methods of university professors were creeping into ASTD.

The ASTD membership was changing. Now there were divisions and special interest groups with representation on the ASTD Board of Directors. In 1974, the Women's Caucus was represented on the Board of Directors, as were special interest groups, black caucus, sales training division, organization development division, community development, media division, and international division.

The ASTD Board of Directors has since been restructured, and none of the groups mentioned above are represented on the Board. The 1974 Board of Directors was an unwieldy Board. Everyone had his own special interests, but the input from the grassroots of ASTD was terrific.

Some memories are best if they are forgotten, or not mentioned at all. On the other hand, bad memories can be very valuable if a lesson has been learned from them. I have a bitter memory of a special ASTD Board meeting being scheduled on December 8, 1973. The purpose of the meeting was to inform the Board of Directors that ASTD had a disastrous financial year. ASTD was going to finish the year with a loss of about $87,000. That would be quite a shock to a Board of Directors who thought everything was running smoothly.

The Board had not been told about a great loss at the Miami Conference or losses on seminars that ASTD sponsored. The organizing efforts for IFTDO had been successful, and AID was paying the bills, but there was no profit for ASTD.

The $87,000 loss became even more critical when the Board of Directors was told that the total assets of ASTD, including its building and office equipment, was worth about $125,000. With another disastrous month or two, ASTD would be bankrupt.

The Board of Directors faced up to the challenge. They became more interested in finances. All programs proposed by the ASTD staff had to be submitted for Board approval. The Board wanted to know the cost of each program, what the income was expected to be, and what the bottom line was. ASTD did a $240,000 turnaround the next year, and has shown a profit ever since that time. ASTD is now financially stable.

Changes Over the Years

How has ASTD changed over the years? We are a mature society now. Communication has improved. ASTD holds international conferences located in the United States. ASTD is still working with federal, state, and municipal governments to further the objectives of training. The *T+D Journal* is published monthly and gives members up-to-date information on what is happening and what is new. In addition, computers have given us instant access to the ASTD home office. The first *ASTD Training and Development Handbook* was published in the 1970s, and now we are using the third edition.

ASTD has a bookstore, which makes books on training available to trainers. ASTD keeps abreast of technology. A great amount of information can be obtained from ASTD, using the Internet. ASTD is financially stable. ASTD is doing a good job of carrying out the vision of our founding fathers, except for one thing: many chapters are decreasing in size. Some chapters are not in business anymore. My own chapter has gone belly-up, even though the chapter is listed in the ASTD network. I think that ASTD could support the chapters more than they do, or perhaps reestablish the regions as they once existed, with a regional vice president, who has contact with the chapters in his or her region. I miss the exchange of information that I get at chapter meetings.

Even though I am ninety years old, there is something good about keeping in touch with your past. Regardless of my feelings about chapters, I will be attending national conferences as long as I can get there, and I will be in touch with ASTD through the Internet and the *T+D Journal*.

Vincent A. Miller *is vice president, MMT International, Ltd., a consulting firm specializing in management, motivation, and technical training. He was the 1974 president of ASTD and served on its board of directors from 1971 through 1979. He was the principal organizer and first director of the ASTD International Division. He was one of the organizers and first secretary-treasurer of the International Federation of Training Organizations (IFTDO). Mr. Miller is the recipient of two prestigious awards from ASTD: the Gordon M. Bliss Award in 1974 and the International Trainer of the Year Award in 1979. He is the author of three books, including* The Guidebook for Global Trainers. *Mr. Miller turned ninety in February 2007 and still attends all ASTD conferences.*

Introduction
to the Inventories, Questionnaires, and Surveys Section

Inventories, questionnaires, and surveys are valuable tools for the HRD professional. These feedback tools help respondents take an objective look at themselves and at their organizations. These tools also help to explain how a particular theory applies to them or to their situations.

Inventories, questionnaires, and surveys are useful in a number of training and consulting situations: privately for self-diagnosis; one-on-one to plan individual development; in a small group to open discussion; in a work team to help the team to focus on its highest priorities; or in an organization to gather data to achieve progress. You will find that the use of inventories, questionnaires, and surveys enriches, personalizes, and deepens training, development, and intervention designs. Many can be combined with other experiential learning activities or articles in this or other *Annuals* to design an exciting, involving, practical, and well-rounded intervention. Each instrument includes the background necessary for understanding, presenting, and using it. Interpretive information, scales, and scoring sheets are also provided. In addition, we include the reliability and validity data contributed by the authors. If you wish additional information on any of these instruments, contact the authors directly. You will find their addresses and telephone numbers in the "Contributors" listing near the end of this volume.

The 2008 Pfeiffer Annual: Training includes two assessment tools in the following categories:

Consulting, Training, and Facilitating

Human Resource Development Liability Indicator, by John A. Sample

Leadership

Helping Leaders Learn to Lead, by Homer H. Johnson

Human Resource Development Liability Indicator

John A. Sample

Summary

Instructional designers, training and development specialists, chief learning officers, and human resource management personnel should be aware of the negative effect that faulty design, incompetent facilitation, and lack of transfer of learning may have on an organization. This paper provides several case examples of litigation involving the training and development function. A summary of essential steps for reducing the threat of liability is provided. The Human Resource Development Liability Indicator provides a quick summary of the potential liability for organizations.

Some readers will recall three significant industrial accidents that focused public attention on the importance for training employees and managers. The nuclear power accidents at Three Mile Island (U.S.A. in 1979) and Chernobyl (Ukraine in 1986) and the devastating chemical spill in Bhopal (India in 1984) were horrific to imagine—much less experience. The Challenger Space Shuttle disaster in 1986, the Columbia breakup in 2003, and the 1996 crash of a ValuJet plane into the Florida Everglades are additional examples of human and technological interfaces that may combine to produce deadly systemic outcomes.

A very active U.S. Congress during the 1960s and 1970s enacted groundbreaking legislation that included the Civil Rights Act of 1964 and the Occupational Safety Act of 1970. The Americans with Disabilities Act followed in 1990. Dozens of other state and federal acts have been enacted during the intervening years, many of which require or imply compliance to specific training (Sample, 1997). The financial scandals beginning in the mid-1990s led eventually to the Sarbanes-Oxley Act of 2002. More recently, a set of complex and confusing requirements have been added to the Federal Sentencing Guidelines for organizations convicted of federal crimes.

Representative Court Cases

The following case examples provide the reader with a glimpse of the kinds of training-related cases that may be litigated in state or federal courts. These cases are clearly not the expected norm for the human resource development profession; however, they do exemplify what may occur when incompetent design and facilitation occur in our training and development programs.

Adults Behaving Badly in Sales Training

A multi-state security business conducted a sales training program in which the employer was sued for violation of California's sexual harassment and gender discrimination laws, assault, battery, sexual battery, and intentional and negligent infliction of emotional distress. Both men and women sales personnel were routinely spanked during weekly sales training sessions for arriving late and other reasons by managers who conducted the training. These spankings were administered with a sign from a competing alarm sales business, caused bruising and tissue damage, and were used as a motivational tool in several offices over an extended period of time. Vulgar and sexist language by both managers and co-workers accompanied the spankings. The director of human resources for the employer, a certified California attorney, testified that if both men and women were spanked, it would not be considered sexual harassment! The plaintiff recovered damages of $500,000 plus punitive damages of $1,200,000 (*Orlando V. Alarm One Inc., 2006*).

Adventure-Based Training

An independent contract trainer hired by a telecommunications company conducted an adventure-based training program for craft-union personnel. The focus of the program included team building using various outdoor challenge exercises. The "swinging log" required that a team of employees stand on a suspended log. The team was responsible for making the log sway back and forth. A fifty-nine-year-old female employee fell off the log and broke her leg. She sued her employer and the contract trainer for damages. The trainer testified for about eight hours on behalf of his employer. The telecommunications company was found negligent and the trainer was not held liable by the jury (Sample & Hylton, 1996).

Federal Prosecution for Negligent Training

ValuJet flight 592 crashed over Florida in 1996. The airline's maintenance contractor, SaberTech, Inc., was responsible for safely disposing of used oxygen canisters. A detonating device on each canister had to be disabled by removal before being transported for recycling. Through a series of supervisory missteps, several boxes of canisters were loaded into the cargo hold of Flight 592, along with several large aircraft tires. A detonating device on one of the partially filled oxygen canisters accidentally ignited, causing a fire in the cargo hold that spread quickly to the tires. Smoke from the burning tires engulfed the plane quickly, and 110 people perished in the crash. SaberTech, Inc., and three employees were prosecuted at the federal and state levels. The lynchpin issue for the federal prosecution of this incident as a criminal case was failure to adequately train maintenance employees *(U.S. v. SaberTech, 2001)*.

Flip Charts and Participant Notes in Evidence!

One of the largest mini-market chains in California was sued by African-American women alleging discrimination in promotions to management. One of the exercises used in a managerial training program required that groups of men and women identify stereotypic behaviors and attitudes. The results of these exercises were captured on flip charts and participant notes that were later uncovered as part of the pre-trial discovery process. The comments by men as a group, captured on flip charts, were deemed evidence of discrimination. This case raises the importance for developing a records retention and destruction policy *(Stender V. Lucky Stores, 2001)*.

Essential Steps to Follow to Prevent Liability

By no means comprehensive, the following steps lay the foundation for current statutes and case law impacting the training and development function in organizations. These steps are consistent with best practices advocated by Eyres (1998), Mathiason and de Bernardo (1998), and Sample (1997, 2007). Industries vary by scope and depth of legal compliance requirements. The essential steps discussed below will apply to most organizations in the private and public sectors. Discuss the situation with an attorney if you believe that your organization may be subject to any special compliance or legal requirements.

Conduct Needs Assessments and Performance Analysis

Use a systematic and structured process to assess and document needs and analyze performance problems by individuals, teams, and units within an organization. Identify and systematically track internal trends that predict litigation (on-the-job accidents, insurance payouts, safety violations, complaints of harassment and violence, union grievances, complaints of differential treatment, etc.). Instruction must be adequate to the task and certainty for liability. The courts will use a test of reasonableness and fore-seeability to determine need for and adequacy of training.

Participate in national forums, professional and business associations that track and report litigation trends. The recent accounting and business scandals should not have been a surprise to anyone. Survey vendors and suppliers as to their continuing and developing liabilities.

Identify Training Goals of Strategic Importance

Continually review compliance and regulatory statutes for mandated training requirements. Identify "implied" or "hidden" training requirements from statutes and case law; consider implications for disparate impact and differential treatment in selecting who attends training. Do not deny training to those who must make decisions based on content of training, especially in the areas of safety, ethics, and federal compliance laws (EEO, ADA, OSHA, among others). Do not rely on "one shot" training experiences to satisfy compliance requirements. Strategically integrate compliance into the cultural fabric of the organization. The HRM (human resource management) and HRD (human resource development) functions must operate as partners—not adversaries!

Design Effective Training

Use a proven approach to design training that systematically links each of the fundamental phases of the process—analysis, design, development, implementation, and evaluation. Match the design of instruction to job-related requirements; insist that instructional goals and objectives drive the design process. Evaluation begins with the design phase. Incorporate performance testing as well as knowledge-based assessments of learning. Consider the legal implications of pre-testing participants. Harassment prevention training should cover all types of illegal harassment, not just harassment based on race or sex. Certain forms of training may invite litigation. Examples include non-traditional, new age, and adventure-based training. Accommodate the religious beliefs of participants when using "visualization" techniques that may impact personal beliefs and world views on work requirements. Certain types of exercises, such as role plays and simulations, if not expertly designed and facilitated, may give rise to litigation. Consider the legal effects of using English-language versions of instructional material with non-English-speaking employees, especially with safety-related and federal compliance laws.

Be aware that training may create a higher standard (or duty) of care in the performance of job tasks. Effective training may be a "trade secret" and/or appropriate for copyright registration. Establish a records retention and destruction policy; decide to what extent flip charts, participant notes, reaction ("smile sheets") evaluations, and test scores should be archived.

Select Qualified Instructors

Compliance-related training requires qualified instructors; examples include harassment prevention and safety-related training. The courts have held organizations responsible for incompetent and inappropriate behaviors of instructors, as was the case in the Alarm One Inc. case cited above. Review skills and formal qualifications (degrees, licenses and certifications) for recency and instructional competency; require periodic updating of qualifications.

Monitor Training

Monitor training sessions on a periodic basis to ensure conformity to learning objectives and lesson plans and organizational legal requirements. Inappropriate remarks during training by instructors or participants may form the basis for litigation; review instructional materials for evidence of bias. Failure to intervene by the trainer may result in litigation (addressing discriminatory comments and behaviors, threats of violence). Keep accurate records of attendance, location, and state of the physical training premises. Maintain copies of instructional objectives, lesson plans, and credentials of instructors. Training that causes death or injury may result in criminal penalties, including prison.

Ensure that records required by statute and administrative rules (such as OSHA, FEMA, Nuclear Regulatory Commission, and others) are maintained, accurate, and accessible. Ensure that those who require mandated training are not denied opportunities for training. Consider having an attorney conduct any training during which participants may voice biases that could be interpreted as evidence of discrimination or where incidents of liability may be identified and discussed. This strategy should maintain the attorney-client privilege.

Evaluation and Transfer of Learning

For compliance-related training, design evaluation processes that focus on expected job performance and the extent to which training resulted in compliant performance on the job. Ensure that managers and supervisors regularly monitor employee performance, including records of performance. Decide the extent to which reaction-level evaluations are useful. Discriminatory biases and allegations of liability could be written on these kinds of evaluations, all of which are discoverable. Consider alternative evaluation processes, such as having a trained instructor use a checklist of expected training behaviors to evaluate instructors. Immediately remediate and document if someone fails a competency standard related to safety or other areas of liability.

Theory Underlying the HRD Liability Indicator

The Human Resource Development Liability Indicator is designed to alert chief learning officers and related managers to the potential liability associated with the training and development function within their particular organizations. The items for the survey are drawn from research of state and federal statutes and court decisions, as well as information from scholarly and applied journals, including law reviews, and therefore meet the fundamental requirements for content validity. The HRD Liability Indicator has been used in graduate classes in human resource development and in conjunction with presentations to professional associations, such as The American Society for Training and Development.

The items do not reflect all possible training-related legal issues, only those that are most likely to be encountered in private- and public-sector organizations. Each organization has a responsibility to be aware of any special state and federal compliance laws that impact the safety and health of its employees, contractors, and the general public. Always seek competent legal counsel if there are any questions or lingering doubts.

Administering the HRD Liability Indicator

The human resource manager for small- and medium-sized businesses may use the Indicator to identify potential legal issues involving the training and development function. Larger organizations may want to use the Indicator with line managers as a tool for educating them to the potential liabilities associated with the training and development function, including on-the-job training and coaching activities.

Administration of the survey takes five minutes or less. Respondents are directed to read each item and to check those items that apply. The Indicator may be completed and retrieved without discussion and the data analyzed at a later time. The Indicator may also be used as part of a "lunch and learn" activity designed to remind managers and employers about their legal responsibilities. Finally, the indicator may be used as an icebreaker for an extended discussion on legal issues impacting the training and development function.

If the Indicator is used as a needs assessment tool, it is highly recommended that the results be discussed with a senior-level manager, the organization's human resource manager, manager for workplace learning and organization development, or corporate counsel. Consult with a competent attorney if unresolved questions pose potential liability.

The results of the survey should be considered highly confidential and proprietary. Disgruntled employees and plaintiffs' counsel may use such information in ways detrimental to an organization. Remember that such information may be requested as part of the pre-trial discovery process. Do not discuss the results of this survey outside the organization.

Disclaimer

This publication is designed to provide descriptive and illustrative material on general concepts and practices as they may apply to human resource development programs in business, government, and not-for-profit associations. While this information is timely and accurate, it does not constitute legal advice. *Readers are advised to consult competent legal counsel for specific advice on legal questions involving their organizations.*

References

Bennett-Alexander, D.D., & Hartman, L.P. (2001). *Employment law for business* (3rd ed.). New York: McGraw-Hill.

Eyres, P. (1998). *The legal handbook for trainers, speakers, and consultants.* New York: McGraw-Hill.

Mathiason, G.G., & de Bernardo, M. (1998). The emerging law of training. *The Federal Lawyer, 45*(4), 2536.

Sample, J.A. (1997). Liability and the HRD practitioner. In J.W. Pfeiffer (Ed.), *The 1997 annual: Developing human resources* (pp. 321–330). San Francisco, CA: Pfeiffer.

Sample, J.A. (2007). *The legal reference for human resource development and adult educators.* Melbourne, FL: Krieger Publishing.

Sample, J.A. & Hylton, R. (1996). Falling off a log and landing in court. *Training, 33*(5), 66–69.

John A. Sample, Ph.D., SPHR, *is a principal in Sample and Associates, a Tallahassee, Florida-based consulting firm that assists clients with a variety of performance-based solutions. Dr. Sample's text,* The Legal Reference for Human Resource Development and Adult Educators *(2007) explores issues and solutions for preventing or reducing litigation associated with the HRD function. He is also an associate professor in the graduate human resource development program at Florida State University (www.fsu.edu/~adult-ed/).*

Human Resource Development Liability Indicator

John A. Sample

The questions below are designed to help you to better determine potential liability associated with the training and development function for your organization. Read each statement and check those statements that are accurate for your organization. If you are not sure, check with the appropriate people in your organization to decide whether the statement applies. Each potential area of liability is linked to specific laws and court cases.

Refer to Interpretation of the Results for a brief summary of each area of potential liability.

If checked	**Refer to**

This organization. . .

_____ makes decisions about who will or will not attend training and development programs.	A
_____ has had an EEO investigation that alleged unfair practices regarding methods used to select who will attend training programs.	A
_____ uses qualifying tests as a predictor for successful completion of training and development programs.	A
_____ uses evaluation of participant learning as a predictor to validate employee or promotional selection methods.	A
_____ will likely have participants who have learning or physical disabilities apply for and attend HRD programs.	A
_____ has a history of complaints from OSHA alleging unsafe business practices.	B
_____ requires employees or contract personnel to perform tasks that are deemed hazardous by industry standards or regulatory agencies of the government.	B
_____ requires employees or contract personnel to use equipment or machinery that could result in serious injury or death if not used properly.	B

If checked   **Refer to**

This organization. . .

_____ requires employees to have contact with chemicals, hazardous materials, or blood-borne pathogens.	B
_____ has a history of litigation alleging negligent selection, retention, training, or supervision.	C
_____ has a history of claims for Workers' Compensation and other types of insurance claims.	C
_____ pays a higher percentage rate for Workers' Compensation insurance compared to other similar organizations.	C
_____ mandates adventure-based training programs for developing employees and managers.	D
_____ uses experiential exercises in a classroom setting in which participants may be expected to reveal and discuss personal beliefs and values.	D
_____ uses business practices or processes considered proprietary or secret.	E
_____ has subscriptions to magazines and technical, trade, or academic journals.	E
_____ develops training and development programs using print, computer-based instruction, multimedia applications, or e-learning software applications.	E
_____ has employees who are required to follow strict ethical guidelines in the performance of job duties.	F
_____ has officers, managers, or employees who could engage in criminal activities, such as fraud, embezzlement, and crimes against the environment, and so forth.	F

Interpretation of the Results

This interpretation key links responses from the HRD Liability Indicator to the following brief summary of statutes and related case decisions. Consult resources such as Eyres (1998), Bennett-Alexander and Hartman (2001), or Sample (2007) for more in-depth explanations for each of the following:

A. *Equal Employment Opportunity Act, Americans with Disability Act, Family Medical Leave Act.* As of 1999 the Equal Employment Opportunity Commission has mandated "periodic" training of managers and employees on laws related to illegal discrimination, particularly all forms of harassment. The various states have equivalent protections that may differ from the federal laws. California and Connecticut have mandatory harassment prevention training requirements. The ADA and FMLA have just as much litigation potential as violations of EEO laws.

B. *Occupational Safety and Health Act.* OSHA and related state laws governing health and safety have required and hidden requirements for compliance training. Different industries may have additional statutory requirements, such as the Nuclear Regulatory Commission, U.S. Centers for Disease Control, and the Department of Labor Mine Safety and Health Administration.

C. *Negligent Training.* Negligence is a private civil action arising out of the laws of torts and is governed in the various states by statutes and case law. Most instances of negligence are based on carelessness and other unintentional conduct that result in injuries to a person, although there are acts of intentional negligence and provisions for criminal negligence. Workers' Compensation statutes are a no-fault option for settling work-related injuries due to employer or employee negligence. It is not unusual for claims of negligent training to be positioned with allegations of negligent hiring, negligent supervision, and negligent retention.

D. *Adventure-Based and Experiential Learning.* Outdoor adventure programs that use challenge exercises (high- and low-ropes courses) for groups and individuals run the risk of physical injury if not expertly designed and managed by trained personnel. Such programs purport to increase self-esteem, confidence, and teamwork, for both individuals and groups. Experiential learning based on principles of radical psychology and extreme confrontation may result in allegations of negligent and intentional emotional distress. Certain Constitutional provisions regarding privacy and religious freedoms may be abridged if organizational facilitators delve too deeply into personal values and beliefs.

E. *Copyright and Trade Secrets.* Intellectual property includes copyright, trade secrets, patents, and trademark laws. Copyright and trade secrets are the most relevant for consideration by training and development personnel. Fair use of copyrighted materials for those in the private sector differs from those in not-for-profit educational institutions. An instructional designer or trainer in a corporation must obtain permission to use copyrighted materials. An instructor in a school or college has a limited fair use privilege that allows spontaneous use of certain materials for classroom instruction. Businesses should consider copyrighting their training and development materials, instructor manuals, and any other materials of proprietary importance. Such programs can be sold to other businesses. Trade secrets bind employees to secrecy regarding proprietary business methods, processes, and procedures that are unique to a business. Employees in the public sector are often required to sign non-disclosure agreements. Training and development materials can be included as a trade secret.

F. *Federal Sentencing Guidelines for Organizations.* Financial scandals during the past ten years have led to a revision in the sentencing requirements for organizations convicted of federal crimes. Organizations cannot be sentenced to prison; however, they may be fined, required to pay restitution, and placed on probation. Fines range from $5,000 to $72,500,000. Organizations found to be criminal enterprises can expect to be fined in such sum as to completely exhaust their assets, therefore closing down the business. Fines can be increased up to 400 percent or decreased by 95 percent, depending on the extent to which an organization complies with a 7-point set of compliance requirements. One of the requirements includes the development of an effective ethics compliance program. These guidelines have spawned a new industry of "ethics" and "compliance" officers, as well as consultants ready to provide training and documentation procedures.

Helping Leaders Learn to Lead

Homer H. Johnson

Summary

When successful executives are asked to identify their most important leadership learning experiences, their responses focus primarily on job challenges (e.g., new assignments) or hardships (e.g., failure to be promoted). Thus learning leadership seems to be highly related to job experiences. However, the data also suggest that, while successful leaders adapt and learn from such experiences, unsuccessful leaders do not and are often derailed by them. Thus, a crucial question is how we can assist leaders to better learn from their experiences, that is, how can we assist leaders to learn to lead. A questionnaire is presented that identifies eight strategies that will improve leader learning and assist leaders in learning to lead.

"Leadership can be learned, but cannot be taught," is an often-quoted adage. The message is that one cannot be taught leadership by the more traditional modes of instruction, such as classroom teaching, workshops, lectures from the boss, and others. Rather, leadership development comes through experience, particularly challenging experiences and hardships, together with reflecting on, and learning from, these experiences. Moreover, the evidence now suggests that successful executives are those who best learn from these challenging experiences and have the ability to adjust and adapt their behavior to better meet the demands of more complex and challenging situations.

As an example of this line of thought, consider one of the seminal studies by McCall and his associates at the Center for Creative Leadership (Lindsey, Holmes, & McCall, 1987; McCall, Lombardo, & Morrison, 1998). In this study, successful executives were asked to list their most significant leadership learning experiences. The results were quite consistent: The two highest-ranking types of significant learning experiences were "hardships" and "challenging experiences." "Hardships" included business failures, failure to obtain an expected promotion, and being fired. Interestingly enough, also included in this category were personal traumas such as divorce and a death in the family. The other high-ranking category, "challenging experiences," consisted of experiences such as building an operation from scratch, managing a turnaround operation, being part of a task force, and being given increased responsibility in terms of people or functions.

A surprising finding of this study was the low ranking that executives gave to educational programs such as conferences, workshops, in-house training programs, and graduate degree programs. Many of these programs, such as in-house training programs, are specifically designed to develop leaders. Given the ubiquity and volume of these educational activities, it seems important to ask the question: When in the leadership development process would these activities have the greatest impact on developing leader skills?

Several other studies have found similar results. For example, Ready (1994) asked leaders to identify their top learning experiences. Job assignments, projects, and task forces ranked number one. These experiences look very similar to the "challenging experiences" reported above. The category that ranked second was "coaching and performance feedback," which could also challenge a leader's ways of operating, as well as encourage a critical reflection of one's management style. As with the McCall studies, traditional management education programs did not score very high on the list of important learning experiences. For example, university executive education programs ranked very low as important learning experiences, and in-company programs were reported to have little usefulness except in developing understanding of the company's strategic vision.

Ready concluded that "to develop leadership capacity one must be presented with challenging opportunity and must be ready and capable of acting on it. The lessons gained from this opportunity will be leveraged considerably when the individual is offered honest, thoughtful, and timely feedback on his or her performance. In addition to opportunity and feedback, the person must have the time and capacity to reflect on this feedback, to internalize it, and to transfer the lessons learned to day-to-day behaviors" (p. 27).

Using a slightly different approach, Leslie and Velsor (1996) looked at why executives derail. These researchers found that the most important factor for the success of their group of successful executives was their ability to adapt and develop. Respondents described successful leaders as "growing" and "maturing over time" as the job or the organization expanded. Successful leaders were also characterized as "learning from mistakes" and "learning from direct feedback." In contrast, the leading cause of executive derailment (executives who were fired or demoted) among the unsuccessful executives was their failure to adapt and change their management styles. While both successful and unsuccessful executives were provided ample challenges, the unsuccessful executives were unable to learn from these experiences.

These studies strongly suggest that one key component in the development of leaders is the opportunity to experience new and challenging job assignments and duties. However, a second crucial component is that the leaders or potential leaders must be able to "learn from" these experiences. Challenging experiences in themselves are not enough to foster leader development, as is evidenced by the numbers of leaders who "derailed" after facing new challenges. Whether the leader or potential leader also learns from these experiences seems to be critical for the development of leadership.

The important question is how we can help leaders better learn from their experiences. As the research cited above indicates, leaders have to take responsibility for their own learning. Not only do they have to seek new opportunities for growth, but they have to employ learning strategies in those new opportunities, strategies that will help them learn and grow as leaders.

The Managing Your Learning Questionnaire

In order to assist managers and leaders to develop their learning capabilities, a questionnaire was developed that covers eight key strategies for how managers and leaders can manage their own learning. The questionnaire looks at whether the person uses personal development plans, seeks new experiences, utilizes feedback, learns from criticism, uses reflective learning, and creates a learning environment. Each of the eight strategies included on the questionnaire has been found to relate to effective leadership development.

Briefly summarized, the eight strategies are:

1. *Utilizes personal development goals and plans.* Do you set personal development goals? Do you have a personal development plan that you review and update regularly? Do you review your growth with your manager and others and use this input to update your plan?

2. *Seeks new experiences.* Do you seek out assignments that will develop your skills in areas in which you lack experience or competence? Do you seek assignments that push you out of your "comfort zone" and expose you to new people and challenges?

3. *Approaches decision making as learning.* Do you approach new experiences with an open mind? Do you obtain broad input from key people before making a tough decision? Do you approach new situations as learning opportunities?

4. *Seeks and utilizes feedback.* Do you ask for feedback on your performance during and after a new or difficult assignment? Do you ask for advice on how you can become more effective from those you work for and with?

5. *Learns from the negative.* Do you avoid responding defensively when some-one criticizes your work; do you instead use the criticism to improve your behavior? Do you discuss your failures with others to obtain their input on how you might learn from them?

6. *Uses reflective learning.* Do you reflect on important events at work or home with the goal of improving your decisions or behavior? Do you analyze your success and failures for ideas for your personal improvement?

7. *Reflection–action–feedback loop.* Do you use the process of reflecting on a pre-vious situation to help improve your behavior in a similar situation, then try the new behaviors when that situation arises again, and then ask for feed-back on your effectiveness in the situation, again reflecting on the outcomes?

8. *Creates a learning environment.* Do you create a "learning environment" with co-workers in which information and knowledge are openly shared? Are you open and honest with others regarding their performance and behavior and expect the same from them?

Scoring the Learning Questionnaire

The recommended method for scoring the questionnaire is to score each of the eight strategies individually and not to calculate an overall or total score. The purpose of the questionnaire is to have the respondents begin thinking about how they can learn from their experiences. Typically, the respondents fill out the questionnaire to ex-amine their current use of each of the strategies; then there is a discussion of each of the strategies with examples of their use; and finally the respondents are asked to develop action plans to increase their use of the behaviors described in each strategy.

Using the Questionnaire

As noted above, the overall purpose of the questionnaire is to assist the leader or po-tential leader to begin thinking about learning from experience. The list of strategies covered by the questionnaire is not meant to be definitive, but rather is designed to begin a discussion on how one can use one's experiences to become a more effec-tive leader.

For example, the questionnaire has been used in a mini workshop on "How Lead-ers Learn to Lead." The participants in the workshop are first given a brief description of the McCall and Lindsey studies noted above and asked to guess which of the categories were ranked the highest by successful executives as their most important leadership learning experiences. The participants are also asked to explain why they make their choices. After completing that exercise, the results of the study are presented and discussed.

Following that exercise, the Leslie and Velsor study (also cited above) is reviewed to emphasize that experience itself is not sufficient. The other critical component is to learn from experiences. Many leaders have difficulty learning from, and adjusting to, challenging experiences and consequently may derail because of these experiences. Thus, for some leaders, challenging experiences enhance their leadership development, while for those who fail to adapt and learn, the experiences are the cause of their derailment.

This leads into a brief discussion of how leaders learn. Next, the participants complete the questionnaire. Following that, each of the eight strategies is discussed. A final part of the workshop is a discussion of how the participants might increase their use of each of the learning strategies covered in the questionnaire (or other areas may be suggested), and then the development of action plans to accomplish these goals.

The format of the workshop varies with its purpose. In one variation, the workshop is used in conjunction with receiving a 360-degree feedback report, with an emphasis on the need for managers to take control of their own development and suggesting the eight strategies as a means for doing this. In another variation of the workshop, the final part of the workshop is a module on "reflective learning," in which the participants are taught both reflection and journaling techniques and how to apply these techniques to the development of their leadership skills.

References

Leslie, J., & Velsor, E. (1996). *A look at derailment today: North America and Europe.* Greensboro, NC: Center for Creative Leadership.

Lindsey, E.H., Holmes, V., & McCall, H.M., Jr. (1987). *Key events in executive lives.* Greensboro, NC: Center for Creative Leadership.

McCall, M.W., Jr., Lombardo, M.M., & Morrison, A.N. (1998). *Lessons from experience.* Lexington, MA: Lexington Books.

Ready, D. (1994). *Champions of change.* Lexington, MA: International Consortium for Executive Development Research.

Homer H. Johnson, Ph.D., *is a professor in the School of Business Administration at Loyola University, Chicago, where he teaches courses in leadership and strategy. He is the author of numerous books and articles and is the case editor of the* Organization Development Practitioner. *His most recent book (with Linda Stroh) is titled* Basic Essentials of Effective Consulting *and was published by LEA in 2006.*

Managing Your Learning Questionnaire

Homer H. Johnson

Instructions: For each statement below, write a number in the blank that best describes how often or consistently you believe the statement is true for you.

4 = true all of the time   3 = true most of the time   2 = sometimes true   1 = generally not true

Utilizes Personal Development Goals and Plans

_____ I set personal development goals for myself that are tied to work performance.

_____ I have a personal development plan for myself, which I review and update regularly.

_____ I periodically review my growth as a manager or employee with my manager and use this experience to set personal improvement goals.

_____ I keep a personal journal to record my reflections and learning.

Seeks New Experiences

_____ I seek out jobs and assignments that will develop my skills and experience in areas in which I lack competence or experience.

_____ I seek out assignments and jobs that have a high degree of personal responsibility and that challenge my skills as a leader.

_____ I enjoy assignments in which I am challenged to deliver a high level of performance both personally and for my unit or project.

_____ I look for assignments that will push me out of my "comfort zone" and expose me to new people and challenges.

Approaches Decision Making as Learning

_____ I approach new experiences with an open mind and don't assume I have the answers.

_____ I obtain broad input from key people before making a decision, but having made the decision, I take full responsibility for the consequences.

4 = true all of the time   3 = true most of the time   2 = sometimes true   1 = generally not true

_____ When approaching a new decision situation, I first get a good understanding of the situation and the options before making a decision.

_____ I approach new situations as learning opportunities for me to better understand the dynamics of leadership and decision making.

Seeks and Utilizes Feedback

_____ I ask for feedback on my performance during and after finishing a new or difficult assignment.

_____ I ask for advice on how I can become more effective from the people who work for and with me.

_____ I use my performance appraisal and other reviews as a constructive opportunity to learn how I might improve.

Learns from the Negative

_____ I readily admit and take responsibility for my mistakes and do not blame others.

_____ I don't respond defensively when someone criticizes my work; rather, I use this as a basis to improve what I have been doing.

_____ I discuss my failures with others to obtain their input on how I might learn from them.

_____ I quickly recognize when I am getting angry or frustrated or defensive and take steps to avoid negative consequences.

Uses Reflective Learning

_____ I reflect on important events at work or home with the goal of improving my decisions or behavior.

_____ If a meeting or project doesn't go well, I review what happened and use this to improve my actions.

_____ I analyze my successes and failures for ideas for improvement.

_____ After finishing a meeting/project, I ask myself what I learned that will improve my skills or thinking.

4 = true all of the time   3 = true most of the time   2 = sometimes true   1 = generally not true

Reflection–Action–Feedback Loop

_____ If warranted, I will change my perspective and my behavior based on what I learned through reflecting on a situation.

_____ Based on reflection and analysis, I am willing to make significant changes in my thinking and behavior, even though they might be difficult or painful.

_____ When I attempt new behaviors, I look at whether they were effective or not and take that into consideration in deciding whether to try those again.

Creates a Learning Environment

_____ I help create a "learning environment" with co-workers in which information and knowledge are openly shared.

_____ I am open and honest with others regarding their behavior and performance and expect the same from them—the goal being to help each other improve.

_____ People in my work unit are good about sharing their observations and ideas about how we can improve our unit performance.

Introduction

to the Articles and Discussion Resources Section

The Articles and Discussion Resources Section is a collection of materials useful to every facilitator. The theories, background information, models, and methods will challenge facilitators' thinking, enrich their professional development, and assist their internal and external clients with productive change. These articles may be used as a basis for lecturettes, as handouts in training sessions, or as background reading material. This section will provide you with a variety of useful ideas, theoretical opinions, teachable models, practical strategies, and proven intervention methods. The articles will add richness and depth to your training and consulting knowledge and skills. They will challenge you to think differently, explore new concepts, and experiment with new interventions. The articles will continue to add a fresh perspective to your work.

The 2008 Pfeiffer Annual: Training includes fifteen articles, in the following categories:

Individual Development: Developing Awareness and Understanding

**Changing Attitudes and Behaviors, by Mel Silberman

Individual Development: Personal Growth

Assertiveness: A Skill for Today's Workplace, by Narendra Kardam, Nikhil Kulshrestha, and Shruti Jain

Individual Development: Life/Career Planning

**Turbulent Change: Imagining the Future, by Peter R. Garber

Individual Development: Change and Risk Taking

**Living on the Edge: Leading Software Training Projects, by Brooke Broadbent

---

**Topic is change focused

Individual Development: Stress and Burnout

> Measurement of Stress in Organizational Roles: Revalidating the Framework, by Avinash Kumar Srivastav and Udai Pareek

Communication: Coaching and Encouraging

> Managing with Social Styles™: Ten Strategies, by Mary J. Buchel

Problem Solving: Change and Change Agents

> **Getting Smart About System Change: Developing Whole System IQ™, by Sherene Zolno

Groups and Teams: Techniques to Use with Groups

> The W.I.T. Model for Debriefing Team Initiatives, by Cher Holton

Consulting/Training: Organizations: Their Characteristics and How They Function

> **A Champion's Role in Sustaining a Distance Learning Program, by Aynsley Leigh Hamel and Zane L. Berge

Consulting/Training: Strategies and Techniques

> **Is Anyone Doing Formative Evaluation? by James L. Moseley and Nancy B. Hastings

> Trainer's Guides Revisited, by George Hall

Facilitating: Theories and Models

> **Applying Action Learning in Assessing Facilitation Skills: An English National Health Service Case Study, by Catherine Guelbert

Facilitating: Techniques and Strategies

> **Move It or Lose It: Using Interaction to Engage Adults, by Gail Hahn

Leadership: Strategies and Techniques

> Learn-Ability: A Leader's Most Important Competence, by Aviv Shahar

Leadership: Top-Management Issues and Concerns

> Customer Dynamics: Utilizing Customer Feedback to Improve Your Organization's Performance, by Carol Ann Zulauf and Karl E. Sharicz

Although focused primarily on change, this section includes a wide variety of other topics as well. The range of articles presented encourages thought-provoking discussion about the present and future of HRD. We have done our best to categorize the articles for easy reference; however, many of the articles encompass a range of topics, disciplines, and applications. If you do not find what you are looking for under one category, check a related category. In some cases we may place an article in the "Training" *Annual* that also has implications for "Consulting" and vice versa. As the field of HRD continues to grow and develop, there is more and more crossover between training and consulting. Explore all the contents of both volumes of the *Annual* in order to realize the full potential for learning and development that each offers.

Changing Attitudes and Behaviors

Mel Silberman

Summary

Most individuals and organizations feel that they could be more effective. However, this typically entails change, and many people are resistant to change. This article explores some of the areas most resistant to change initiatives and presents a process designed to help individuals and organizations successfully implement change.

Arenas of Change

In every organization, there are attitudes and behaviors among leaders and employees that reduce its effectiveness. These attitudes and behaviors cluster in what I would call "arenas of change." Following are six arenas in which uncertainties, tensions, and resistance often occur:

1. *Customer Service.* Any organization that must attract and retain its customers needs its members to embrace a customer orientation. If customers are seen as individuals to be taken for granted or merely tolerated, those customers will become dissatisfied and go elsewhere with their business. Moreover, an indifferent stance toward customers is dangerous, even in circumstances in which customers do not have a choice as to where a need is fulfilled. This typically occurs in the public sector, such as with a governmental agency, a public educational institution, and so forth. Not happy with their experience, customers become less appreciative and hence less supportive of the organization.

2. *Safety.* Safety is a paramount concern in any organization where harmful events can happen to employees and customers. To ensure safety, procedures have to be followed that minimize danger. (A simple example is the wearing of a hard hat at a construction site.) Often, these procedures are unappealing. They

may create personal discomfort, add time and stress to work assignments, and require extensive knowledge acquisition and training.

3. *Teamwork.* Much of an organization's work occurs through small teams. Unfortunately, collaboration does not come easily. It takes a long time for a team to become high-performing. Also, it is often frustrating to work effectively with others and many people prefer to "do it themselves." Individual styles and temperaments also interfere with teamwork. If a person is impatient or needs personal space to be effective, he or she will be a hindrance to a project team.

4. *Process Improvement.* In order to improve quality and efficiency, many organizations need to rethink how they do things. The rub is that most people don't like change. They are used to "business as usual," preferring the familiarity of continually doing things the way they've always been done. Furthermore, they are afraid of the risks involved in committing to what's not yet been "proven." Some hold back and others actively resist the changes being suggested or mandated.

5. *Diversity.* Increasingly, the workplace has become more culturally diverse in terms of differences in gender, race, ethnicity, country of origin, special needs, age, and many other aspects. The mix can make some people uncomfortable. Some people find it difficult to understand people who act, speak, and perhaps value things differently than they do. Moreover, status issues abound. Who's in the majority? Who's in the minority? Who are the leaders? Who are the followers?

6. *Role Expectations.* Traditional roles of managers and employees allowed for clear expectations. One group's members were the leaders, and the other the followers. Nowadays, employees are encouraged to be self-directing learners and take greater initiative and are empowered to make more decisions on their own. In turn, managers are expected to be coaches, team leaders, and facilitators, as opposed to controllers. This change in role expectations leads to confusion and resistance in many organizations. Even when the change is embraced, people are not sure how to adapt.

The Steps in Changing Attitudes and Behaviors

If you are charged with the responsibility to help promote change in the arenas just cited (or in many additional ones), you need a process that will guide your efforts. I would like to suggest a five-step process:

1. Create Openness

2. Promote Understanding

3. Consider New Attitudes and Behaviors

4. Experiment

5. Obtain Support

Create Openness

The first challenge is to "get your foot in the door," as opposed to "getting the door slammed in your face." Recognizing that the people you are hoping to change may be resistant to your efforts, you want to be seen as open and trustworthy, without an agenda that imposes change. In these initial attempts to build receptiveness to change, the first order of business is to get people to feel open to getting their concerns "out on the table" and to validate them. It's important for people to realize that you are interested in their feelings and points of view and that you see them as "real." That can't happen unless they feel safe enough to express themselves and you can empathize with their feelings and acknowledge the kernels of truth in what they believe. Here are some concerns that might surface if you do this.

Trying to understand someone who is difficult implies that you're sympathetic or even forgiving. When interpersonal skills training encourages participants to "seek to understand before being understood," some participants are concerned that doing so will give a person who has done something unacceptable the impression that the behavior is okay. These participants have difficulty seeing that understanding does not imply acceptance. Rather, it is an attempt to figure out the best way to deal with people instead of writing them off or being angry with them.

Some safety procedures do not really protect us. Sometimes, employees object to safety requirements, such as wearing ear plugs to avoid hearing injuries, because they may lead to other problems, such as not being able to hear a co-worker.

Customers get the idea that they can treat us any way they want. Such a conclusion is often the belief of participants in a customer-service training program in a context in which they have already experienced considerable abuse from customers.

The team concept means that you can't take any initiative without checking in with others. Often, people resist team training because they think it will rob them of personal control.

If beliefs such as those just cited are freely aired, it is now possible to examine them and perhaps find non-threatening ways to challenge the assumptions behind them. This creates some openness to considering new attitudes and behaviors. If, instead, these attitudes and behaviors are simply "urged" by the training program, they may fall on deaf ears.

Promote Understanding

Once participants are open to examining and challenging their beliefs, they will be more willing to accept new information and make shifts in the way they see things.

For example, people previously resistant to teamwork may now be open to the fact that it takes a while for a team to form, storm, norm, and eventually perform. As a result, they may become more patient about the trials and tribulations of their own work teams. Or customer service trainees may now become impressed by the fact that fewer than 10 percent of all unhappy customers complain. They come to realize that active attempts to assist customers and obtain feedback from them is vital to an organization's ability to retain them as clients. Or participants may be made more open to seeking feedback from their bosses when they become aware that such an action is often viewed favorably. Seeking feedback (but not fishing for compliments) shows that you are interested in your own development and want to take the initiative in improving your performance.

Consider New Attitudes and Behaviors

The next step is to invite participants to engage in experiences in which they see new attitudes and behaviors in action. Those experiences can be had through a variety of methods, from real-world activities to simulated ones. When well-crafted and well-debriefed, these experiences can often develop a positive motivation to try out new ways.

Typically, participants in these experiences need to feel safe. While it is important to eventually up the challenge level to master new approaches and skills, participants tend to be more open to exploring new ones if they don't feel judged or embarrassed as they "try them on for size." They also need some time and space to get used to them. Therefore, rushing this stage often leads to resistance.

Experiment

If the experiences in the previous steps have been insightful, motivating, and confidence-building, then the work of change can really go forward. At this juncture (usually when the training is over or between sessions), people can select new activities and commit themselves to applying them back on the job. I like to suggest that this process be called "an experiment in change," instead of the more mundane term "action plan." People are more open to this back-on-the-job application if *they* view it as an experiment in which they find out how useful the new attitude or skill is to *them.* We shouldn't kid ourselves. Most people will not persist with a change unless they find that it is successful. Experimenting allows people to test their wings and find initial success to sustain themselves for further application.

Often, people leave a good training program with so much enthusiasm that they make the mistake of going for broke and then fizzle out when results don't come quickly. Therefore, it's vital to encourage participants to try on a small change first and see what happens. *Less is more.*

Obtain Support

Changes don't last unless they are "lived." Even if people are pumped up about a change in attitude or behavior, they usually find that, while making some headway, they quickly relapse. Real change comes only by overcoming obstacles that are in the way in our daily life.

In this last critical step, people need help in identifying their ongoing needs for support. In particular, they need help in identifying the assistance they need and how to request it and maintain it.

Conclusion

Changing behavior is never an easy process. However, the payoff for individuals and organizations can be great if more effective and productive behaviors are implemented. By considering those barriers that must be overcome and utilizing the five-step process presented in this article, you can put yourself and your organization on the road to greater success.

Mel Silberman *is a psychologist known internationally as a pioneer in the areas of active learning, interpersonal intelligence, and team development. He is also president of Active Training, a provider of products, seminars, and publications in his areas of expertise. He has more than thirty-five years of experience creating and honing techniques that inspire people to be people smart, learn faster, and collaborate effectively. Mel is a regular speaker at conferences of the American Society for Training and Development, the International Society for Performance Improvement,* Training *magazine, and the North American Simulation and Gaming Association. Mel received his Ph.D. in educational psychology from the University of Chicago. His book,* 101 Ways to Make Training Active, *was voted one of the five best training and development books of all time by* Training *magazine. Mel has served as editor of* The ASTD Training and Performance Sourcebook *and* The ASTD OD and Leadership Sourcebook, *both leading annual collections. He is also editor of* The Handbook of Experiential Learning.

Assertiveness
A Skill for Today's Workplace
Narendra Kardam, Nikhil Kulshrestha, and Shruti Jain

Summary

Assertiveness is the ability to express thoughts and feelings in a way that clearly states your needs and keeps the lines of communication with others open. It's about finding win/win solutions. It is about standing up for personal rights and expressing thoughts, feelings, and beliefs in direct, honest, and appropriate ways that do not violate another person's rights. After describing how to identify assertive behavior, the authors provide an opportunity for readers to assess a variety of behaviors. They then present their tuning fork strategy for developing assertiveness skills.

Assertiveness: The Broad Concept

Each and every individual, during the course of his or her life, from one scenario to another, from one situation to another, goes through four life positions. These four life positions (from the transactional analysis discipline), shown as a grid in Figure 1, are known as the "OK Corral." The quotation in each box typifies the attitude of each life position. And individuals who conform to these attitudes are classified as shown in the italics.

People move around the grid depending on the situation, but have a preferred position that they tend to revert to. This is strongly influenced by experiences and decisions in early life.

Figure 1. The OK Corral: Life Positions and Attitude

I'm Not OK, You're OK

This is the "get away from" position. These people feel sad, inadequate, or even stupid in comparison to others. They undervalue their skills and contribution and withdraw from problems. The trait reflected here is called passiveness or passivity.

Passive people express their feelings, thoughts, and beliefs in a manner easily disregarded by others. The basic message is, "My feelings don't matter; only yours do. My thoughts aren't important; yours are the only ones worth listening to. I am nothing; you are superior."

I'm Not OK, You're Not OK

This is the "get nowhere" position. These people feel confused or aimless. They lack clarity of focus. They don't see the point of doing anything, and so usually don't bother. The trait reflected here is called confusion or sometimes manipulation.

I'm OK, You're Not OK

These people are in the "get rid of" position. They tend to get angry and hostile and are smug and superior. They belittle others, whom they view as incompetent and untrustworthy, and are often competitive and power-hungry. The trait reflected here is called aggressiveness or aggression.

Aggressive individuals' goal is to get their own way, no matter the cost to others. The basic message is, "This is what I think; you're stupid for believing differently. This is what I want; what you want is not important." The "feel-good" factor of getting one's way, though, is usually short-term.

I'm OK, You're OK

These people are in the "get on with" position. They're confident and happy about life and work, and interact by collaboration and mutual respect, even when they disagree. The trait reflected here is called assertiveness.

All four positions have bearing on an individual's thinking and communication. For the purposes of this article, we will focus on the "assertive" box.

Assertiveness Defined

Assertiveness is the ability to express one's thoughts and feelings in a way that clearly states one's needs and keeps the line of communication open with the other (Ryan & Travis, 2004).

Assertiveness entails conduct that enables an individual to think in a positive manner about himself or herself and others, to be open to ideas and suggestions, and be willing to accept change if the need so arises.

Assertive people . . .

1. See everyone as equals with equal rights and equal responsibility.

2. Find win/win solutions.

3. Stand up for personal rights and express thoughts, feelings, and beliefs in direct, honest, and appropriate ways that do not violate another person's rights.

4. Are willing to express themselves: "This is what I think. This is what I feel. This is how I see the situation."

5. Focus on communication and mutuality: to give and get respect, to ask for fair play, and to leave room for adjustment and compromise when the rights and needs of two persons conflict.

Advantages

What are the advantages of assertiveness? What do you gain by its use? Assertiveness. . .

- Is a necessary skill for human survival;
- Is a reflector of positive mental health;
- Increases the chances of our needs being met;
- Allows us to remain in control;
- Brings greater self-confidence;
- Lets us have greater confidence in others;
- Reduces conflicts and arguments;
- Reduces stress; and
- Increases the likelihood that we will lead a happy personal and professional life.

Myths

What are some common beliefs about assertiveness that are not true?

Myth 1: "I will get what I want."

Not necessarily. Assertiveness is not a form of manipulation; otherwise no mutual respect would exist. Rather, it is based on the concepts of communication, negotiation, and compromise.

Myth 2: "There is a need to be assertive in all situations."

Not true. You may choose to be non-assertive when:

1. Dealing with overly sensitive individuals who become threatened when faced with open communication.
2. Unusual circumstances call for special understanding and compassion.
3. Chances of misinterpretation are high.

Myth 3: "Others will be assertive if I am assertive."

Not necessarily. Others may respond with confusion, passivity, or aggression or they may withdraw completely.

Indicators of Assertiveness

Assertiveness within an individual can easily be identified. Use of phrases like, "Take my word for it," "Trust me," and "I have no doubt about it" to a great extent make it easier to recognize assertive individuals. By considering those factors shown in Column 1 of Table 1, an individual can be identified as assertive or not, based on the indicators described in Column 2.

Table 1. Indicators of Assertiveness

Factors to Be Observed	Manner of Approach
Sense of responsibility	Share praise
	Shoulder blame
	Not passing the buck
Motivation	Develop positive attitude in self and other
	Act as a catalyst
Keen interest	Ask questions for clarity of the objective
	Listen attentively
Honest and direct in manner	Don't take the easy way out
	Adopt a tough but acceptable path
	Establish sender credibility
Performance commensurate with abilities	Whole-hearted effort for success
	Act as a catalyst

How Assertive Are You?

1. Do you often find that others compel you into thinking their way?

2. Is it difficult for you to express your feelings openly and honestly?

3. Do you sometimes lose control and become angry with others?

4. Do you yell at your teammates when they don't agree with your ideas?

5. Do you say "yes" when you actually want to say "no"?

If you responded to any of these in the affirmative, you lack assertiveness.

If you answered "no" to all of the questions, you probably behave with some level of assertion. Understanding how assertive you are requires answers to questions like the ones that follow:

- Am I saying what I really wanted to say? And how often?

- Am I clear and understandable?

- Am I being direct and unapologetic in what I say?

- Do I maintain good eye contact?

- Do I make appropriate use of gestures and facial expressions?

- Do my listeners agree with the message?

- Do I use a level, well-regulated, non-threatening voice?

- Do I avoid whining, pleading, or sarcasm?

- Do I express myself honestly and accept responsibility for the message?

- Do I feel pleased and rewarded by being able to express my thoughts and feelings?

- Do I select the appropriate time to be assertive with others?

Assesing Behavior

The situations presented below will give you an opportunity to test your level of understanding about assertion and other behaviors. For each situation, indicate whether the response is passive, aggressive, assertive, or confused. The answers are provided in Table 2 at the end of this section.

Situation 1

Your friend has just complimented you on how well dressed you are and how nice you look. You feel pleased, and you say:

   a. "Oh come on, you're just saying that to be nice. You probably say that to everybody."

   Assertive   Aggressive   Passive   Confused

b. "Thank you."

Assertive   Aggressive   Passive   Confused

c. "Oh, I bought this on sale."

Assertive   Aggressive   Passive   Confused

d. "Yeah, life is full of fun."

Assertive   Aggressive   Passive   Confused

Situation 2

Your family has just criticized you because they didn't like what you prepared for the evening meal. You say:

a. "Oh I didn't know that the food was bad. Anyway, I will not cook any more of it in the future."

Assertive   Aggressive   Passive   Confused

b. Nothing

Assertive   Aggressive   Passive   Confused

c. "Shut up! If you don't like what I cook, you cook it yourself!"

Assertive   Aggressive   Passive   Confused

d. "I think your criticism is unfair. Tell me what you like that I can cook next time."

Assertive   Aggressive   Passive   Confused

Situation 3

You bought a shirt and, when you brought it home, you found it to have a flaw in it. You don't want the item as it is, so you've returned it to the store. The clerk has just said, "It's sale merchandise. Besides, no one will ever notice it." You say:

a. "Well, I still want to return this one and either get my money refunded or exchange it for one that is not defective. I do not want this one."

Assertive   Aggressive   Passive   Confused

b. "Look, give me my money back. I don't have all day for you to waste my time."

   Assertive   Aggressive   Passive   Confused

c. "Well, I suppose I can keep it, if you're sure it won't show."

   Assertive   Aggressive   Passive   Confused

d. "I think you have cheated me. I will just call the police."

   Assertive   Aggressive   Passive   Confused

Situation 4

You and your partner are dining out at a moderately expensive restaurant. You have ordered a medium-rare steak. When the steak is served, it is rather over-done. You:

a. Grumble to yourself but eat the steak and say nothing to the waiter. When you pay the bill and the cashier asks, "How was everything?" You say, "Fine."

   Assertive   Aggressive   Passive   Confused

b. Say to the waiter, "I ordered my steak to be cooked medium. This is over-done. Please bring me one cooked medium."

   Assertive   Aggressive   Passive   Confused

c. Get up and complain to the cashier about the poor service. "If people can't cook what I order, I am not going to eat here!"

   Assertive   Aggressive   Passive   Confused

d. You yell at the waiter and walk out of the restaurant.

   Assertive   Aggressive   Passive   Confused

Table 2. Correct Responses to the Situations

Option	Situation 1	Situation 2	Situation 3	Situation 4
A	Passive	Confused	Assertive	Passive
B	Assertive	Passive	Aggressive	Assertive
C	Passive	Aggressive	Passive	Aggressive
D	Confused	Assertive	Confused	Confused

If you missed some of these answers, you may wish to review the earlier explanation of the OK Corral.

The Tuning Fork Strategy

The strategy that we propose is called the Tuning Fork Strategy of assertiveness development. We have named it that because, like a tuning fork, it has two main aspects: when one arm of a tuning fork vibrates, the other also starts vibrating a little later and ultimately both get in sync to produce a holistic effect.

Preview

There are two main phases of the strategy—visualization (preparation) and realization (implementation). Each has two sub-steps.

1. Visualization of the goal or situation

    A. You understand and summarize the facts of the situation.

    B. You indicate your feelings about the situation.

2. Realization of the goal or situation

    A. You state your requirements, reasons, and benefits to the other party.

    B. You motivate others to find the best solution.

The Strategy in Detail

Visualization/Preparation

    A. Make sure you understand and can summarize the facts of the situation for yourself.

    - Create a positive first impression.

        Short and sweet introduction for establishing a good rapport

        Draft a brief written account of the issue

    - Be thoughtful about your use of language.

        Clear and direct

        Receiver-oriented

Lucid and winning

Holds the listeners captive, if not spell-bound, for example: "We would love to. . ." (state mutually beneficial purpose)

B. Be able to describe your feelings about the situation.

- Present with empathy.

  Showcase your ability to understand

  Maintain interest, perhaps through use of anecdotes, fables, or shared experiences

  Use a confident approach

- Focus on "How" of a statement rather than "What" to bring clarity. For example:

  "I feel comfortable. . ."(state feelings)

  "I want to. . . ."

  "I don't want you to. . . ."

  "I liked it when you asked about. . . ."

  "Would you like to be a part of. . . ?"

Realization/Implementation

A. State your requirements, reasons, and benefits to the other party.

- Clear statement of the problem

- Clearly stated requirements

- Clear-cut benefits to others

- Understandable and plausible reasons, for example, "I would like to . . . (state requirements). In this way, we will be able to work together more productively (benefits to other party) because this will increase our production (reasons)."

B. Motivate others to find the best solution.

- Throw open the presentation for discussion and brainstorming.

- Provide an equal platform for all to express their thoughts and ideas freely.

- Encourage everyone to participate.

- Utilize past experience by asking questions.

- Take an occasional break, using a "Stop-Breathe-Look-Listen-Feel" process to assess the progress of the session.

- Use statements that express your thoughts and encourage others to respond, for example:

   "I have mixed reactions. I agree with these aspects for such and such reasons, but I am disturbed about this particular aspect."

   "How do you see this situation?"

   "What do you want to do?"

- "Own" your message.

- Personalize with "I" parlance, for example, say, "I have a different opinion," not "You are wrong." Say, "I would love to have some strategy from you," not "You really should show me some work, you know."

Practicing Assertiveness

In the day-to-day work environment, there are many opportunities to use assertive behavior. In this section, we'll provide an example of how to present criticism assertively. We'll then go on to describe some do's and don'ts and some mental blocks that need to be overcome when practicing assertion.

Providing Criticism

Begin by commenting on specific actions, not generalities. Say, "You missed the deadline for that report" rather than "You are absolutely hopeless at managing your time."

Follow up with reasons for your comments. For example, "You missed the deadline for that report, probably because you have been spending more time on telesales than we planned. Perhaps we should discuss how you should allocate your time in the future."

Do's and Don'ts

Some do's and don'ts for assertive communication are listed in Table 3.

Table 3. Do's and Don'ts for Assertive Communication

Do	Don't
Provide logic and reason	Say "no" at the start
Have something else in the offing	Give excuses
Be ready to accomplish the task at a later stage	Dilly-dally
Accept or reject at the first instance	Waver in your decision making
Use "umbrella campaign" tactics, that is, appeal to the largest possible audience	Promise and then retreat

Mental Blocks

Early in childhood, we are usually taught certain "rules" that can create mental blocks when we get older. Inability to break loose of these blocks limits our thought processes and creativity. Assertiveness, however, necessitates that one consider ideas and actions beyond this limited scope. Table 4 lists a few of the rules we may have been taught and the subsequent problems that may result if we can't eliminate these blocks.

Table 4. Mental Blocks and Resulting Problems

"Rule"	Resulting Problem
There is only one right answer	Not being open to views
That is not logical	One's intellect is brought into question
Follow the rules	Restrictive; people feel "penned" in or as if they are being treated as children
Be practical	Demoralizing; limits creativity
To err is wrong	Fear of making a mistake
Don't be foolish	Fear of looking stupid in front of peers
Avoid ambiguity	Limits ability to consider options

Conclusion

When considering the need for communication and creativity in today's global business world, we believe that assertiveness is a key attribute for success in these areas. By learning what constitutes assertiveness, recognizing the worth of assertiveness skills, utilizing the tuning fork strategy, and practicing assertion, today's workers can greatly increase their own value in the workplace.

Reference

Ryan, S.R., & Travis, J.W. (2004). *The wellness workbook.* Berkeley, CA: Celestial Arts.

Narendra Kardam *is a PGDM (IIM, Calcutta), M. Phil (Bus. Admin.), PGDAC (CDAC), and B Tech (IIT, Delhi). He has total industry experience of more than eight years in top Navratna, such as IOC, CONCOR, and eGuru cool.com. He has taught in educational institutes such IPM, Ghaziabad, and eGurucool.com and is currently working as a faculty member with the department of marketing management at NIILM School of Business. He is an active contributor to various journals, magazines, and newspapers.*

Nikhil Kulshrestha *is a PGDBM (HRD & OB). He has an MBA and a master's in sociology. A respected faculty member in the area of OB and HR, he has completed a diploma program in export management. He has eight years' experience and is currently studying the BPO sector of Delhi and NCR region. He has actively contributed to various journals and newspapers. He serves on the faculty at NIILM School of Business in the HR area.*

Shruti Jain *recently submitted her thesis, "Trade Promotion and Expansion under WTO Regime-India's Gains and Concerns," for her Ph.D. She has a master's in foreign trade management (M.F.T.M.), a post-graduate diploma in management (P.G.D.I.M.), and a professional diploma in international business (P.D.I.B.). She has been in academia for three years and is currently serving on the faculty at NIILM School of Business in the International Business wing.*

Turbulent Change
Imagining the Future
Peter R. Garber

Summary

Much has been written and discussed about changes occurring in the workplace today, but relatively little about dealing with changes in the workplace tomorrow. Changes in the future will be much different than those we deal with today. Undoubtedly these future changes will be even more turbulent than today's. The better you prepare yourself for these future changes today, the easier and more effectively you will be able to deal with them when they arrive. Liken this process to the announcement from the pilot on an airplane experiencing bumpy weather: "Ladies and gentlemen, we are expecting some turbulence. Please hold on because it is going to be a rocky ride ahead!" Okay, maybe the pilot isn't quite that dramatic (or honest), but that essentially is the message. The same will certainly apply to the ride we are about to take into the future. The ability to quickly adapt to change will become one of the most important skills a working person can have in the future, second only to the ability to learn a new job or skill.

Change Redefined

The new millennium has become an overused cliché. The fact is that the changes that the new millennium brought with it already started before the turn of the 21st Century. The exact date is not important or even identifiable. What we are talking about is a new age measured not so much by the calendar as by events or turning points in history. These come as a result of cumulative, not single, events. One builds on and enables another. For example, the development and popularity of the personal computer set the stage for the Internet to become a common, really an essential, household technology. The Internet is enabling a whole host of changes to begin that will dramatically impact life in this new century.

Change will become more radical and immediate. The electronic age will usher in new ways of life that we cannot even begin to envision. Imagine what our great, great grandparents would think about what we have available to us today. The changes that our great, great grandchildren will take for granted will be even more phenomenal. Not only will our lifestyles be vastly different as this new century fully unfolds, but the workplace will change as well. Obviously, predicting the future is an inexact science. This article is not intended to have very much to do with science, or at least the science of predicting the future. The ideas presented here are based more on current observations and intuitions about what it might be like a few decades from now. They are intended to make the reader think about some of these possibilities and the likelihood of their reality. Some of the things suggested might make you laugh. Some may even scare you. Other things that may sound preposterous today may become commonplace tomorrow. In any case, we all need to begin to prepare ourselves for the possibilities, both positive and negative, that are really just around the corner as we travel on the information superhighway and make a few rest stops along the way.

Are We There Yet?

Children love to ask their parents in the first few minutes on a long car trip, "Are we there yet?" This is a question that may be difficult if not impossible to answer. We indeed will never "get there" when it comes to arriving at the future. The future and what it will bring will constantly be slipping ahead just slightly out of our grasp. Future generations will continue to try to visualize what the next changes will be. Even with all of the advancements and new tools they will have to work with that we cannot even conceptualize today, they may be no more accurate in their predictions. And so it goes, each generation trying to understand what the next might be like. The following are just a few of the possibilities that the future may hold:

Computer Bosses. The computer will be the ultimate boss in the future. You may be working for a massive microchip someday, a computer program. *"The computer won't let us do that"* may be the most limiting factor future generations face at work. "Boy, the computer was a real tyrant today," a future working person may commiserate to his or her spouse at the end of the workday. "I don't think that this system likes me very much. I know that it has been giving all the really good assignments to Joe, who just started on this network. He's such a suck-up (there will still be such people in the future), always feeding the computer new data all the time. He doesn't think I know what he's been up to, but I've seen his data input into the computer."

Organizational Change. Organizational changes will be so complex that there will have to be computer programs written to understand them, and even then no one really will. Organizational charts of the future will have to include computer systems hierarchies as well. Computers will hold actual positions, but won't receive salaries or take vacations or join labor unions until the latter half of the 2000s. A change in reporting structure in your organization of the future may mean that you log onto a different website in the morning or work on a different computer server or network. These changes will still be traumatic and turbulent.

Virtual Conferences. Teleconferences will replace physical business travel. The technology will become so advanced that it will be virtually impossible to distinguish between actually being at a meeting and teleconferencing. High definition will become so realistic that you won't be able to distinguish real life from TV. You may keep bumping into your TV, it will be so real. Future business conventions will also be virtual experiences. Everyone will simply attend the three-day event via new teleconferencing technology from his or her home office. Drinks and cocktails will be provided at each person's home to serve as a "mixer" so everyone can get comfortable with one another at the beginning of the convention. Attendees will be able to isolate conversations with one particular person through this technology, allowing for private discussions, flirtation, and other traditional convention behaviors and activities.

Language Skills. These will be less important as universal business language becomes more and more accepted. Business English will become even more dominant and universal. Business English will become different from regular English—no slang or acronyms.

The ability to communicate your thoughts/feelings in writing (email) will become less important due to its many inherent limitations and one-dimensional aspect. Too much gets lost in the translation. Email will be replaced by live-mail clips (LMCs). These LMCs will be stored video audio clips that you open, save, forward, and reply to the same as you would emails today. But you must be able to quickly get your point across to the receiver. People will have to dress up to send messages to one another. You will also be able to receive a written transcript from a voice recognition system. It will be just like a computer dating service.

Data Access. The ability to access data will become the most powerful force on earth. Data will be even more closely regulated and controlled because of its power. The Internet will become highly regulated and controlled by the government. New world governing data (NWGD) agencies will cause a bureaucratic nightmare on the Internet. Internet taxes and codes will be controlled by a NWGD agency. There will be such a thing as Internet jail, including punishments of denial of access to data. This will set the stage for very powerful lessons in future justice. Email will take over the world, and the U.S. Postal Service will take over email. You won't be able to receive email on Sundays or federal holidays (there will be twenty-seven in the future). But tell your pet dogs not to despair; someone still needs to physically deliver all of the things that everyone is buying online to people's homes. Fido will still be able to get in a good bite or two in the future into unexpected visitors to your home bearing packages.

Paperless Society. Everything will be electronic: newspapers, books, letters, notes, reports, etc. "Dilbert" comics and other office humor publications will be provided in electronic form into which the reader can insert his or her own real-life office characters. The comics will become a lot more fun and realistic.

Corporate Universities. These will begin to take over the education process in society. They will become the *think tanks* of the future. They will become more influential than traditional universities. These institutions of higher learning will begin developing curriculum for future employees. The curriculum will be less theoretical and more business-related in all disciplines. It will emphasize teamwork and collaborative thinking, rather than individual achievement. All training will be offered online in a variety of creative formats. The virtual classroom will surpass the traditional live experience. It will provide learners with the optimal learning environment. For instance, if you are studying world economies, you will be in a simulated environment that takes you to the various countries to experience first-hand how they live, work, and spend their money. You could find yourself working in a rice field in the Asia/Pacific region of the world or on a fishing boat in the North Atlantic as you learn about why the U.S. dollar is currently so weak in the world economy or why moving business investments to the Pacific Rim would be a wise thing to do. These colleges will still have football games—probably virtual, with the contests played via computer games with theoretical plays and calculated outcomes. Sixty thousand students will log on to each of these autumn weekend events, and then all get drunk afterward and start sending incomprehensible slurred messages to one another and try to see how many people they can stuff online into a small website.

Redefining the Workplace. The likely future workplace will be your home, where you can work online from your home computer system. We will have virtual workplaces with no buildings or physical property except computer and telecommunications equipment. All meetings will be teleconferenced. Employees will work remotely from home or a central transmittal center as part of organizational website systems. Most commercial buildings will be replaced by computer data banks. Commuting to work will become almost extinct in the future. Traffic congestion will be on the information superhighway, not the thruway. Business casual will be your bathrobe and slippers. A whole new clothing line will appear called *Business Loungewear*—pajamas you can work in. Executives will wear wing-tipped bedroom slippers and have pinstriped pajamas with company logos on their bathrobes. There will be commuting simulators, even equipped with construction delays, to make you feel you have driven to work in the morning. These simulators will put you in the right mind frame (frustrated and angry) when you begin working.

SharedNetUserGroups or SNUGS. Future employees will work in shared file units. Work groups will be defined by who has access to a particular file base. The future version of a job transfer or change might be being reallocated to a different access group or web-site. This can be as traumatic as being physically transferred. The family moves its data access as well. There will be tearful good-byes to chat-room buddies, even though you may never actually have met. Employees will ask to not be virtually transferred until teenage children graduate from their virtual home high school.

Electronic Corporate Image. Business wear will be judged on how good it looks on a computer screen. Instead of looking at how a new outfit looks in a dressing room mir-ror, you will inspect yourself via a video camera projecting it on a monitor. New fabrics and styles will emerge designed to make you look thinner on computer monitors.

Virtual Mergers and Acquisitions. Continued mega-mergers and acquisitions will lead to far fewer major corporations than there are today. These mega-corporations will become so dominant that virtually everyone's employment will be connected in some way. These mega-corporations will be more powerful than the government. Cer-tainly they will be much more efficient.

Corporate Computer Wars. Wars in the future will be fought by these mega-corpora-tions over access to information. Government referees will be called in to officiate these battles. Information will become more important than territory or boundaries. Casu-alties will be measured in terms of destroyed or captured electronic data.

Career/Life Total Integration. Where careers and personal lives begin and end will be-come far less distinct. The whole family unit will become more involved in the par-ents' careers. Your email address will become more important than your street address. The future will create even more obtrusive ways of getting messages to you. There will be no escape. The Dick Tracy wristwatch will become an unfortunate reality—a tiny, complete computerized communications device capable of sending and receiving mes-sages any place, any time. Everyone will wear one. It will be a great aid to the elderly; "I've fallen off-line and can't get back on the system" will be a common message to Network Emergency Response workers from this growing segment of our population.

Return to Home Center Lifestyles. History once again will repeat itself, as it will be like going back to an agrarian society; only in the future the cash crop will be information. Future societies will become more home-centered both physically and intellectually. Fu-ture homes will be designed with this lifestyle in mind. Home information centers will include host computers that will control everything in the home. Today we have redun-dant independent systems: TV, VCR, doorbells, telephones, TV cable, telephone lines, computerized microwaves and ovens, thermostats, cell phones, and so on. In the future these will all be combined into one central system. Home computers will take over many of the parenting responsibilities while parents work, such as daycare. Sensors activated by toxic smells or moisture content in the room will tell you when to change diapers. Employment terminations will be simply a denial of password access into the network. Without that you're finished.

Some Unexpected Stops Along the Information Superhighway

The following are some scary possibilities that might exist in the future that we may not presently be fully prepared for:

- Handwriting will become a lost art form. Toddlers will be taught keyboard skills instead of how to print their ABC's. We will have to go to museums (virtual of course) to see handwriting examples like Egyptian hieroglyphics.

- Computers will be personal in the sense that they will be customized to complement your particular strengths, weaknesses, and personality. Personal computers will become personal assistants. They will truly make you a more effective person. People will be judged less on their own personal strengths and weaknesses than on those of their personal computer assistants. Promotions in the future will involve obtaining more powerful personal computer assistants that are programmed to succeed. They will give you advice on how to get ahead. PCs will be more of an extension of you, a conscience, like Hal in the movie *2001*. Downgrading your personal computer assistant will be the future equivalent of being demoted.

- If you do have to leave your home for some reason, an automated response tracking (ART) system will control the drive in your hydrogen powered transport unit (HPTU). Traffic accidents will be programmed out of existence. Our future cars will become smarter than we are. "Didn't you mean to take a left at that light?" ART will inquire, as you try to fake out the system as you head for the (virtual) golf course instead of staying home and working on that report due next Tuesday. "Mr. Johnston is going to be very upset with you. He was expecting that report to be completed on time," ART warns you as you pull into the clubhouse parking lot and begin to get your golf game virtual experience (GGVE) computer program out of the car. "I'm afraid that I'm going to have to report this behavior to Mr. Johnston. It's part of my programming." You begrudgingly shove your GGVE back in its compartment and head back home thinking of ways to disable ART.

- Virtual hazardous data waste sites will be monitored by government agencies that will regulate data storage in the future for viruses and other dangerous infectious traits that could corrupt other systems.

- Websites will have specific costs associated with them, as hotels and resorts do today. People with higher-level positions in mega-corporations will have access to the most expensive and exclusive ones. The less privileged you are, the less access you have, and the class system cycle continues. Poverty in the future will be redefined by what sites you have access to. It will be more of an intellectual definition than physical or material.

- There will be no physical money, just electronically programmed money cards. Every financial transaction will require just a swipe of a card.

- The government may need to regulate what occupations/services need to be provided online and which can still be performed live in-person. In an effort to reduce pollution, the government may issue work permits for those who are allowed to leave home to work. This will save billions in road maintenance and other infrastructure costs.

- Longer lives will lead to longer working careers. This career longevity will be made even more possible by advances in medicine as well as the ability to work from home. Normal retirement ages will get later and later. Someday the normal retirement age could be as old as eighty-five, but you could qualify at the young age of eighty-two if you wanted to go out early.

- The first child conceived over the Internet (they will find a way) will become a reality by the second half of the 21st Century. With all the sex that is constantly taking place on the Net, it was bound to happen sooner or later!

What Can You Do?

The future always seems to come before we are ready for its arrival. It can seem like a thief that sneaks in during the night and makes everything seem different the next day. Open your mind to new possibilities. Anticipate change. The ability to learn and adapt will continue to be the most important skills in the future. What will career development mean to you in the future? What form will it take? You will have no choice but to adapt to change in the future. It will move so fast there will be no past to hold on to.

How well positioned are you for these possible changes? Are you ready for these possibilities? If not, what can you do about it today? You need to open your mind to new possibilities. You need to accept the fact that future value systems may be different than they are today. Think about many of these possibilities might occur in the future and see how many of them come to fruition. What other possibilities can you think of that may exist tomorrow? Thinking about the future in this way can help make it less turbulent for you.

Peter R. Garber *is manager of employee relations for PPG Industries, Inc., Pittsburgh, Pennsylvania. He is the author of a number of management books, including* Turbulent Change: 10 Natural Forces for Business Success, Winning the Rat Race at Work, *and* 100 Ways to Get on the Wrong Side of Your Boss, *and more than forty other articles and training tools.*

Living on the Edge
Leading Software Training Projects
Brooke Broadbent

Summary

Developing an organizational learning strategy is both an honor and a head-ache. It may be a smashing success or a dismal failure. This article examines the case of a large-scale software rollout and provides advice to ensure the success of the accompanying learning strategy.

Your Assignment—If You Accept It

"Pat, we have a huge opportunity for you. I want you to develop a learning strategy for a complex, organization-wide software implementation. You have several years' experience consulting on various learning projects and some small software under-takings. I know that you have never participated in a complex software rollout; here's your opportunity. I want you to step up to the plate."

What would you do if you were in Pat's shoes? Stress out? Seek new employment? Or swing into action?

Decision-Making Tips

Here are a few tips to help you decide whether you should bite the bullet. First, the good news. If you are an accomplished training leader, you have what it takes to handle the training side of big software projects. For example, if you have a successful track record with training needs identification and you have had success in other training and con-sulting endeavors, you have a firm foundation to lead this assignment. If you don't have solid training needs identification skills, instructional design skills, and consulting skills and you are tempted to take on this project, I suggest that you find team members who do have the required background and expertise. You'll need them. It also helps to have very strong communication skills and to have some change management strategies up your sleeve.

A second thought—the not-so-good news. Software projects in large organizations cause big headaches. They follow a treacherous road with potholes and dead ends. They have the capacity to nose-dive into oblivion or to soar over budget. As a result of the pressure to meet deadlines and budgets, members of the project team become frustrated, irritable, and stressed. They are absorbed by complex change requests, failed beta tests, budget overruns, missed deadlines, configuration catastrophes, conversion glitches, and the like. Faced with challenges from many directions, members of the implementation team will not be available to meet with you to discuss training. Or if they do agree to meet you, don't count on having their undivided attention for very long.

As a result of the state of affairs described above, training plummets to the bottom of the priority list in the early phases of software projects. Don't worry. Later, when rollout is in sight, training will suddenly be heralded as the shining savior of the project. When that happens, you will have everyone's ears. And they will want yours. (Better your ear than your head.) Resources that were not available earlier will materialize. People will actually ask to meet with you. And offer to help. Needless to say, you will want to develop a credible learning strategy—quickly. It's now your turn to feel stressed and under pressure.

If you were in Pat's shoes, would you take on this assignment based on what you've read so far? Not sure? Here are more considerations.

Mitigating Your Personal Risks

Developing a learning strategy for an expensive software rollout is a high-risk activity. If team leaders are not confident in your knowledge, skills, and attitudes, you could be shown the door or placed on the shelf before you think you have finished your work. The tips and guidelines presented in this article, combined with old-fashioned hard work, will help you keep your job and actually enjoy the challenge of supporting software implementation through developing a rock-solid approach to learning.

Learning Strategy Questions

The learning strategy that needs to be developed will address many questions. Following are a few that we'll consider in this article:

1. Why is the software being implemented?

2. Is its use mandatory?

3. What's in it for me, as a user, as a manager, as a specialist?

4. How does it impact the way that I do my work?

5. How do I use it?

6. What training is available?

7. Where do I go for help?

8. What's the fastest way to learn it?

Change Management

You will probably find that the driving force behind questions 1 through 4 is the tendency of humans to resist change. Your level of success will increase if you accept the reality of resistance to change and simply do what needs to be done to mitigate the resistance. When people ask why the software is being implemented and want to know if its use is mandatory, they are often coming from a place of "I'll use it if you make me." What do you do about this potential stonewalling? Maybe resistance to change does not sound to you like a classical "training" issue of identifying and teaching knowledge and skills. You might simply prefer to say that it's someone else's problem. But the reality is that change-management issues must be dealt with before, during, and after training. If you don't address change-management issues, your training efforts could be wasted. It's simple. With effective change-management activities, uptake of the new system will be faster. It could also be relatively painless.

For some skilled training leaders, attention to change management comes automatically. It's part of successful instructional design and delivery. For others, change management is a separate activity, left to change-management experts. In any case, it pays for training leaders to be conscious and intentional about developing approaches that mitigate resistance to change.

That's where the tools of change management come in handy. You should start on change-management approaches as soon as possible. May I now assume that you would take on the project if you were Pat? After all, it does present many interesting challenges. Wondering about change management? Table 1 examines elements of change-management activities that I've seen put to good use on enterprise-wide software systems training—on projects like Pat is being asked to lead. They can, however, work for all training implementations.

Table 1. Change Management Strategies That Work

Activity	Tips	Results
1. Undertake full consultation with stakeholders.	Be open. People need to vent. They have good ideas, so listen intently.	Knowledge for all, mutual understanding, and potential buy-in from stakeholders.
2. Map out how the new software will affect work processes.	Identify the existing ways of working and how they will change.	People will gain practical information on how to use the software.
3. Identify and foster champions and trainers from throughout the workplace.	Work with these people to provide the knowledge and skills they will require to take on new responsibilities.	This group will become leaders before, during, and after implementation.
4. Engage trainers from the workplace.	Make sure to help trainers develop their training delivery skills.	Having in-house experts adds huge credibility to the project.
5. Identify the benefits of using the new software.	Be honest. Acknowledge that the new software means learning new ways to work.	Awareness. Credibility. Positive thoughts.
6. Identify the pitfalls of using the new software.	Be honest. Explain what's being done to address pitfalls.	Credibility. Engagement from stakeholders.
7. Develop a clear training plan.	Focus on the issues that arose during consultation.	Shared understanding of the issues and the solution.
8. Design and deliver training based on specific roles.	Keep the training job-oriented with specific workplace-related examples.	As a result of this training, people will feel competent to use the new software.
9. Meet with stakeholders to explain the training plan.	Be honest about risks, possible results, and deadlines.	Reasonable expectations from the training.
10. Create a simple explanation of the change process.	Use a cycle such as "deny, resist, explore, and commit" to help people understand the process.	People accept and understand what is happening.
11. Distribute information bulletins.	Give real-life examples of what is happening.	The changes that are coming will move from being abstract to concrete.
12. Develop job aids.	Use the job aids during the training sessions.	Learners will know how to use the job aids and will use them after the training.
13. Send emails, videos, and other communications from senior management mandating use.	Balance mandated usage with the provision of training to ensure that people know how to use the software correctly.	Clear understanding of management's expectations.

Instructional Possibilities

Our baker's dozen of change-management activities examined in Table 1 will help you deal with resistance to change. While addressing change-management issues, training will rise to the surface. For example, if you are holding a change-management meeting to discuss how the software will impact roles, attendees will no doubt ask what training is available. Let's develop some ideas about how you might answer that question.

Returning to our original list of eight questions several paragraphs above, we have addressed the first four. But what about questions 5 through 8? They were:

5. How do I use it?

6. What training is available?

7. Where do I go for help?

8. What's the fastest way to learn it?

These four questions relate to training and information, not change management, although dealing with them and providing successful training will help to alleviate resistance to change. Your challenge is to recommend which instructional approach to take. A few years ago there were just two options for conducting instruction: instructor-led in a classroom and self-study using printed materials. Today there are various options for instructor-led training and for self-study using the technology of computers and the World Wide Web. Following is an annotated list of twelve options that you should consider when developing your approach, whether it is instructor-led or self-study. Remember, people learn in different ways. Your favorite approach to learning works for you—it's not going to work with everyone.

1. Hands-on instruction in a live training environment

    - Closest to using the application in the workplace, if you use it to replicate real-life situations

    - Ensures that the learners have received instruction

    - Can be combined with job aids and user guides so that people learn how to use these tools during training, which could increase the likelihood they will use their support tools after the training

    - Can also be conducted as a follow-up to a call made by a user to a help desk

- Can focus on power users who will coach others, rather than on all potential users

- Requires a well-designed instruction package, skilled instructors, classrooms, and careful loading of data and management of the training environment

- May be impossible to implement with a big bang enterprise-wide roll-out, since there are probably not enough classrooms and instructors

- Needs to be conducted close to the go-live date in order for learners to retain information

- Can be subject to downtime when the system is not available

2. Pre-recorded demonstrations (sometimes called demos, simulations, or sims)

    - Close to reality in that they show the software at work while avoiding the challenges of setting up and maintaining a live training environment

    - Is totally passive; learners do not use the application so they do not have an active learning experience

    - A good back-up if you are using hands-on instruction and the system is not available

    - These pre-recorded materials can be used in a classroom or over the Web

    - Relatively inexpensive to produce

    - Demonstrations can be stopped and re-started and combined with quizzes built into the demonstrations so that learners use their keyboards in exercises that replicate hands-on training

    - Can be used by an instructor or a learner

    - If demos are made available, there is no guarantee that people will use them, unless you use them in a controlled learning lab environment

3. Computer-based training (CBT)

    - Is delivered from a computer's hard drive or a CD-ROM

    - Can combine key text, quizzes, and possibly demos

    - High-quality CBT is expensive to produce but cost-effective if there are a large number of participants

- If CBT is made available, there is no guarantee that people will use it, unless you use it in a controlled learning lab environment

- Difficult, if not impossible, to update after the CBT is distributed

4. Web-based training (WBT)

- Similar to CBT but delivered over the Internet or an intranet

- Can combine key text, quizzes, and possibly demos

- High-quality WBT is expensive to produce but cost-effective if there are a large number of participants

- If WBT is available, no guarantee that people will use it, unless you use it in a controlled learning lab environment or build in a mandatory online test that all participants must take in order to establish their qualification to perform certain types of work

- Users access the material without downloading it, so updates relatively easily

5. User guides

- Help instructors prepare to conduct sessions

- Act as a reference for power users

- Labor-intensive to maintain in the early life of the software when it is still being modified

- Can be used during face-to-face training sessions to support instructors

- Less expensive to develop than CBT and WBT

- No guarantee that people will use them unless the guides are used in training sessions

6. Job aids

- Consist of short text and graphics for a quick summary of how to use the software tools

- Can be used during face-to-face training sessions to support instructors

- Less expensive to develop than CBT and WBT

- Can be used by learners during training to help them follow instruction

- After training, help users to recall instruction received during the training session

- No guarantee that people will use them

7. Webinars

- Live or pre-recorded presentation over the Web with the possibility of voice, graphics, and software demonstrations

- Requires that learners have the proper computer, Internet access, and either a headset or a telephone

- Can be recorded and played back "any place, any time"

- Large numbers of people can participate from their desktops

- A new way of teaching that requires instructors to develop their skills

- Helpful to have more than one person conducting the session

- If live sessions are sufficiently engaging, some assurance that people are listening

- If session are dull, participants distracted and do other activities during the webinar

8. Games

- Can engage learners and create memorable experiences

- Complex to develop and require specialized skills, knowledge, and software

- Expensive to create and to maintain

- Can be worth the effort when there are large groups of potential participants

9. Electronic performance support systems (EPSS)

- Information that is available on the Web to help people perform specific tasks

- Like online help, people have a tendency to not consult EPSSs

- Less expensive to develop than WBT, webinars, and games

- Can use the wide distribution network of the Internet or an intranet

10. Portal websites

- Used to create a central clearinghouse when there are many good sources of information that individuals might not find on their own

- Can include links to training materials and courses

- One of the more inexpensive options to develop

- Needs to be maintained because linked URLs change

11. Online Help

- Normally a searchable index of topics about software features

- Inexpensive and effective, but users have a tendency to not consult

12. FAQs

- Frequently asked questions, with answers

- Inexpensive to develop

- Boring to read

- Best if built on real questions and concerns that users have, rather than as a tool to propagate management's message

Costing

These twelve instructional options can vary greatly in cost. The final costing will depend on labor rates in your market and how elaborate you make your initiative—no matter which approach you use. The time it takes, which will shape the final amount of effort required and the cost, will be governed by the skills of the people who work on the project, whether they are employees or consultants.

You can help manage costs by having a detailed work plan that you carefully develop and monitor. Careful piloting of test modules, as discussed below, will also help you to ensure effectiveness and eliminate excessive revisions.

Considerations When Selecting an Approach to Learning

How would you or Pat select the best learning tools from the twelve options cited above? In addition, once you have chosen an option, how will you gauge the effectiveness of that approach? Two types of pilot testing will help you as you move along. After you develop a test module, have it reviewed by people who know the software, in an alpha test. They will tell you whether the material is accurate. Once you have accurate information, you can conduct a beta test with users. Watch them use the tools. Assess whether they learned what the training was attempting to convey.

Let's step back. How do you select your option or mix of options in the first place? Frankly, it's rather daunting to have twelve choices. Your deft consulting skills are about to rise to the surface. Knowing the options and knowing their mechanics is science. Sensing how to apply them is an art. The first rule of consulting is to do it "with" your client, not "to" your client. In other words, full, open, frank consultation is the only path to follow. This consultation should touch on a number of considerations, including the budget for training, past experiences with instruction on similar projects, expectations on the part of management and workers, people who can help you, the culture or cultures of learning that permeate the organization, availability and skills of trainers, and anything else that people want to talk about—and might surprise you. Also, an effective consultant helps shape a consensus on the rollout strategy. People might not have thought seriously about this, so here is an opportunity for leadership. If it's an all-at-once approach to launching the software, your learning strategy will be different from the one for a gradual rollout from one unit or geographical region to another.

Remember, a combination of approaches will apply to several preferred learning styles.

Gather Information from Thought Leaders

You will need to open a wide window on the organization. Find out who the thought leaders are in the training, information, communication, and change management areas. Work intently with managers. What's their vision? What have they tried to date? With what results? What's possible now? Who can help? What exists already? Share your observations, ideas, and hypotheses with management. Listen to theirs. Identify the organization's conventional wisdom about training. Nail down what thought leaders believe. Find out what a broad spectrum of people thinks about what approach will work best. Speak to members of the software team, managers, employees, and folks who have been involved with similar projects. What is available from the software provider? How has training been done in other organizations similar to yours?

Learning Plan Versus Learning Strategy

The process we have been going through of getting all the training facts and selecting which of the twelve approaches to use leads to a learning plan. This is essentially an instructional design exercise. The output is a document listing learning objectives, a curriculum with high-level content, and an explanation of selected training methods and tools, as described above. It can be a big undertaking to write a learning plan for any situation. It is even more challenging to write a learning plan for a complex, organization-wide software implementation.

You have to conduct solid research to determine who is being trained, when, how, where, and with what tools. And there is more if your challenge is to write a learning "strategy." That's what Pat has been asked to undertake.

An effective learning strategy is about using your consulting skills, your leadership qualities, your consensus-building skills, and wordsmithing. As a consultant, internal or external, your assignment is to move the organization forward. Your role is to consult fully, to help formulate options, to challenge where necessary, and to provide your feedback. You will also lead people along new paths, build a consensus, and articulate the vision in such a way as to ensure understanding. As we saw with the change-management strategies above, it's crucial that you clearly articulate your strategy and gain full support from management by explaining the approach to relevant decision-makers on the management team.

A Key Document

The learning strategy that you write will become a key document, generate clear direction, spearhead conclusions about crucial areas, weave practical solutions, and pinpoint concrete examples. Your report will speak of results, risks, risk mitigation strategies, and an evaluation plan. This level of detail will help build mutual understanding and confidence. A clearly written report spells out the issues you uncovered and addresses them. All of this casts the die of an effective learning program.

Conclusion

It's a huge responsibility and honor to develop a learning strategy. Remember, conducting training sessions is only part of the story. Some of the learning gaps can be bridged by providing solid information in simple job aids. Also, don't try to sweep the change-management issues under the carpet. It won't work. Put change management front and center. Distinguish among change-management solutions, effective instruction tools, and a learning strategy. Sharpen your consulting and communication skills. If you identify gaps in your skill set for this work, find team members to fill them. Develop training tools that will work with the population you are dealing with. Engage management. And be positive.

Just think! If you succeed with this assignment, you will be entitled to take a break and then accept another assignment that's just as demanding—or more so. And, on the next assignment, you will have another chance to tweak your approach. You will continue to enjoy living on the edge as you lead complex software training projects.

Brooke Broadbent, M.A., *has led the training component of several software implementation projects. He wrote* The ABCs of e-Learning *(Wiley, 2002) and authored over one hundred articles and books about training and personal growth. He lives in Ottawa, Canada, where he is also a certified business coach.*

Measurement of Stress in Organizational Roles
Revalidating the Framework
Avinash Kumar Srivastav and Udai Pareek

Summary

In this article we review developments in the measurement of stress in organizational roles. In particular, we examine two previously published instruments, *Organizational Role Stress* (ORS) and *ORS–Scale*, developed by Pareek in the 1980s. Confirmatory factor analysis of fifty items of the ORS Scale measured on 453 randomly selected respondents in a public-sector industry has thrown new light on the conceptual framework of the ORS. Eight out of the ten subscales and thirty-seven out of the fifty items on the ORS Scale have acceptable validity. *Self-Role Distance* (SRD) has not emerged as a clear factor; however, the SRD subscale definitely needs to be redesigned. *Role Erosion* (RE) is being merged with *Role Stagnation* (RS); the two concepts need to be separated; RE subscale needs to be worked on. This study points to the existence of an additional type of role stress, namely *Role Underload* (RU), for which a new subscale has to be developed.

Understanding Stress

Changes are taking place in the environment at a faster pace every year. Unexpected events, either challenging or threatening, are facing us more frequently. While the pressure for higher performance is ever-growing, there is less and less time available to prepare and react. All this makes fertile ground for creation and magnification of *stress* (Pestonjee, 1999, pp. 15–34). We are living in the "Age of Stress." Understanding the meaning of stress, its causes and determinants, containing the level of stress, and functionally coping with the stress experienced are becoming increasingly important.

Derived from the Latin word, *Stringere,* in the 17th Century, stress meant hardship, straits, adversity, or affliction. Its meaning evolved to denote force, pressure, strain, or strong effort with reference to an object or person (Hinkle, 1973) in the 18th and 19th Centuries. In physics, stress came to be known as the internal restoration force generated within a solid body as a result of an external force tending to distort the body. The concept of stress developed by physicists and engineers was passed on to the social scientists (Cooper & Marshall, 1978).

Selye (1936, 1974) made the first reference to stress in the human system, conceptualizing and defining stress as *a nonspecific response of the body to any demand made upon it.* Lazarus, Cohen, Folkman, Kanner, and Schaefer (1980) brought out that stress is not merely a response but also a function of an individual's appraisal of the situation. People do not respond directly to a stimulus, but to the meaning of the stimulus in relation to their own perceptions of the environment. In other words, events by themselves are not stressful, unless they are perceived by the individual as threatening. The stress experienced is determined by the appraisal of what is at stake and the analysis of the resources available to meet the demand. The notion of appraisal broadens the concept of stress to include some of the psychological factors, such as personality variables like the *need for power* and *locus of control.* What one person sees as a threat another may see as a challenge. The current view on the subject is that stress is the result of a lack of fit between a person (in terms of personality, aptitudes, and abilities) and the environment, along with a consequent inability to cope effectively with the various demands it makes on him or her (Harrison, 1976). Stress can be defined (Robbins & Sanghi, 2006) as a dynamic condition in which an individual is confronted with an opportunity, constraint, or demand related to what he or she desires and for which the outcome is perceived to be both uncertain and important.

Stress in Organizational Roles

The effectiveness of an organization is dependent on the effectiveness of its people (Pareek, 1993, 2004). Even the most competent and motivated people may not perform well when there are problems in their organizational roles. The following are some examples of role-related problems in organizations (Srivastav, 2006b):

1. The role has requirements that are basically against the role occupant's requirements, values, nature, or what he or she strongly likes.

2. The role faces conflicting demands from the significant people in the organization (role occupant, boss, peers, and subordinates).

3. The role occupant cannot have the required interaction and communication with those in the related roles.

4. There are inadequacies in the availability of internal and external resources that are required for performing the role.

5. The role occupant is not clear about what the significant people in the organization expect from his/her role.

Organizational role represents an assigned position in the organization, which is defined by the expectations of the significant people. The role occupant performs in the organization to fulfill his/her role expectations (Pareek, 2004). Organizational roles have an in-built potential for stress. Stress resulting from the occupation of an organizational role and performing or not being able to perform therein is known as *Organizational Role Stress* (ORS) (Pareek, 1983).

Evolution of the Role Stress Framework

Kahn, Wolfe, Quinn, Snoek, and Rosenthal (1964) identified three dimensions of organizational role stress, viz., *Role Conflict, Role Ambiguity,* and *Role Overload,* briefly described below.

- *Role Conflict*: Comprises the following four elements.
  - *Inter-Sender Conflict* (arising due to incompatible demands from different senders in the role set)
  - *Intra-Sender Conflict* (arising due to contradictory demands from a single role sender)
  - *Inter-Role Conflict* (arising due to contradictions in expectations from different roles)
  - *Person-Role Conflict* (arising when role expectations are in conflict with person's self-concept, values or beliefs)
- *Role Ambiguity*: Arises when role expectations are not clear.
- *Role Overload*: Arises when there are too many demands in too little time.

Based on the work of Kahn, Wolfe, Quinn, Snoek, and Rosenthal (1964), Rizzo, House, and Lirtzman (1970) developed scales for the measurement of role conflict and role ambiguity, comprising fourteen items (eight representing role conflict and six representing role ambiguity). Although Rizzo, Hosue, and Lirtzman's scales have been used very extensively for research, they are not free from controversies about their validity. McGee, Ferguson, and Seers (1989) called for a moratorium on Rizzo's scales, while Kelloway and Barling (1990) argued that the call for this moratorium was premature.

The Role Overload scale, comprising three items, was developed by Beehr, Walsh, and Taber (1976). For many years thereafter, only the three above-mentioned types of role stress were identified. Organizational role stress researchers remained confined to role conflict, role ambiguity, and role overload, even though the three continued to ill-represent the complexities of role performance problems encountered.

Pareek (1982) made an important contribution to organizational role stress research by identifying eight types of organizational role stress that closely represented most problems encountered in organizational roles. He developed a forty-item instrument known as *Your Feelings About Your Role* to measure eight types of role stress: *Inter-Role Distance* (IRD), *Role Stagnation* (RS), *Role Ambiguity* (RA), *Role Erosion* (RE), *Role Overload* (RO), *Role Isolation* (RI), *Role Inadequacy* (RleIn), and *Self-Role Distance* (SRD). Test-retest reliability for different types of role stress was verified to be significant at the 0.001 level (Pareek, 1993, p. 51).

Your Feelings About Your Role was improved further by Pareek. Factor analysis of data collected using the forty-item instrument in question revealed the need to split *Role Ambiguity* (RA) (the old version) into a new version of *Role Ambiguity* and *Role Expectation Conflict* (REC) and to split *Role Inadequacy* (RleIn) into *Resource Inadequacy* (RIn) and *Personal Inadequacy* (PI). This was followed by the development of a fifty-item instrument known as *Organizational Role Stress* (ORS) (Pareek, 1983) to measure ten different types of role stress.

ORS Scale

The ORS scale (Pareek, 1983) comprises fifty items divided into ten subscales for measuring the following ten types of role stress. It makes use of 5-point Likert scale for scoring each item (0 for the least likely situation and 4 for the most likely situation). Each type of role stress is scored in the range 0 to 20. The total ORS, which is the sum of the ten types of role stress, is scored in the range from 0 to 200. The ORS scale has been extensively used for role stress research (Aziz, 2004; Pestonjee, 1999; Srivastav, 2006a, 2007). The instrument is reproduced as an exhibit at the end of this article.

Inter-Role Distance (IRD)

In general, a role occupant plays more than one role (typically an organizational role and a non-organizational role). If one of these roles is excessively demanding, the other role suffers. IRD arises when the role occupant is unable to balance between two of his or her roles. For example, the role of a son in the family may interfere with his role as a marketing manager when his father is critically ill.

Role Stagnation (RS)

A role occupant feels insecure in taking up a new role if he or she lacks the required skills. In such a condition, the role occupant keeps on stagnating in the older role, which is more familiar, secure, and comfortable. This gives rise to RS. For example, a quality manager of long standing would experience RS upon being promoted to a general manager if he does not have the general management skills. RS can also be experienced due to lack of opportunities for growth.

Role Expectation Conflict (REC)

A role occupant experiences REC if there are conflicting expectations from his or her role senders. For example, if the marketing manager expects the R&D manager to introduce product updates at a fast pace, and the production manager expects him not to introduce product updates without adequate lead time, the R&D manager would experience REC.

Role Erosion (RE)

If the credit for one's accomplishment in the role is given to some other person in another role or some important function belonging to one's role is performed by some other person in another role, the role occupant feels deprived and experiences RE. RE is commonly encountered in organizations under restructuring or technology upgrading.

Role Overload (RO)

Role overload is experienced on encountering either too many or too high expectations. If the role occupant lacks empowerment or when his or her actual performance is far below the expected performance, he or she experiences RO. For example, if a quality manager is expected to ensure a quality acceptance rate of 99.99 percent when he or she is able to achieve only 95 percent after best efforts have been put in, he or she would experience RO.

Role Isolation (RI)

When the role occupant does not have the required frequency or ease of interaction with others in her role set, RI is experienced. RI may be due to geographic separation of role set members, due to systems not permitting the required level of interaction. For example, RI may result from a boss maintaining a distance from the subordinates, lack of coordination at the peer level, or project team members not relating to each other.

Personal Inadequacy (PI)

PI is experienced when the role occupant lacks the necessary knowledge, skills, or experience needed for her effective role performance. For example, a software design engineer with inadequate competence for handling software design would experience PI.

Self-Role Distance (SRD)

SRD is experienced when the role occupant does not find his role interesting, when his special skills remain unutilized, or when there is a conflict between his image/needs/values and those of his role. For example, when an introverted person is given a sales executive's role or when an extroverted person is given a role confining him to his office desk, he will experience SRD.

Role Ambiguity (RA)

RA is experienced when the role occupant is not clear about expectations from her role or she has doubts about certain responsibilities, functions, or activities. RA can arise because expectations may not have been defined in the first instance, or they could have changed with time. RA is commonly experienced by occupants of newly created roles or process roles having lack of concretely defined activities.

Resource Inadequacy (RIn)

RIn is experienced if the resources external to the role occupant are not available for carrying out the role responsibilities. Personal competence of the role occupant represents his internal resource, captured in PI. External resources could include human resources, buildings, infrastructure, materials, machines, tools, equipment, books, documents, and information necessary for successful performance in the role. For example, a production manager in a manufacturing company will experience RIn if he or she does not have the adequate number of operators and testing equipment.

Objectives of the Study

1. To revalidate the framework used for the ORS scale;

2. To find out the validity of its items and subscales; and

3. To identify the scope for possible enhancement of item and subscale validity;

Methodology

A large, multi-unit, multi-location, multi-product Indian public-sector industry having a diverse organizational culture was selected for the study. Workshops were conducted explaining the significance and implications of the ten types of role stressors at the individual and organizational level to motivate the participants to participate in the exercise with an open mind, without fear or apprehension, to minimize data errors due to defensive behavior and manipulation by the participants. Participants were promised that their individual role profiles would be made available to them with necessary solutions for their possible adoption. Due care was taken to include participants representing all the diversity (age/gender/hierarchical level/functional allocation) present in the organization. The ORS was administered to collect role stress data from the participants. The organizational role profile was discussed with the participants in the group. Individual role profiles were separately discussed with the individuals. ORS scoring sheets with completed and valid data constituted 453 ORS samples.

Individual scores on each of the fifty items corresponding to 453 respondents were subjected to Confirmatory Factor Analysis to extract ten factors (corresponding to the ten subscales of the ORS), using the SPSS package. Seven types of factor extraction followed by four types of rotation for each type of extraction were carried out. The best interpretable extraction–rotation combination was used for determining the validity of items and subscales. Loadings of less than 0.3 were taken as low. Loadings of 0.5 or more were taken as high. Loadings equal to or more than 0.3 but less than 0.5 were taken as moderate.

The validity of each item was studied and categorized. Item validity was considered to be high when the item clustered only under the desired factor with a high or moderate loading. It was seen as moderate and acceptable when its loading on other factors was significantly lower than that on the desired factor (high on the desirable factor and medium on the other factors or moderate on the desired factor and low on other factors). It was labeled as marginal and acceptable when its loading on the desirable factor was higher than that on the other factor, but loading on both desirable and undesirable factors fell under the same category, that is, high or medium. It was seen as unacceptable when the item was being scattered to several factors, with its loading on the desirable factor not being significantly higher.

A validity index was calculated for each subscale. A *subscale validity index* is the ratio of the number of expected items actually clustering in the subscale (with acceptable high/medium loading) and the total number of items in the subscale.

Results and Discussion

Table 1 furnishes the loading of the individual items of the ORS scale on the ten factors extracted through *principal component* factoring and *equamax* rotation. Forty-nine point eight percent of variance in role stress could be explained by these factors. The results reflected the validity of the subscales and individual items, as described below.

Factor I: Role Ambiguity (RA)

Four out of five items related to RA (refer to the exhibit), items 9, 29, 39, and 49, cluster in Factor I. This factor explains 18.8 percent of variance in role stress. RA subscale has a validity index of 0.8. Items 9, 29, 39, and 49 thus have high loadings. Item 9 (lack of clarity) has an additional moderate loading on Factor VI (REC). This is understandable. Lack of clarity of scope and responsibility may also lead to experiencing REC. Item 19 (unawareness of expectations), not clustering in this factor, also has a moderate loading on Factor VI (REC). It signifies that unawareness of expectations may lead to REC. This item is very weak and needs to be redefined. Items 29, 39, and 49 have high validity. Item 9 has moderate and acceptable validity. Item 19 has an unacceptable validity.

Factor II: Role Stagnation (RS)

Four out of five items related to RS, items 2, 22, 32, and 42, cluster in Factor II. This factor explains 6.3 percent of variance in role stress. The RS subscale has a validity index of 0.8. Items 2, 32, and 42 have high loadings, but item 22 has a moderate loading. Item 12 (inability to prepare for higher responsibilities) does not cluster in this factor and is scattered with moderate loadings on Factor X (SRC) and Factor III (PI); it signifies that lack of preparedness for taking on higher responsibilities may result in experiencing SRC and PI; the item is very weak and needs to be redefined. Item 22 (lack of time and opportunities) is scattered, with moderate loading on two other factors, Factor V (RO) and Factor IV (IRD). It signifies that lack of time and opportunities leads to RO and IRD. This is also a weak item needing redefinition. Item 32 (lack of scope for personal growth) is scattered, with a moderate loading on Factor VII (RI);

this is explainable. Lack of scope for personal growth also connects with RI; when one isolates oneself from other roles in one's role set, one cannot experience growth in one's role. Two of the five items, numbers 2 and 42, have high validity. Item 32 has a moderate and acceptable validity. Items 12 and 22 have unacceptable validity.

Factor III: Personal Inadequacy (PI)

All the five items related to PI, 7, 17, 27, 37, and 47, form a strong cluster in Factor III. This factor explains 4.3 percent of variance in role stress. The PI subscale has a validity index of 1.0. Item 7 has a moderate loading. Items 17, 27, 37, and 47 have high loadings. Item 7 (lack of knowledge) has an additional moderate loading on Factor VI (REC); this is also explainable, as lack of knowledge may result in the perception of conflict in role expectations. Items 17, 27, 37, and 47 have high validity. Item 7 has a marginally acceptable validity.

Factor IV: Inter-Role Distance (IRD)

All five items related to IRD, 1, 11, 21, 31, and 41, form a strong cluster in Factor IV. This factor explains 4 percent of variance in role stress. The IRD subscale has a validity index of 1.0. Item 1 has a moderate loading, but other items have high loadings. Items 1 and 31 (both representing conflict between organizational/non-organizational roles) also have moderate loadings on Factor X (SRC); this is understandable. Item 21 (lack of time for family) also has a moderate loading on Factor V (RO), which is to be expected. Items 11 and 41 have high validity. Items 21 and 31 have moderate and acceptable validity. Item 1 has a marginal and acceptable validity.

Factor V: Role Overload (RO)

All the five items related to RO, 5, 15, 25, 35, and 45, cluster in Factor V. This factor explains 3.4 percent of variance in role stress. The RO subscale has a validity index of 0.8. Items 5, 25, and 45 have high loadings. Item 15 (workload influencing work quality) has a moderate loading; it has an additional (moderate) loading on Factor X (SRC); this is explainable, as the role occupant finds himself unable to maintain the desired work quality because of work overload. Item 15 has a marginally acceptable validity. Item 35 (need for reducing the role) has a low loading; it has an additional (moderate) loading on Factor I (RA). The need for reducing the role overload may be felt due to perceived ambiguity in role expectations. This item is very weak and needs to be redefined. Item 35 has an unacceptable validity.

Table 1. Confirmatory Factor Analysis of ORS Items

Items	Factor I RA	Factor II RS	Factor III PI	Factor IV IRD	Factor V RO	Factor VI REC	Factor VII RI	Factor VIII RIn	Factor IX RE	Factor X SRD
9	0.63					0.30				
19						0.42				
29	0.68									
39	0.57									
49	0.52									
2		0.55								
12			0.30							0.47
22		0.36		0.30	0.31					
32		0.51					0.33			
42		0.58								
7			0.40			0.36				
17			0.72							
27			0.59							
37			0.72							
47			0.65							
1				0.46						0.39
11				0.68						
21				0.66	0.31					
31				0.59						0.33
41				0.66						
5					0.63					
15					0.41					0.38
25					0.67					
35	0.36				(0.27)					
45					0.66					

	9.38	3.14	2.17	1.98	1.72	1.44	1.40	1.31	1.20	1.17
3						0.51				0.46
13						0.62				
23						0.60		0.35		
33						0.32		0.45		
43						0.47				0.34
6							0.40			
16							0.64			
26							0.68			
36							0.55	0.30		
46	0.33						0.47			
10	0.46						0.33			
20		0.53			0.33			0.46		
30		0.46			0.52			0.35		
40								0.51		
50								0.64		
4								0.33	(0.23)	
14									0.76	
24									0.69	
34									0.69	
44										
8										0.58
18		0.49								
28		0.61								
38	0.30					0.34	0.33			
48	0.31			0.34						
Eigen Value	9.38	3.14	2.17	1.98	1.72	1.44	1.40	1.31	1.20	1.17
% Var	18.8	6.3	4.3	4.0	3.4	2.9	2.8	2.6	2.4	2.3

Factor VI: Role Expectation Conflict (REC)

All the five items related to REC, 3, 13, 23, 33, and 43, cluster in Factor VI. This factor explains 2.9 percent of variance in role stress. The REC subscale has a validity index of 1.0. Items 3, 13, and 23 have high loadings. Items 33 and 43 have moderate loadings. Item 3 (inability to meet conflicting demands from seniors) has an additional (moderate) loading on Factor X (SRC); this is understandable. Item 23 (inability to meet conflicting demands from clients) has an additional (moderate) loading on Factor VIII (RIn); perhaps the conflict is arising because of inadequate resources. Item 33 (conflict in expectations of seniors with those of juniors) has a higher (moderate) loading on Factor VIII (RIn); perhaps the conflict is arising because of inadequate resources. Item 33 is weak and needs to be redefined. Items 13 and 43 have high validity. Items 3 and 23 have moderate and acceptable validity. Item 33 has an unacceptable validity.

Factor VII: Role Isolation (RI)

All five items related to RI, 6, 16, 26, 36, and 46, cluster in Factor VII, items 6 and 46 with moderate loadings and the other three with high loadings. The RI subscale has a validity index of 1.0. Item 6 (lack of getting others' attention and time) has an additional (moderate) loading on Factor X (SRC); this is logical to understand. Item 36 (absence of teamwork and collaboration) has an additional (moderate) loading on Factor VIII (RIn); RIn is felt because the role occupant is working without receiving help from others. Item 46 (lack of response from other roles) has an additional (moderate) loading on Factor I (RA). This is natural; lack of response enhances the perception of ambiguity. Items 16 and 26 have high validity. Item 36 has a moderate and acceptable validity. Items 6 and 46 have marginally acceptable validity.

Factor VIII: Resource Inadequacy (RIn)

Four out of five items related to RIn, 20, 30, 40, and 50, cluster in Factor VIII. Items 20 and 30 have moderate loadings. Items 40 and 50 have high loadings. The RIn subscale has a validity index of 0.8. Item 10 (lack of information) does not cluster on this factor; it is scattered with moderate loadings on Factor I (RA) and Factor VII (RI). It means that lack of information accentuates the perception of ambiguity and isolation. This item is very weak and needs to be redefined. Probably, "I do not get" needs to be replaced by "I do not have." Item 20 (lack of resources) has an additional (moderate) loading on Factor V (RO), meaning that lack of resource leads to experiencing overload. Item 30 (lack of people) has an additional (high) loading on Factor V (RO), meaning that lack of people leads to experiencing overload. Items 40 and 50 have high validity. Item 20 has a marginally acceptable validity. Items 10 and 30 have unacceptable validity.

Factor IX: Role Erosion (RE)

Only three items related to RE, items 24, 34, and 44 cluster with high loadings under Factor IX. The other two items, 4 and 14, cluster under Factor II (RS), with high and moderate loadings, respectively. The RE subscale, therefore, has a validity index of 0.6. RE items have a clear split. The two items clustering under Factor II (RS) represent deprivation or erosion. On the other hand, the three items clustering under Factor IX (RE) represent the desire to take on additional responsibilities. Item 14 (depriving the role) also has a moderate loading on Factor VIII (RIn) and a low loading on Factor IX (RE); this is surprising. This may be due to the perception of the role occupant that resource inadequacy is resulting from transfer of some of the important functions from his or her role to other roles. Items 24, 34, and 44 have high validity. Items 4 and 14 have unacceptable validity.

Factor X: Self-Role Distance (SRD)

Only one item related to SRD. Item 8 clusters in Factor X with a high loading. The SRD subscale has a validity index of 0.2. It is a thorough mixup of items from seven different subscales and needs a thorough re-examination and redesign. Items 18 (inability to use own expertise) and 28 (uninteresting work) cluster with moderate and high loadings, respectively, on Factor II (RS). This means that inability to use own expertise or compulsion to do uninteresting work is driving the role occupant not to take up the new role and keep on stagnating in the older role. Item 38 (compulsion to work against one's will) is scattered with moderate loadings on Factor I (RA) and Factor VII (RI). This means that compulsion to work against will is resulting in the feeling of ambiguity and isolation. Item 48 (value conflict) is scattered, with moderate loadings on Factor I (RA) and Factor VI (REC). This means that conflict in values is creating the perception of ambiguity and conflict in expectations. Item 8 has a high validity. Items 18, 28, 38, and 48 have unacceptable validity. Items 12 (lack of preparedness due to preoccupation), 1 (conflict between role and family life), 31 (conflict between organizational and non-organizational roles), 15 (inability to maintain work quality due to work overload), 3 (inability to meet seniors' conflicting demands), and 6 (lack of attention from other roles) also have moderate loadings on Factor X. Most of the items clustering in Factor X are representing some kind of conflict between the self and the role, but most of the SRD items are not clustering in this factor. Hence this factor can be named Self-Role Distance (SRD).

Conclusion and Recommendations

Table 2 furnishes the validity of items in the ORS scale. It can be seen that thirty-seven out of the fifty items have acceptable validity. Twenty-four items have high validity. Seven items have moderate (acceptable) validity. Six items have marginal (acceptable) validity. Thirteen items have unacceptable validity. Items with unacceptable validity need to thoroughly examined, substituted for, or modified to ensure their validity. Items with marginally acceptable validity may also be looked into for improving their validity.

Table 2. Item Validity

High-Validity Items	Moderate (Acceptable) Validity Items	Marginal (Acceptable) Validity Items	Unacceptable Validity Items
11, 41	21, 31	1	12, 22
2, 42	32	15	33
13, 43	3, 23	6, 46	4, 14
24, 34, 44	36	7	35
5, 25, 45	9	20	18, 28, 38, 48
16, 26			19
17, 27, 37, 47			10, 30
8			
29, 39, 49			
40, 50			

Item wording issues, such as (a) use of comfort items versus stress items, (b) positive statements versus negative statements, (c) simple sentences (which are easy to understand) versus complex sentences (which are not so easy to understand), and (d) offering a single option (seeking single response) verses offering multiple options (seeking multiple responses) under the same item, need to be carefully considered.

Table 3 furnishes the validity index for the constituent subscales of the ORS scale. It can be seen that eight out of the ten subscales have acceptable validity. The validity index for four subscales is 1.0, and for another four subscales it is 0.8.

Self-Role Distance (SRD) has not emerged as a clear factor. The SRD subscale needs to be completely redesigned.

Table 3. Subscale Validity Index

Sub–Scales	Validity Index
PI, IRD, REC, RI	1
RA, RS, RO, RIn	0.8
RE	0.6
SRD	0.2

Role Erosion (RE) is being split into two parts, namely *deprivation* (or erosion) and *desire to do more* (or under-load). RE items representing deprivation are clustering under *Role Stagnation* (RS). RE and RS are thus being merged; the two concepts need to be separated. The RE subscale, therefore, should be thoroughly worked on.

Strong clustering of RE items representing the desire to do more reflects that role occupants are experiencing *Role Under-Load* and want to have additional responsibilities. The study therefore points to the existence of an additional type of role stress, namely, *Role Under-Load* (RU), for which a new subscale has to be developed.

Acknowledgment

Thanks are due to Dr. K.S. Gupta for his valuable feedback on the pre-final version of the manuscript.

References

Aziz, M. (2004, October). Role stress among women in the Indian information technology sector. *Women in Management Review, 19*(7), 356–363.

Beehr, T.A., Walsh, J.T., & Taber, T.D. (1976). Relationship of stress to individually and organizationally valued states: Higher order needs as a moderator. *Journal of Applied Psychology, 61*, 41–47.

Cooper, C.L., & Marshall, J. (1978). *Understanding executive stress.* London: Macmillan.

Harrison, R.V. (1976). *Job stress as person-environment misfit.* Presented at the Annual Meeting of the American Psychological Association, Washington, D.C.

Hinkle, L.E. (1973). The concept of stress in the biological and social sciences. *Science, Medicine and Man, 1*, pp. 31–48.

Kahn, R.L, Wolfe, D.M., Quinn, R.P., Snoek, J.D., & Rosenthal, R.A. (1964). *Organizational stress: Studies in role conflict and ambiguity.* Hoboken, NJ: John Wiley & Sons.

Kelloway, E.K., & Barling, J. (1990). Item content versus wording: Disentangling role conflict and role ambiguity. *Journal of Applied Psychology, 75*(6), 738–742.

Lazarus, R.S., Cohen, J.B., Folkman, S., Kanner, A., & Schaefer, C. (1980). Psychological stress and adaptation: Some unresolved issues. In H. Selye (Ed.), *Selye's guide to stress research* (Vol. 1). New York: Van Nostrand.

McGee, G.W., Ferguson, C.E., & Seers, A. (1989). Role conflict and role ambiguity: Do the scales measure these two constructs? *Journal of Applied Psychology, 74,* 815–818.

Pareek, U. (1982). *Organizational role stress scales.* Ahmedabad, India: Navin Publications.

Pareek, U. (1983). Organizational role stress. In L.D. Goodstein & J.W. Pfeiffer (Eds.), *The 1983 annual.* San Francisco, CA: Pfeiffer.

Pareek, U. (1993). *Making organizational roles effective.* New Delhi: Tata McGraw-Hill.

Pareek, U. (2002). *Training instruments in HRD and OD.* New Delhi: Tata McGraw-Hill.

Pareek, U. (2004). *Understanding organizational behavior.* New Delhi: Oxford University Press.

Pestonjee, D.M. (1999). *Stress & coping: The Indian experience.* New Delhi: Sage Publications India Private Limited.

Rizzo, J.R., House, R.J., & Lirtzman, S.I. (1970). Role conflict and ambiguity in complex organizations. *Administrative Science Quarterly, 15,* 150–163.

Robbins, S.P., & Sanghi, S. (2006). *Organizational behavior.* New Delhi: Dorling Kindersley (India) Pvt. Ltd.

Selye, H. (1936). A syndrome produced by diverse nocuous agents. *Nature, 138,* 32.

Selye, H. (1946). The general adaptation syndrome and the diseases of adaptation. *Journal of Clinical Endocrinology, 6,* 117.

Selye, H. (1974). *Stress without distress.* New York: New American Library.

Srivastav, A.K. (2006a, June). Role stress in public sector. *Management & Change.*

Srivastav, A.K. (2006b). *Process-based role analysis and design for organizational development: An Indonesian case study.* Global Organizational Development Summit, Mysore, India, September 18–20.

Srivastav, A.K. (2007, September). Achievement in public sector: A cross-functional study on relationship with stress and coping. *IIMB Management Review.*

Dr. Avinash Kumar Srivastav *has an MS in electronics and communication engineering and a Ph.D. in management in organizational behavior. He is the associate dean (research) at ICFAI Business School, Bangalore, India. He has four decades of experience, including thirty years in different kinds of industries in India and Indonesia, having occupied top-level executive and advisory positions. He has served as an external consultant to International Labor Organization; executive director, ITI Ltd., Bangalore; and an OD advisor, change management advisor, and HR director in Jakarta. He has authored forty national and international publications on different aspects of organizational behavior and development. He was the editor of the book titled* R & D Management, *published by Tata McGraw-Hill, New Delhi. He is the consulting editor for the* ICFAI *Journal of Organizational Behavior. He was awarded at the national level in India for his achievements and contributions in research and development and in quality and standardization.*

Udai Pareek, Ph.D., *is the distinguished visiting professor at the Indian Institute of Health Management Research, Jaipur, India. He is the advisory member, human resource development international and on the academic advisory board for the Global Committee on the Future of Organization Development. He is the only Asian to become a Fellow of the National Training Laboratories (NTL). He has been US-AID HRD/OD advisor to the Ministry of Health, Government of Indonesia. He is the editor of the* Journal of Health Management *and has been the consulting editor of the* Journal of Applied Behavioral Science. *He has authored or edited fifty books and 350 research papers. He has received several national awards in India.*

Organizational Role Stress (ORS) Scale

Udai Pareek

1. The Instrument and Its Administration

The organizational role stress (ORS) scale is used to measure ten role stresses, inter-role distance, role stagnation, role expectation conflict, role erosion, role overload, role isolation, personal inadequacy, self-role distance, role ambiguity, and resource inadequacy. The ORS uses a 5-point scale (0 to 4), containing five items for each role stress and a total of fifty statements. Thus the total scores on each role stress range from 0 to 20. Responses are given on an answer sheet [not included in this exhibit].

2. Scoring

The answer sheet is also used for scoring. The total scores on each role stress range from 0 to 20. To find the total scores for each role stress, the ratings given are totaled horizontally (for five items). The ten rows, respectively, rate the following:

Row	Stress
1	Inter-role distance (IRD)
2	Role stagnation (RS)
3	Role expectation conflict (REC)
4	Role erosion (RE)
5	Role overload (RO)
6	Role isolation (RI)
7	Personal inadequacy (PI)
8	Self-role distance (SRD)
9	Role ambiguity (RA)
10	Resource inadequacy (RIn)

3. Answering Guidelines

Do not write anything on the questionnaire. Give responses on the Answer Sheet only; read instructions carefully before responding.

People have different feelings about their roles. Statements describing some of them are given below. Use the Answer Sheet to write your responses. Read each statement, and indicate in the space beside the corresponding number on the Answer Sheet, how often you have the feeling expressed in the statement in relation to your role in the organization. Use the numbers given below to indicate your own feelings.

If you find that the category to be used in answering does not adequately indicate your own feelings, use the one closest to the way you feel. Do not leave any item unanswered. Answer the items in the order given below.

Write 0 if you never or rarely feel this way.

Write 1 if you occasionally (a few times) feel this way.

Write 2 if you sometimes feel this way.

Write 3 if you frequently feel this way.

Write 4 if you very frequently or always feel this way.

ORS Questionnaire

_____ 1. My role tends to interfere with my family life.

_____ 2. I am afraid I am not learning enough in my present role for taking on higher responsibility.

_____ 3. I am not able to satisfy the conflicting demands of various people above me.

_____ 4. My role has recently been reduced in importance.

_____ 5. My workload is too heavy.

_____ 6. Other role occupants do not give enough attention and time to my role.

_____ 7. I do not have adequate knowledge to handle the responsibilities in my role.

_____ 8. I have to do things in my role that are against my better judgment.

_____ 9. I am not clear on the scope and responsibilities of my role (job).

_____ 10. I do not obtain the information needed to carry out responsibilities assigned to me.

_____ 11. I have various other interests (social, religious, etc.) that are neglected because I do not have time to attend to these.

_____ 12. I am too preoccupied with my present role responsibilities to be able to prepare for taking on higher responsibilities.

_____ 13. I am not able to satisfy the conflicting demands of my peers and juniors.

Write 0 if you never or rarely feel this way.

Write 1 if you occasionally (a few times) feel this way.

Write 2 if you sometimes feel this way.

Write 3 if you frequently feel this way.

Write 4 if you very frequently or always feel this way.

_____ 14. Many functions that should be a part of my role have been assigned to some other role.

_____ 15. The amount of work I have to do interferes with the quality I want to maintain.

_____ 16. There is not enough interaction between my role and other roles.

_____ 17. I wish I had more skills to handle the responsibilities of my role.

_____ 18. I am not able to use my training and expertise in my role.

_____ 19. I do not know what the people I work with expect of me.

_____ 20. I do not get enough resource to be effective in my role.

_____ 21. My role does not allow me enough time for my family.

_____ 22. I do not have time and opportunities to prepare myself for the future challenges of my role.

_____ 23. I am not able to satisfy the demands of clients and others, since these are conflicting with one another.

_____ 24. I would like to take on more responsibility than I am handling at present.

_____ 25. I have been given too much responsibility.

_____ 26. I wish there was more consultation between my role and others' roles.

_____ 27. I have not had the right training for my role.

_____ 28. The work I do in the organization is not related to my interests.

_____ 29. Several aspects of my role are vague and unclear.

_____ 30. I do not have enough people to work with me in my role.

_____ 31. My organizational responsibilities interfere with my extra organizational roles.

_____ 32. There is very little scope for personal growth in my role.

_____ 33. The expectations of my seniors conflict with those of my juniors.

_____ 34. I can do much more than what I have been assigned.

_____ 35. There is a need to reduce some parts of my role.

_____ 36. There is no evidence of several roles (including mine) being involved in joint problem solving or collaboration for planning action.

_____ 37. I wish I had prepared myself well for my role.

_____ 38. If I had full freedom to define my role, I would be doing some things differently from the way I do them now.

_____ 39. My role has not been defined clearly and in detail.

_____ 40. I am rather worried that I lack the necessary facilities needed in my role.

_____ 41. My family and friends complain that I do not spend time with them due to the heavy demands of my work role.

_____ 42. I feel stagnant in my role.

_____ 43. I am bothered with the contradictory expectations different people have from my role.

_____ 44. I wish I had been given more challenging tasks to do.

_____ 45. I feel overburdened in my role.

_____ 46. Even when I take the initiative for discussions or help, there is not much response from the other roles.

_____ 47. I need more training and preparation to be effective in my work role.

_____ 48. I experience a conflict between my values and what I have to do in my role.

_____ 49. I am not clear what the priorities are in my role.

_____ 50. I wish I had more financial resources for the work assigned to me.

Managing with Social Styles™
Ten Strategies
Mary J. Buchel

Summary

Managers are constantly interacting with and influencing their direct reports. One of the most powerful and important skills for managers is what Daniel Goleman (2006) identifies as *social intelligence*. This article addresses ten situations where managers can apply social intelligence to improve results.

Introduction

An approach to developing social intelligence is *social styles* training. Socrates said, "Know thyself," and that is where social styles training begins, with *self-awareness*—being aware of how one's social style is viewed by others during interactions.

Self-awareness leads to *self-management,* or the ability to control and adapt the expression of feelings and of assertiveness.

Next, managers develop *social awareness*—the ability to understand another's needs, based on that person's social style.

Finally, managers apply social intelligence or social styles awareness in *relationship management*—managing relationships in order to influence others in organizational situations such as coaching, developing others, managing change, and teamwork.

This article provides a brief overview of social styles training, then describes ten situations in which managers can apply their knowledge and skill regarding social styles in day-to-day management situations. The information in this article is useful to social styles trainers as they describe management situations in which social styles knowledge and skills can be vital.

Social Styles Training Overview

Social styles training focuses on self-understanding along two dimensions:

1. The extent to which a person is more tell assertive (direct) or ask assertive (indirect); and

2. The extent to which a person controls feelings and emotions or expresses them.

These two dimensions form a matrix that identifies four social styles: Driving, Expressive, Amiable, and Analytical. (See Figure 1.) This model, researched and developed by Merrill and Reid (1981) is the basis for (1) a self-profile and (2) a multi-rater profile. The multi-rater profile provides insights for managers about how they are viewed by others. These insights are vital if managers are to be effective.

Once managers learn the strengths and challenges of their own styles, they begin to explore interaction situations with others with styles that are similar to or different from their own. Ultimately, managers develop self-management, social awareness, relationship management, and versatility skills in adapting their own styles to ensure that interactions with others are productive.

The advantage to managers of social styles training is that they will have greater awareness and heightened sensitivity to (1) the impact of their own styles on others and (2) how best to appeal to the needs of others' social styles. In interactions with others, they can apply strategies to be more effective and more influential.

Strategies for Managing with Social Styles

Following are ten situations where knowledge and skill regarding social intelligence and social interaction can be applied by managers to interact more productively and to make better decisions. For each situation, there are examples and suggestions. It should be noted that these suggestions simplify the intricacies and depth of understanding that results from training in social styles.

1. *In recruiting and attracting people to a position,* advertising can appeal to the social style desired for the position by describing the job in terms that reflect that style's behavior. For example, if the situation or the team would benefit from Driving characteristics, the ad can include terms such as *decisive, action-oriented,* and *work independently.* If the situation or the team would benefit from someone who has an Amiable style, use terms such as *relationship expert* and *someone who can provide support and coaching to others.*

Figure 1. Social Style Model™

For an Analytical style, words that appeal include *conscientious* and *maintaining high standards.* To appeal to an Expressive, use words such as *enthusiastic, high-energy,* and *creative.*

2. *In making a decision to hire or promote* into a position, a manager may have two or three finalists, each meeting qualifications. The deciding factor can be a candidate's social style.

For example, if one of the four styles is underrepresented in a work group, the hiring manager can choose a candidate with that style. Or if one of the two dimensions—Control/Emote or Ask/Tell—is over-represented, the hiring manager can opt for someone who complements styles of current work group members.

Note that style can be approximated during interviews by observation and through self-report. It is not recommended that the hiring process include a paper-and-pencil assessment of social style. This may raise legal questions about the validity of the hiring process.

Also, note that social styles can play a part in making a hiring or promotion decision *only after* a manager has determined that all final candidates meet other knowledge, skill, and ability requirements for a position.

3. *While setting performance expectations,* standards, and goals for direct reports, a manager can appeal to the preferences of each style in framing expectations. For the Analytical style, emphasize the importance of fact-based decisions, precision, accuracy, and minimizing risks. With an Expressive, talk about how important the work is to the chief executive. Emphasize incentives and public recognition upon achievement of a goal or project. Set expectations with a person whose style is Driving; let them know in what areas they'll be able to work independently and talk about challenges they'll face. With an Amiable, map out the timeframe and let them know about aspects that require teamwork and coordination.

4. *When delegating or assigning projects,* think about what each style considers important. For instance, when delegating long-term project coordination to an Amiable, describe the link between the project and teamwork within the work group or among work groups.

Delegating a similar project to someone with a Driving style, emphasize challenges to be overcome, such as time frame or breakthrough aspects of the project.

Delegating to Analyticals works best when there are plans and milestones, as well as clear criteria for success.

Expressives respond when they know their personal contribution will be valued as they take on a project.

5. *In introducing change and managing change* with direct reports, keep in mind that change causes stress. Each style has an initial reaction to an announcement of a change.

Amiable and Analytical styles tend to become more ask assertive, to withdraw, or to acquiesce without talking through the change. With Amiables and Analyticals, a manager's role is to provide forums for reflecting on the change and working through the change with others in the work group.

Expressive and Driving styles tend to become more tell assertive, challenging, or even dogmatic. Effective managers provide a forum for Expressive and Driving styles to vent, then engage them in shaping the change.

After a change has been announced, there is ongoing communication that is group-wide or organization-wide. In planning this communication, it is useful to consider what each style looks for and appreciates when going through a change.

- Amiables appreciate sincerity and a team approach.

- Expressives appreciate enthusiasm; they look for acknowledgement of their past and present contributions.

- Driving styles appreciate a goal focus, commitment, and momentum.

- Analyticals look for data-based decisions and a step-by-step approach.

6. *Handling resistance or pushback from direct reports* can demand a manager's best skills. Pushback from Expressive and Driving styles tends to be more vocal and immediate. Provide *floor time* and recognition of the points these styles raise.

Resistance from Analyticals and Amiables takes longer to surface. When managers get little or no reaction or pushback from these styles, they need to probe and question to assist these styles in surfacing their concerns.

Working with all styles of direct reports through a change, effective managers find ways to honor and incorporate direct reports' issues and concerns in planning a change.

7. *Recognizing direct reports* is more effective when a manager considers social styles. Analyticals appreciate serious praise that is based on the facts of their accomplishments. Driving styles like praise for a significant accomplishment. Both Analytical and Driving styles prefer accolades that are concise, not overdone.

Expressives thrive in an atmosphere of recognition. They are comfortable in the limelight. Amiables and Expressives both enjoy the approval of others, so let these styles know who noticed and liked what they accomplished.

8. While *leading problem solving and decision making* with a group of direct reports, managers can capitalize on different styles at various points in the process.

The Analytical style will be most helpful in developing a precise statement of the problem. In addition, Analyticals excel at data gathering. Expressives support problem solving with their intuitive approach and big-picture thinking. Driving styles tend to be action-oriented, so their style will be especially helpful in moving from decision to implementation. Amiables can assist in building relationships with key stakeholders during implementation of a decision.

9. *When coaching direct reports on their interaction skills,* a manager can add value to the coaching session by discussing social styles.

For example, a direct report may be having difficulty with a customer. A manager can coach the direct report to consider that the customer's style may be more tell assertive or ask assertive than the direct report's. Or the customer may be someone who controls feelings and emotions—or expresses them—to a greater extent than the employee. Once these style differences are laid out, the manager can assist the direct report to develop strategies for more effective interaction. Managers who have a solid understanding of social styles can coach their direct reports to increase their social intelligence and interaction skills.

There are times when a manager may have two direct reports who are in conflict. The two people need to work together, but they are constantly disagreeing and unable to resolve their differences. The direct reports may describe their differences as a personality conflict.

Social style differences are a part of almost all conflict situations at work. In mediating the conflict as a third party, a manager can present information on each person's style. Then the manager can assist the conflicted individuals to understand and appreciate their own styles and the style of the other person. Focusing on styles is a no-fault approach to mediating and managing conflict between direct reports.

10. *Consider social styles in creating development goals related to interaction, teamwork, and communication* for direct reports. Each style has its own growth challenges.

- Expressives need to remember to consider others' points of view and not overwhelm others with their own ideas and energy.

- Analyticals' challenge is to actively engage in decision-making discussions and to provide a direction or decision.

- Amiables' growth is in learning to make requests of others and in speaking up and disagreeing with others.

- Driving styles can become more effective interpersonally by talking about the benefits of others' ideas.

Caveat

These examples and suggestions are intended as *broad brush* ideas. In applying social styles to various management situations, keep in mind that styles define what people with similar styles generally have in common. Individuals with the same social style can differ markedly from one another.

Conclusion

During social styles training, managers can develop skills in self-awareness, self-management, social awareness, and relationship management. Trainers can help managers to apply their knowledge and skills in social styles as those managers make people decisions and interact with and coach their direct reports. The ten applications of social styles outlined in this article can be part of the discussion a trainer has with managers to assist them in thinking through application of social styles in interactions and decisions involving direct reports.

References

Goleman, D. (2006). *Social intelligence: The new science of human relationships.* New York: Bantam Dell Publishing Group.

Merrill, D.W., & Reid, R.H. (1981) *Personal styles and effective performance.* Radnor, PA: Chilton Book Company.

TRACOM. Available: www.tracomcorp.com

Mary J. Buchel *is a management and organization development consultant with thirty years' experience assisting managers and teams to interact and communicate more productively. She is an expert in team development, process improvement, performance management, and systems thinking. Mary serves on the Board of Examiners for the State of Wisconsin Baldrige program. She speaks Spanish and has worked in Mexico and Latin America. Mary earned a master's degree in organizational communication from the University of Wisconsin-Milwaukee.*

Getting Smart About System Change
Developing Whole-System IQ™
Sherene Zolno

Summary

Business, government, and non-profit leaders are saying that, more than ever before, they need to have exceptional skills and creative new approaches to respond to the complex, systemic challenges facing their organizations. However, structuring a change process to effect whole-system change is a new knowledge area for most of these leaders and for those who consult to them. Identifying this as *Whole-System Intelligence* (WSIQ™), the author presents a model for how to assess and gather data about the whole system, a model that then becomes a tool for ensuring that change intervention is *systemic*. In addition, the author suggests that certain components should be included in the change process to ensure that a critical mass for change is achieved—that the change process is *systematic* as well.

Changes in markets, customers, competition, and technology around the globe are forcing leaders and their organizations to develop new strategies and learn new ways of operating. Most importantly, being a leader today involves knowing how to lead complex, large-scale, system-wide, sustainable change.

New and enhanced leadership capability in whole-system change—what this author calls whole-system intelligence—is required when deeply held beliefs are challenged, when the values that made an organization successful become less relevant, and when legitimate yet competing perspectives emerge. Many efforts to transform organizations through mergers and acquisitions, restructuring, improving processes, or strategy work falter because leaders fail to grasp what it really takes to shift and sustain change throughout their organizations.

Whole-System Intelligence: Core Distinctions

In dealing with new or growing pressure to change, organizations sometimes must integrate demands from a wide range of stakeholders and make changes in their core processes, strategies, and methods of doing business. A *whole-system meeting* (often called a "conference" or "summit") is sometimes used when high levels of participation and cooperation are required to accomplish the needed changes. Usually all stakeholders, or a significant number of their representatives, attend the meeting and participate in max-mix discussion groups that bypass normal organization boundaries.

A whole-system meeting may be used to launch a change process, marking the end of old and the beginning of new approaches in organizational functioning. Because it affords opportunities for relationship building across functions and levels in an organization, as well as with customers, vendors, and community stakeholder groups, enhanced cooperation is an expected outcome of most of these gatherings.

A *whole-system change process*, on the other hand, is the integrated, system-wide, usually long-term, large-scale intervention that is designed to address the challenge of changing a complex organization and ensuring that the change is sustained. As consultants and researchers, most of us are familiar with the change initiative that doesn't last—kicked off with fanfare and an event (usually a whole-system meeting), followed by a short period of organizational focus, then forgotten as the business crises of the day draw away the leaders' attention.

Unlike that now familiar one-time event model, a well-designed whole-system change process guides an organization as it considers and makes changes in multiple aspects of its system *concurrently* in order to achieve a critical mass of energy toward change, and thus the potential for truly sustainable change. While many organizations have held whole-system meetings, and while those gatherings have reportedly had a positive affect on business processes and results, few consultants seem prepared to support a leader and an organization through major change, start to finish, addressing the organization's different components in a coordinated fashion. This is what we call *Whole-System IQ*™: the ability to guide whole-system change—systematically. Two models that can be used to guide and sustain large-scale change—Field Assessment™ and Whole Field Change™— are presented below.

Field Assessment™

An organization must assess itself as an organization and fully understand its systems in order to create the platform needed for launching a whole-system change process. This may be accomplished using Field Assessment™, a comprehensive model designed

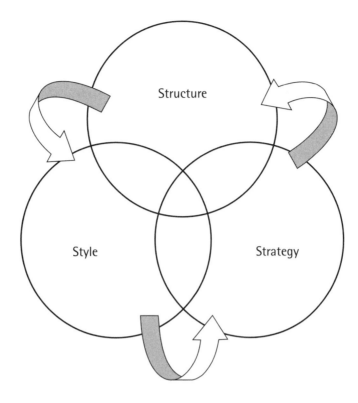

Figure 1. Field Assessment Model

to expand thinking about how organizations can be systemically viewed (system-as-a-whole) and systematically improved or changed (planned, coordinated change to affect the system-as-a-whole). (See Figure 1.)

Field Assessment illustrates the interconnectedness of elements that define the organization. Using the model, and thinking of each of the three frames as a window through which to gaze into the organization's life, a leader and his or her team can analyze the organization as a system with interrelating parts. Three frames comprise the whole (the field):

- *The Style Frame.* The style frame is focused on assessing an organization based on the cohesiveness of its culture and the strength of its shared values.

- *The Strategies Frame.* The strategies frame focuses one's view on the organization's vision, mission (or purpose), and its intentions.

- *The Structure Frame.* The structure frame concerns one with viewing and understanding the organization by assessing how it aligns its goals, formal roles, systems, and technology, that is, the organization's methods for deploying its human and other resources in achieving its purpose and intention.

To be effective, an organization must have a high degree of fit, or internal alignment, among these three frames. What goes on in each frame must be consistent with and reinforce what is going on in the others. Thus, to improve an organization, one would have to pay attention to all of the frames at the same time, giving you a truly systemic way of seeing the parts and how they are adding up to the whole.

Theoretically, all three frames are interrelated—there is no starting point or implied hierarchy—so a change in one would have a ripple effect on all others. It would be impossible, therefore, to make a change in one area of organizational life (by changing the organization's strategy, for example) without having an effect on all other areas. To change a system, the intervention must be designed to impact all three frames concurrently. Creating an entirely new organization is, therefore, not just a matter of devising a new strategy, restructuring various internal systems, or of changing management style, but of doing all three at the same time in a coordinated manner.

Whole Field Change™

Implementing a sustainable, large-scale change process may require commitment of from one to three years and include analysis and learning, meetings, seminars, coaching, process alignment training and conversations, and whole-system conferences, both internally and externally focused. Leaders will need to bring the entire organization together in different group sizes and configurations to identify the system's limitations and reframe them, to figure out how to access new levels of productivity, to begin creating provocative ideas about their future, and to generate new strategies for positively impacting the environment.

The components of a Whole Field Change™ process, generally speaking, must be co-created, organized, and delivered within the timeframe in a coordinated, systematic process. Figure 2 suggests how these might be sequenced. Meetings with different groups are indicated above the twelve-month timeline; coordinated leadership development programs are indicated below the timeline.

Some of the structures for change that should be considered for inclusion in a Whole Field Change™ process are described below:

1. Off-site meetings for members of the board to align their support for the change process.

2. Having representatives of the board, as liaisons but also as stakeholders, participate in leadership development and in other components of the process.

3. Chartering a group composed of representatives of all organizational levels and key departments to guide the transformational change process. Some-

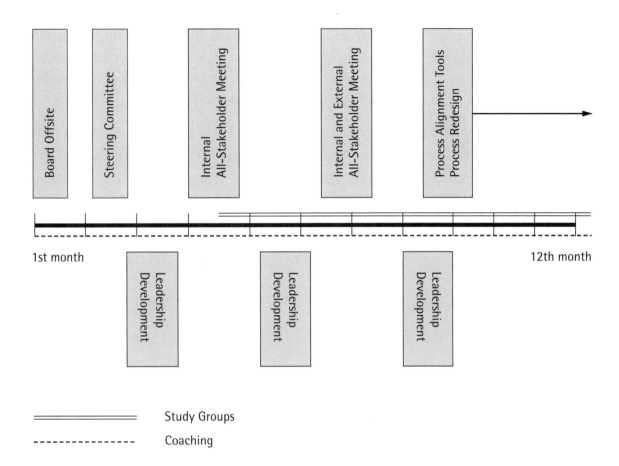

Figure 2. Suggested Timeline for Whole Field Change

times referred to as a steering committee, its members are asked to focus on the entire system, rather than on the pieces they face operationally day-to-day. To do this they should be given the leadership tools for understanding, supporting, and sustaining change. This occurs in the leadership development programs.

4. Stakeholder gatherings, both internal and external, to launch the change process, enhance cooperation, and build relationships across functions and levels and with community stakeholder groups. Since leaders must give employees a strong sense of the history of the enterprise and what's good about its past, while driving toward an as-yet-obscure future, these gatherings assist the leader in solidifying change commitments. In preparation for these gatherings, the leader's job is to frame the key questions and issues.

5. Process alignment, the translation of new vision and intention into concrete mechanisms, such as policies, procedures, and work processes, that form the organization's infrastructure. How people are participating in the organization,

how they are being acknowledged and rewarded, how partnerships are established and supported, and how results were achieved—all are demonstrations of alignment, or misalignment, with a newly stated strategic intention and thus an appropriate subject of a process alignment team's scrutiny.

6. Providing ongoing coaching and learning via study groups deepens participants' understanding of and ability to apply the tools and concepts presented, add velocity to the accomplishment of specific objectives, develop personal leadership, especially in "blind spots," and address specific issues within the leadership team. Study groups become the vehicles for discussion and deeper inquiry into the concerns and questions raised during the change process. Each person's study group becomes the center for practice and application of new ideas and a resource for building resilience during the change.

The Leader's New Intelligence

It takes understanding itself as a system and building the capacity to think systemically and act systematically for an organization to be ready to be a powerful player in the global business of delivering quality products and services. A leader with a high whole-system change IQ makes this possible, for this leader has learned how to structure the process of change to include *concurrent* lines of inquiry and process redesign. This leader can assure that the organization takes its place at the table of those who've achieved success at transforming themselves.

As consultants and coaches to these leaders, we need to build our own change design capabilities. When we do, the stories of whole-system change that have succeeded will far outstrip the stories of those that have failed.

Sherene Zolno, RODC, *is a researcher, educator, and consultant whose expertise includes working with leadership teams to ready them for the future and assisting organizations in identifying strategic intentions, improving operations, and transforming culture. Her research-based* New Century Leadership™ *program and* Timeline for Tomorrow™ *process form the foundation for whole system change in several major organizations. She served on ASTD's OD Professional Practice Area Board. Her writing has been published in ASTD's* Research Monograph *and OD Network's* OD Practitioner *and* VisionAction Journal, *in Pfeiffer's* 2000 *and* 2002 Annuals, *as well as in numerous other professional publications.*

The W.I.T. Model for Debriefing Team Initiatives

Cher Holton

Summary

This article presents and describes the W.I.T. Model, which can be used to ensure successful and productive debriefs of training activities.

It has been said that participants never question their own data. That's what makes the debriefing phase of any team activity the most crucial to a facilitator's success. If the activity is just fun, participants will leave saying, "Sure it was fun, but what was the point?"

As a facilitator, you can never assume that participants will "get it." The debriefing phase is what separates the pros from the rookies, and the best of the best know how to draw the magical "aha's" from the participants themselves.

The W.I.T. Model is a simple, yet powerful way to facilitate the debriefing of a team activity. It is easy to remember because the word W.I.T. reminds you that you have to keep a sense of humor! Here's how it works:

W = What (Specific Descriptions)

Encourage participants to begin processing what happened during the activity. For example, how did the team respond to the instructions? How did the team approach the activity? What roles emerged, and who filled them? What was the level of involvement and commitment to success among team members? How did team members communicate with one another?

The goal during this phase of the debriefing is to start people talking about the activity in a risk-free way, generating observations of what happened.

I = Impact (How the "Whats" Affected the Result)

During this phase, participants begin discussing how the actions and behaviors of team members impacted the overall result. For example, what behaviors helped the team achieve success? Where were the "aha" moments, and how were they incorporated into the work of the team? What communication issues created problems? How were disagreements and diverse opinions handled? What worked—and why? What got in the way—and how could it be avoided in the future?

The goal during this phase is to create a deeper discussion, helping team members to recognize the impact of their behaviors on each other and on the final result.

T = Transfer (How This Is Like What Happens at Work)

This is the most critical phase of the debriefing, and the one most often overlooked by inexperienced facilitators. This is where the rubber meets the road! During this phase, participants discuss how what they have learned relates back to the "real-life" work situations. For example, where do team members see similar behaviors in a work setting? What did team members learn from this experience that could transfer back to the job setting and help them work more effectively and productively?

With each phase of the W.I.T. debriefing process, the level of intensity and risk increases. As a facilitator, your job is to let the participants "lead the dance," and to be responsive to whatever input they provide. Your role is to craft the debriefing session so participants leave recognizing they have been involved in a powerful experience that transforms the way they approach their work. By using the W.I.T. Model, you can achieve this while maintaining your wonderful sense of humor! And that's really when the best learning takes place, after all!

Cher Holton, Ph.D., *president of The Holton Consulting Group, Inc., is an impact consultant focusing on bringing harmony to life: with customers, among team members, and in life. In addition to being one of fewer than a handful of professionals world-wide who have earned both the Certified Speaking Professional and Certified Management Consultant designations, she has authored several books, including* The Manager's Short Course to a Long Career, Living at the Speed of Life: Staying in Control in a World Gone Bonkers!, *and* Crackerjack Choices: 200 of the Best Choices You Will Ever Make.

A Champion's Role in Sustaining a Distance Learning Program

Aynsley Leigh Hamel and Zane L. Berge

Summary

This paper reviews the role, tasks, and characteristics of a distance learning (DL) champion in sustaining a distance learning program, with the conclusion that a DL champion can have a significant role in the sustainability of a program.

It takes a great deal of resources, time, and work to bring a distance learning (DL) program live in any organization, regardless of size and culture. However, once it is moving, how does an organization keep the DL program going? A number of factors can contribute to the continuation of a successful program, including a champion who will take a significant leadership role. This article examines what that champion needs to do. While a champion may look a little different in every organization, he or she must take on some common tasks and have some key characteristics.

Attributes of a Champion

The DL champion may be an instructor who finds that the current system contains some good components but sees room for improvement. She may be a middle manager who is very impressed with the results of the current program and wants more. She may be a vice president who witnessed how the program transformed a mediocre employee into one who was enthusiastic about work and wanted to learn more. It might even be the project manager who worked diligently to make the program happen in the first place, and now wants to keep the momentum going. The champion may come from any number of places within the organization.

However, champions share some common characteristics and conduct similar activities. First, a DL champion needs to see both the small and large picture through an environmental scan to see the current issues and opportunities. Champions assess what did work and market those elements (Gold, 2005). They examine what good the program has already done and look to expand on it. The champion will look beyond just the financial savings that the program garnered for the company to see the effectiveness and who benefited (Berge & Kendrick, 2005). In addition, the champion engages personnel and the leaders who need to be involved in order to keep the momentum going.

The champion must be a visionary charting a new course and explaining why the DL program should go in this direction. As will be demonstrated later, working with senior leadership can provide new opportunities for the champion to show how the DL program can be utilized in different facets of company life.

Even if the program is successful in the beginning, the DL champion must understand what made it that way. Was it just the novelty of the program? Was it mandated, meaning that everyone was required to participate, even if they were reluctant? Was it the department that offered to experiment with it first? "The single biggest danger in business and life, other than outright failure, is to be successful without being resolutely clear about *why* you are successful in the first place" (Collins, 2001, p. 213). This means going beyond just collecting data that demonstrates cost-effectiveness to seeing a picture of more employees trained, the use of more tools to make more sales, or whatever the initial goals of the program promised to deliver in a given time frame. The DL champion understands that the program cannot rest on its laurels, but rather needs to continue to innovate, reach out to new people, and garner new resources. As stated in Berge (2001, p. 14), "Organizations are similar to individuals in that they also engage in new tasks and the implementation of new processes, so they are not static in terms of their experiences and the accumulation of new knowledge." Therefore, the champion is much more than just one who keeps the program at its current place. The champion is engaged in finding new markets, understanding what the program has going for it and what forces are against it, and deciding what it will take to overcome new obstacles.

From Novelty to Acceptance

A new program brings excitement partially because of its novelty, but the excitement can fade as it becomes a part of the landscape of the organization. How does the DL champion continue to engage people in DL? The first way is to match up what DL can do in order to assist the organization in reaching new goals. Assuming that it has been decided that DL will do more than just collect dust in the server room, a strategic plan must be built. It has to include goals, policies, programs, actions, decisions, and additional resources (Berge & Kendrick, 2005). In addition, "Don't go crazy trying to determine your company's investment; devote energy toward finding the best value for the e-learning enterprise" (Gold, 2003, para. 27). This means that, instead of determining how much money DL saved the training department, see where it was beneficial in terms of training a large number of staff in a short amount of time and how it made a project that seemed impossible possible. The DL champion needs to show where DL has recently added value to the company and where it can do so in the future.

The champion must engage the current leadership in learning what DL has done and its potential in the future. For example, at Deloitte Consulting, the chief learning officer (CLO) demonstrated to the rest of the senior leadership what DL could do to a transformation as large as entering into the new market of financial services consulting (Gold, 2003). Deloitte was able to train thousands of employees through a centralized mechanism in a relatively short amount of time. This impressed the CEO with the advantages that DL could leverage if Deloitte opted to enter other new markets or if changes that required training needed to occur quickly. However, unless the CLO had educated the CEO and other leaders as to how DL made the transformation happen quickly and in a centralized manner, this important point could have been lost.

By talking with and listening to senior leadership, a champion can uncover new opportunities to leverage DL for long-term company goals. "Leadership must understand how distance training can assist them in meeting the organization's objectives" (Berge & Kendrick, 2005, para. 24). Rick McAnnally, the director of global talent management and diversity for John Deere, says that one must be engaged in business discussions in order to have an impact: "You can't be disassociated when business discussion is going on—you have to be a part of it" (Davenport, 2006, p. 43). If senior leadership does not know about it, they may bypass DL altogether when determining how best for the organization to reach its goals in the future.

To keep the program going, the DL champion must also communicate effectively with all involved. Are employees aware of the program's existence? In the case of PNC Bank, the simple answer was no. It seemed that only the employees building the DL project were aware of its existence, but those outside of the group did not. Therefore, when the program was launched, the reception was less than enthusiastic. After examining why, the DL group realized that few knew about it, so the group diligently worked with staff at all levels to promote the program. Kodak regularly publicizes its program through success stories in its newsletters, posting information on the company's website, and utilizing company-wide emails to inform employees about new resources within DL (Gold, 2003). Marketing what is going on and what is planned keeps the whole company engaged in DL, making them want more if available and encouraging them to take advantage of it when possible.

The DL champion can also ensure that everyone has continued equal access to the programs. Maybe a program was only tested on a select few individuals at the beginning. If the DL program receives rave reviews through a couple of employees, then others might desire access as well. Just because the senior leadership and a small handful of employees can use it does not mean that the organization is prepared to have everyone start using it (Berge & Kendrick, 2005). Therefore, the DL champion has to leverage the resources necessary in order to ensure that everyone can use the program when they want or need it.

Making Cultural Change Happen

Is sustaining DL in an organization a cultural change that the champion must engage in? Yes. Although the novelty of the program wears off, the champion must demonstrate to all facets of the organization that DL is there to stay and what is in it for them. The champion must show to all employees that learning is a valued component of the organization and that DL can help be a part of this important cultural change.

Demonstrating how DL can directly impact them is one way to foster interest from all staff in the organization. For example, John Deere University's course offerings are tied directly to new employment opportunities within the company. If an employee meets certain criteria, he or she is welcome to apply for any job opportunities of interest (Davenport, 2006). In addition, a tracking system shows what courses employees are taking or are in the process of taking so that the employees can share progress with their supervisors.

Making cultural change happen can be one of the most difficult barriers to knock down when trying to weave DL into the fabric of any organization. If it is perceived that learning is not valued, then any attempts to engage employees in learning will fall on deaf ears. Who wants to engage in an activity that is not valued by the organization? Or if the organization is slow to adopt technology for any reason, then it is very likely that the organization will be very slow to adopt technologically mediated learning opportunities (Berge & Kendrick, 2005). Therefore, a champion must identify any barriers that may persist and ways to go around them or through them. The champion must understand all forces—both those that drive the organization toward the goal (known as driving forces) and those that keep the organization from reaching the goal (known as the restraining forces) (Lifter, Kruger, Okun, Tabol, Poklop, & Shishmanian, 2005). Lifter goes on to state that champions must understand "the most important driving and restraining forces operating on one's organization in order to effect change" (Lifter, Kruger, Okun, Tabol, Poklop, & Shishmanian, 2005, p. 15). Maybe the technological structure cannot support this kind of initiative. Finding the resources for new servers and/or staff might be a step in the right direction. Perhaps the instructors are less than knowledgeable. Therefore, choosing new instructors and making them available for employees to talk with or email may help smooth relations over. While cultural change will take time and resources, identifying what makes staff resistant to change can help pave the way toward a brighter future for DL, and a champion makes that work happen.

Maintaining Momentum

A DL champion must wear a number of "hats" when continuing the momentum behind a DL program. He or she must engage with all members of an organization to see where new opportunities may hide and then exploit them. Examining where the senior leadership wants to take the organization can provide a plethora of opportunities, as illustrated by the earlier example of Deloitte Consulting and also the case of McAnnally from John Deere, who advocates for a champion to be involved with all business discussions and demonstrate how DL can be a part of their future plans. A champion cannot just react, but rather must be *proactive* in continuing to reach for new opportunities, drawing from past successes and demonstrating new uses for DL and related technologies.

Finding out who did not participate before and why may provide many new opportunities in the future. For example, Kodak discovered that many employees were not engaged the first time their DL program was released because they did not want to learn a new software in order to try it. Employees preferred applications that were simple, because learning with certain applications that were more sophisticated meant they had to first learn how to use the application (Gold, 2003). The problem didn't lie specifically with the DL, but with a need for more application training.

In addition to exploring new learning opportunities for employees, it is important to explore other ways to utilize DL that are not restricted to learning new skills. For example, DL could be used to alert employees to the new branding of a company's products. In the case of an acquisition, employees can use it to learn about the newly acquired company and how the acquired company will be integrated into the main corporation. Capital One Financial, Inc., utilizes DL as a way for executives to engage with employees on a variety of subjects in a seminar fashion, discussing current business goals, successes, and challenges (Salopek & Davenport, 2005). DL must be looked at in ways other than just providing courses in a quick and reliable manner; it must be viewed as a tool that can be utilized in many different ways (Rosenberg, 2001).

In addition to seeking new ways to use DL, the champion listens for ways to improve it. Some of the companies mentioned, including Kodak, examined reasons why employees were opting to not use DL and then made necessary changes. A champion can also explore new ways of delivering the learning opportunities, such as more blended learning techniques to better meet the needs of learners and to pique their interest.

While it is important to bring down barriers through more or better resources, sometimes working around them can be just as effective. A DL champion looks for those opportunities and exploits them to meet the goal.

"Sustainable transformations follow a predictable pattern of buildup and breakthrough . . . with persistent pushing in a consistent direction over a long period of time . . . eventually (it will be) hitting the point of breakthrough" (Collins, 2001, p. 186). The DL champion takes on a leadership role that helps to push the organization toward desired goals through the use of DL. The champion recommends that senior leadership consider DL in the future by engaging with them about past successes and future projects and promotes DL to all staff through new initiatives and by demonstrating how it directly affects them. The champion continuously puts out new information about DL opportunities, to make sure that everyone is aware of the program and can participate. In short, the champion is engaged, takes responsibility for his or her role, and constantly evaluates the pace of progress and adjusts accordingly (Carnell & Shank, 2003).

Conclusion

We have shown what a champion of DL can do to overcome various barriers to sustain DL in an organization. While the champion may look a little different in each organization, some of the roles he or she will play are similar. A champion helps to maintain and expand a DL program. A champion can overcome various barriers, including those that are cultural. The sustainability of a DL program in an organization will look different in each one and will take its own unique path.

References

Berge, Z.L. (2001). A framework for sustaining distance training. In Z.L. Berge (Ed.), *Sustaining distance training: Integrating learning technologies into the fabric of the enterprise* (pp. 13–27). San Francisco, CA: Jossey-Bass.

Berge, Z.L., & Kendrick, A.A. (2005). Can interest in distance training be sustained in corporate organizations? *International Journal of Instructional Technology and Distance Learning, 2*(2).

Carnell, M., & Shank, S. (2003). The champion's role in successful six sigma deployments. Retrieved October 11, 2006, from www.isixsigma.com/library/content/c020422a.asp

Collins, J. (2001). *Good to great.* New York: HarperCollins.

Davenport, R. (2006). John Deere champions workforce development. *T+D, 60*(4), 40–43.

Gold, M. (2003, August). Eight lessons about e-learning from five organizations. *Training & Development.*

Lifter, K., Kruger, L., Okun, B., Tabol, C., Poklop, L., & Shishmanian, E. (2005, April). Transformation to a web-based preservice training program: A case study. *Topics in Early Childhood Special Education, 25*(1), 15–24.

Rosenberg, M.J. (2001). *e-Learning: Strategies for delivering knowledge in the digital age.* New York: McGraw-Hill.

Salopek, J., & Davenport, R. (2005, October). 29 organizations that leverage learning to achieve amazing results. *Training & Development,* p. 59.

Aynsley Leigh Hamel *is a 1999 graduate of Gettysburg College in Gettysburg, Pennsylvania, where she received a bachelor of arts degree in history and women's studies. She currently is employed at VISICU, Inc., in Baltimore, Maryland, as an executive assistant to the vice presidents of client services and clinical services. She is also pursuing her master's in distance education at the University of Maryland University College online.*

Zane L. Berge *is an associate professor, Instructional Systems Development Graduate Program, at the University of Maryland System, UMBC campus. His scholarship in the field of computer-mediated communication and distance education includes numerous articles, chapters, workshops, and presentations. He consults internationally in distance education.*

Is Anyone Doing Formative Evaluation?

James L. Moseley and Nancy B. Hastings

Summary

Formative evaluation supports the change process by providing program designers and developers an opportunity to evaluate and improve programs, products, procedures, practices, processes, and other entities while they are still fluid. The Formative Evaluation Checklist (FEC), introduced here, is intended to provide practitioners with a guide to aid in the successful completion of formative evaluation of instructional programs and products.

The FEC is divided into five phases, each sub-divided into four categories. Under each category you will find a series of Yes or No questions. If you can answer Yes to each question included on the checklist, you have successfully completed a robust formative evaluation.

Formative Evaluation

The answer to the question raised in our title is a definitive YES. When Aunt Rose makes her delicious spaghetti sauce, she tastes it as she continues to add her secret seasonings. She repeats the process several times until the sauce is perfection. That's formative evaluation. When your design team decides to limit production of the new safety manual to only 250 copies (rather than the planned 2,000) until the flaws are worked out, that's formative evaluation. When you give your design document to a small group of potential users, listen to their responses to the objectives, content, strategies, and so forth, and make the necessary changes that they suggest, that's formative evaluation. It happens frequently in all kinds of organizations.

Formative evaluation is the type of evaluation that is done while your products, processes, procedures, and practices are fluid. In other words, you can still make the necessary changes before signing off. In instructional systems design (ISD), formative evaluation occurs at all stages: analysis, design, development, implementation, and evaluation. Cronbach said, "Evaluation, used to improve the course while it is still fluid, contributes more to improvement of education than evaluation used to appraise a product already placed on the market" (1966, p. 236).

Although, Michael Scriven (Tyler, Gagne, & Scriven, 1967) coined the term "formative" evaluation, Cambre's early work, in the 1920s and 1930s, showed an interest in formative evaluation in conjunction with the development of film and radio. Many other researchers have also addressed this type of evaluation, offering a variety of terms for the same process. It has been called "developmental testing," "tryout," "learner verification," "storyboarding," "debugging," "prototype evaluation," and "learner validation" (Markle, 1989). The history behind these terms is rich in research and has contributed immensely to the field of educational evaluation.

The Formative Evaluation Checklist (FEC)

The Formative Evaluation Checklist (FEC), provided below, includes a series of questions that should be answered when conducting a robust formative evaluation of an instructional program or product. The FEC is presented in five phases: analysis, design, development, implementation, and evaluation. Each phase corresponds with a stage in the ISD process. The individual phases are subdivided into four categories, each consisting of multiple questions that should be considered when conducting formative evaluation. To use the FEC, simply answer Yes or No to each question in each of the four categories, at each stage in the process. A glossary of terms follows the checklist.

Review your answers. If you have responded Yes to all questions, you have conducted a robust formative evaluation. If you have answered No to one or more questions, you are encouraged to review the question or questions and revisit your formative evaluation plans for that phase.

Analysis

1. Need

    a. Is the program based on a thorough needs assessment that incorporates analysis, front-end analysis, needs assessment, needs analysis, discrepancy analysis, gap analysis, etc.?

    b. Is the planned program a suitable solution for the identified need?

    c. Are the intended outcomes of the program aligned with the output of the needs assessment?

2. Learner

   a. Have you identified the target population for the program?

   b. Does your target population have the prerequisite skills to succeed?

   c. Have you identified relevant characteristics of the target population, such as age, experience, attitude, and motivation, that may affect the design, development, implementation, and evaluation of the program?

3. Environment

   a. Have you studied the performance environment within which learners will be expected to use the knowledge, skills, or attitudes gained in the program?

   b. Have you taken steps to ensure that the performance environment will provide the necessary support for the program and learner?

   c. Have you studied the learning environment and taken steps to align it with the performance environment to facilitate transfer?

4. Alignment

   a. Are the need, the learner, and the environment aligned throughout the analysis phase?

Design

1. Goals and Objectives

   a. Have you identified relevant program goals, aligned with the identified need and the desired outcomes of the program?

   b. Have you completed a goal analysis and developed objectives that identify the audience, behavior, conditions, and degree of accuracy required to demonstrate mastery for each of the steps that must be mastered to attain the desired outcomes?

   c. Have you reviewed the goals, objectives, and proposed course content with the subject-matter expert for accuracy and completeness?

2. Assessment

   a. Have you developed plans to assess learner mastery of the terminal and enabling objectives?

    b. Are your assessment plans aligned with the behaviors, conditions, and degree of accuracy identified in the objectives?

    c. Have you determined when and how the assessment data will be collected and analyzed?

3. Instructional Strategies

    a. Are the instructional strategies matched to the required learning and the available instructional environment?

    b. Are the instructional strategies matched to the characteristics of the target audience to ensure learners remain motivated and engaged throughout the program?

    c. Are the selected instructional strategies matched to the abilities and expertise of the potential instructors?

4. Alignment

    a. Are all the goals and objectives, the assessment procedures, and the instructional strategies aligned for a solid design?

Development

1. Delivery Method

    a. Is the medium selected for the program appropriate for the content?

    b. Does the medium require specific learner skills and/or experiences and, if so, does the target audience possess those skills and/or experiences?

    c. Are there any limitations in the learning environment that may interfere with the effectiveness of the chosen delivery method?

2. Instructional Materials

    a. Have you considered the clarity of instruction regarding vocabulary level, sentence complexity, introductions, elaborations, conclusions, transitions, and directions and the impact of music, color, narration, and synchronization?

    b. Have you constructed a prototype of all instructional materials and piloted it with potential instructors and members of the target audience?

    c. Have you made any identified revisions and repeated the pilot process to test those revisions with potential instructors and members of the target audience?

3. Assessment Materials

   a. Have you considered the clarity of instruction regarding vocabulary level, sentence complexity, and directions?

   b. Have you constructed a prototype of all assessment materials and piloted it with potential instructors and members of the target audience?

   c. Have you made any identified revisions and repeated the pilot process to test those revisions with potential instructors and members of the target audience?

4. Alignment

   a. As the program is developed, are the delivery methods, the instructional materials, and the assessment materials fully aligned?

Implementation

1. Learner

   a. Have you considered the learners' perceptions of the instruction they have received?

   b. Have you considered the impact of the instruction on the learners, e.g., relevance of the instruction, confidence in learning the content, and general satisfaction?

   c. Have you resolved issues raised by learners regarding problematic areas they encountered with the instructional materials?

2. Instructor

   a. Have you sought data from instructors, trainers, managers, administrators, and others involved in the instruction?

   b. Have you provided instructors with all necessary materials, instructions, documentation, etc., to effectively implement the instruction?

   c. Have you resolved issues raised by instructors regarding problematic areas they encountered with the instructional content?

3. Environment

   a. Have you identified discrepancies in the anticipated and actual learning and performance environments and modified the program to accommodate these discrepancies whenever necessary?

    b. Does the learning environment include all necessary equipment, resources, and space to accommodate the needs of the learners and instructors?

    c. Have barriers in the performance environment that may interfere with transfer been identified and addressed?

4. Alignment

    a. Have the learners, the instructor, and the environment been aligned for user-friendly implementation?

Evaluation

1. Plan

    a. Have you developed a full-scope evaluation plan, including the identification of instruments, procedures, and personnel?

    b. Have you developed all instruments that will be used to collect the evaluation data?

    c. Have evaluation plans and materials been reviewed and piloted to identify problems with the evaluation design, including instruments, procedures, and personnel?

2. Data Collection and Analysis

    a. Is the evaluation plan targeted at the collection of meaningful data, and is it aligned with the identified need and the program goals and objectives?

    b. Have you analyzed the results, being mindful of the objectives, methods, and evaluation techniques?

    c. Have you used the evaluation data to decide what needs to be recycled, reviewed, modified, adapted, terminated, etc?

3. Revision

    a. Have you developed a plan to revise the program based on the evaluation data?

    b. Have you developed a plan to evaluate how any revisions made as a result of the original evaluation will impact the overall effectiveness of the program and planned for additional pilot-testing?

      c. Do these plans support ongoing evaluation and continuous improvement?

    4. Alignment

      a. Have the plan, the data collection and analyses procedures, and the revision suggestions been aligned?

Action Plan

Use these questions to guide your formative evaluation. Discuss them with other members of your design team. Your result will be a solid, robust, formative evaluation—one that your organization can support and value.

Glossary of Terms

Alignment: Synchronization of all aspects of the program or product, including methods, means, and tactics; important as a precursor for the success of all phases of formative evaluation.

    Alpha Testing: Very early phases of the pilot-test; prototype phase when the object is first able to run; usually conducted in the developer's office.

    Beta Testing: Later phases of the pilot-test when the object is closer to release and when the program is operating and ready for user feedback.

    Change: Process that occurs when an entity undergoes a modification or a transition; a break in the accustomed patterns and traditional ways of doing things.

    Environment: The context within which the evaluation occurs.

    Field Testing: Formal testing of all object components in the setting in which they are to be used.

    Full-Scope Evaluation: Term referring to the four types of evaluation (formative, summative, confirmative, and meta) that judge merit or value of a program, product, or intervention.

    Instructional Systems Design (ISD): A systematic procedure that includes analysis, design, development, implementation, and evaluation.

    Pilot-Test: Activities designed to try out procedures and make needed changes and adjustments in programs, products, or processes.

    Subject-Matter Expert (SME): The person who is most knowledgeable about the object that is being evaluated.

References

Cronbach, L. J. (1966). The logic of experiments on discovery. In L.M. Shulman & E. Keislar (Eds.), *Learning by discovery.* Chicago, IL: Rand-McNally.

Dick, W., Carey, L., & Carey, J.O. (2005). *The systematic design of instruction* (6th ed.). Boston, MA: Allyn & Bacon. Chapter 10, Designing and Conducting Formative Evaluations, includes an extensive account of the formative process in instructional design.

Flagg, B.N. (1990). *Formative evaluation for educational technologies.* Hillsdale, NJ: Lawrence Erlbaum Associates. The book's foci are on the concept, the practice, and the methods of conducting formative evaluations.

Markle, S.M. (1989). The ancient history of formative evaluation. *Performance & Instruction, 28*(7), 27–29. This is a succinct, informative article on formative evaluation for those readers who appreciate the history behind the concept.

Tessmer, M. (1993). *Planning and conducting formative evaluations.* London: Kogan Page. This book focuses on origins, characteristics, values, and limitations of formative evaluation with special emphasis devoted to the planning phase.

Tyler, R.W., Gagne, R.M., & Scriven, M. (1967). *Perspectives of curriculum evaluation.* Chicago, IL: Rand-McNally. This book is a classic on curriculum evaluation written by three eminent men in the field of curriculum and instruction.

James L. Moseley, Ed.D., LPC, CHES, CPT, *is associate professor of instructional technology in the College of Education at Wayne State University in Detroit, Michigan. He teaches human performance technology courses. He is a licensed professional counselor, a certified health education specialist, and a certified performance technologist. He is the recipient of numerous teaching and service awards, the co-author of five books, the author of a variety of articles and book chapters, and a member of both ISPI and ASTD.*

Nancy B. Hastings, Ph.D., *is a lecturer of instructional technology in the College of Education at Wayne State University in Detroit, Michigan. She teaches both traditional and online courses in instructional technology and has been instrumental in developing a fully online M.Ed. program. She also has extensive practical experience, having worked in corporate training and performance improvement for over fifteen years in both manufacturing and service-related settings.*

Trainer's Guides Revisited

George Hall

Summary

Trainer's guides not only provide the trainer with his or her "lines," but also describe detailed content, transitions, timing, and activities. There are many formats that are used to organize a trainer's guide. Regrettably, these guides are often poorly designed; they are not integrated with the participant's guide, the course PowerPoint slides, or the presentation of flip-chart exercises. Consequently, trainers are forced to create their own set of training materials, which integrate the various components of the course to supplement the trainer's guide. This paper explores how standard conventions regarding the layout of trainer's guides are obsolete and suggests a new standard. The author compares and contrasts features and benefits and concludes by offering a sample lesson plan.

Typical Lesson Plans

Trainer's guides are frequently designed using a standard template that is awkward and ineffective. Novice trainers are confused by this convention, which experienced trainers either ignore, work around, or compensate for by designing their own lesson plans. Typically, the layout of a trainer's guide follows a standard three-column convention. The first column, labeled Time, is for timing and type of activity. The second column, labeled Topic, is for the actual statements, questions, directions, and transitions between ideas. The third column, labeled Materials, lists media, the requisite pages in the participant's guide, and the PowerPoint slide by number (see Exhibit 1).

To deliver a course using a typical lesson plan, the instructor covers the material in the second column in the time frames specified in the first column. The instructor presents course content via PowerPoint slides and class exercises that coincide with the requisite pages in the participant's guide.

Exhibit 1.   Typical Trainer's Guide

Time	Topic	Materials
	Welcome	
20 min	Introductions	Slide 1

- Introduce yourself and the course topic: Value Chain Analysis.
- Tell participants that they are going to start off with a simple exercise.
- Ask participants to turn to page 2 of their Participant's Guide and turn to Class Exercise 1.   PG, page 2
- Answer Key is in Trainer's Guide Appendix page 14.
- Discuss how different words can be used to convey different ideas.   PG, page 3

Transition: We often use the word "value" to describe the contribution of a certain line of business. How can the word "value" be interpreted?

- Ask participants to introduce themselves and to state the first thing they think of when they hear the words "value chain."
- Record comments on flip chart.
- Leave comments on flip chart to discuss later.

To deliver the lecturette in this example, the instructor would have to coordinate the following:

- Read from page 1 of the Trainer's Guide to introduce the course.

- Show slide 1 and review content.

- Flip to the Participant's Guide page 2 and complete an exercise.

- Review content on the Participant's Guide page 3 and transition to next topic.

What frequently happens at this point is that novice trainers get lost in this convoluted series of directions. New trainers completing a train-the-trainer course, for example, will struggle with the challenge of completing these tasks in a poised, confident manner. In practice, what we see is a novice trainer holding the trainer's guide in one hand while painfully flipping to the participant's guide in the other. Things deteriorate further if the novice gets lost or if the unexpected happens, for example if the page numbers in the trainer's guide do not match the exercise outlined in the participant's guide. The connections between slides can become lost; the novice trainer missed the transition to the next slide because he or she was managing so many other aspects of the class. Slide 1, for example, might stay up for 20 minutes while the class members considered other topics in their participant's guides, which should have been reinforced in slides 2 through 4. In other words, the novice trainer is overwhelmed, floundering, or flustered. Participants are forced to move through the material is a disjointed manner, which affects their ability to learn, understand, and appreciate the material. In many ways, you cannot blame instructors for appearing unpolished because the trainer's guide itself (their primary resource) is disorganized and stiff.

Compensating for Design Flaws

Despite the organization of the trainer's guide, most instructors still learn how to lead the course in a poised, professional manner. How, exactly, do professional trainers accomplish this feat? The instructor is often forced to create his or her own notes, which stay true to the outline provided by the trainer's guide in terms of transitions, time spent on delivering content, and the timing of breaks. Professionals have always created their own work-arounds to awkward or unpolished conventions. Eventually, standards change and the convention is improved. The going convention in the design of training materials was adequate at a time when word processing programs, such as Microsoft Word, were state-of-the-art. New programs, notably Abobe Creative Suite 2, offer unparalleled capabilities to design a truly useful trainer's guide. In this next section, we will explore how this technology can be used by trainers to improve their lesson plans.

Revised Lesson Plans

We are needlessly punishing our novice trainers and our staff by designing training guides that read like technical support manuals. We, the training staff, designed the trainer's guide and the participant's guide, and we are ultimately responsible for improving these materials. What would a better trainer's guide template look like? Adobe InDesign, a professional page layout software preferred by publishing and design professionals, is an ideal program to create such a template. This software changes how one thinks about the layout of a trainer's guide. A trainer's guide no longer has to have three columns and be designed as a sequence of single-sided pages. Trainers should not have to flip or fumble around in the trainer's guide to find an appendix or the corresponding page in the participant guide that complements a PowerPoint slide. A new template would be visually appealing and allow the trainer to see (simultaneously) the participant's guide and PowerPoint slide, as shown in Exhibit 2.

Slide 7

Value Chain Analysis

- Technology
- Inbound Logistics
- Operations
- Outbound Logistics
- Marketing
- Service
- Procurement
- Human Resources

Value Chain Analysis

A value chain analysis is integral to understanding the changes that took place at GE under their legendary CEO, Jack Welch.

The Boundary-less Organization

Shortly after becoming CEO in 1981, Welch began removing layers of management and tearing down functional silos.

Welch believed, and rightly so, that silos created walls.

Walls impede the flow of information.
Walls create competition among groups.

GE needed speed and transparency.

The boundary-less organization enabled GE to generate and disseminate information very quickly.

p.4   Participant's Guide

Value Chain Analysis

9:00–9:30 30 Minutes

1. Show slide 7 (Value Chain Analysis)

2. Introduce the topic by asking questions. The following questions can be used:

   Can one say that how a company organizes itself is as important as—if not more important than—its strategy?

   How do companies make certain that strategy and structure are aligned with each other?

3. Make these points:

   At perhaps the most basic level, we can think about a functional structure being organized around a firm's value chain.

   A value chain depicts the relationships among separate activities that are performed to create a product or service.

   A Value Chain Analysis involves looking at the following components:

   - Technology
   - Inbound Logistics
   - Operations
   - Outbound Logistics
   - Marketing
   - Service
   - Procurement
   - Human Resources

   The value chain helps us understand the changes that took place at GE.

4. Refer to the discussion of Jack Welch's ideas about value chain analysis on page 4 of the PG.

p.4   Trainer's Guide

Exhibit 2. Sample Trainer's Guide in InDesign

Although the trainer's guide and the participant's guide are typically thought of as separate documents, they are not. Fortunately, this separation is artificial and merely a convention that can be revisited. Ideally, the trainer's guide and the participant's guide should be designed to work together. A layout involving two facing pages allows for a closer coordination of activities than a series of single-sided pages does. The layout should include the following features:

Trainer's Guide Layout

The trainer's guide page starts on the left-hand side of the book or binder so that the instructor can see his or her own training notes. Ideally, the trainer's guide should be customized so that it reflects the instructor's own speaking voice, tone, and experience. Large margins are used in the trainer's guide to allow space for notes, examples, and stories. Transitions between ideas are made explicit and clear, and the instructor can set the appropriate context because there is no confusion about which slide to show or what topic comes next. The flow and timing of the class is better because there is no confusion about when or how to lead an exercise or take a break. Footers, which include dates and version numbers, are used so that the instructor can have a clear sense of where he or she is in the course at all times.

Participant's Guide Layout

The participant's guide page is placed on the right-hand side of the book or binder so that the instructor can see the corresponding page in the participant's guide. This eliminates the need for the instructor to flip back and forth between the trainer's and participant's guides. The participant's guide page can feature a miniature copy of the corresponding slide so that the instructor can see the slide that accompanies the material. Notes regarding how to run an exercise (e.g., time spent in groups for an exercise, the need for handouts, the use of props or prizes) in the participant's guide can be included in this section as well.

Closing

The most dynamic training departments I work with are continually refining their processes. A colleague once remarked, "Training is a business. We need to run our training departments *as if* we are an outsourced service." I could not agree more with this sentiment. The business environment changes too quickly, and the demands placed on employees have never been greater. In the information era of Peter Drucker's famous "knowledge worker," constantly examining obsolete conventions and revising your training department's materials is critical to a process of continuous improvement.

George Hall, MBA, MS, *a principal in the firm Bracken Najor Hall LLC, consults on workplace learning/performance issues. He teaches in the College of Business Administration at Strayer University and the University of Phoenix. He is the American Society for Training and Development (ASTD) field editor for management development. He can be reached at georgechall@comcast.net.*

Applying Action Learning in Assessing Facilitation Skills
An English National Health Service Case Study
Catherine Guelbert

Summary

This article is a case study in how action learning techniques can be used to assess the skills of facilitators for action learning. The goal of our program was twofold: (1) to create a large number of leaders familiar with action learning who could disseminate and implement changes desired in a national healthcare organization and (2) to find the right caliber of facilitator to support the process.

In my role with the National Health Service in London, I had been assigned the task of selecting facilitators for an action learning program. On one level this was a purely business issue requiring only the drafting of a specification to support a successful recruitment of facilitators. However, an evaluation of the assessment process brought to light a number of observations about action learning and the impact the process itself had on applicants and contributors alike.

The ideas discussed are predicated on the notion that if action learning is a powerful tool for change and leadership development, then the identification of people with the right skills to facilitate and advise action learning groups is crucial to success.

The approach underpinning the practice described here is the classic Revans theory and models for action learning. Reg Revans (1907–2003) is the acknowledged father of action learning, a technique for solving business problems. He developed this in the National Health Service and National Coal Board in the 1960s and subsequently went on to apply the method with huge success in Belgium. As a consequence, action learning is now practiced globally and in all business sectors. People work together in facilitated groups with the goal of addressing intractable problems through critical questioning and dialogue. The role of the facilitator is to enable this process to develop naturally within the group to the point at which facilitation is no longer required.

The work described in this study was evaluated by the Revans Institute for Action Learning and Research at Salford University and resulted in some significant observations about the rate and depth of learning and understanding that can be gained in a short time.

The issues considered here are as follows:

- How can you bring together a bureaucratic process such as recruitment and an intense experiential process such as action learning to create a dynamic and rigorous environment for assessment of practice?

- How can you really judge the quality of practice of facilitators in action learning? What are you looking for and how do you know when you have found it?

- Is it possible for participants who are relatively inexperienced in action learning to assimilate and understand its principles so as to be in a position to judge the quality of facilitation they are receiving?

- What are the learning outcomes, and what impact might they have on individuals and organizations?

Background

The work took place in the context of rapid change in the English National Health Service (NHS) in 2002. Government policies created a momentum for modernization and transformation, which required something different from traditional business methods, and action learning was applied as a means of assisting with transformational change.

As part of this change, the number of strategic-level organizations was lessened, and a new form of front-line organization, the Primary Care Trust (PCT), was created. The aim of the program was to involve all 302 PCTs in action learning groups that would contribute to and support transformational change. The target was to achieve one hundred action learning groups by 2005, each expected to run for twelve months with a membership of six people made up from senior managers and clinical members from three different PCTs.

In the summer of 2002, a joint program team between NatPaCT (National Primary Care Action Team) and the NHS Leadership Centre was established to select the action learning group facilitators. NatPaCT held responsibility for the program and the Leadership Centre provided specialist advice and support.

The recruitment process was conducted according to government procurement procedures. This provided a framework that ensured equity for contractors and clarity of purpose and criteria.

The desired outcome was the selection of facilitators with a very specific skill set who demonstrated a very sophisticated appreciation of action learning.

Setting Out the Specification for Action Learning Facilitation

The first stage of the process was to specify exactly what was required. The challenge was to be clear about what the action learning process would deliver in the context of the goal to bring about transformational change. The case for action learning was predicated on the personal preference of influential advisers whose experience of it had identified the power of the approach in unlocking creative thinking and action. However, a belief in the efficacy of a methodology is not enough in itself. It has to be tested, and there has to be evidence of efficacy. There is widely documented evidence of the success of action learning in the public sector in the UK and elsewhere, in both the public and private sectors. Yet, because it is a qualitative methodology, it is subject to critique because of the lack of outcome-based metrics. In addition, practice in action learning varies so much that it is sometimes difficult to know what one is getting in terms of process and outcome until the practitioner has worked with a group for some time.

The work to scope the specification for this project and to outline the initial design for the action learning process was led by me and the Nat Pact lead director for change. We were very clear that we had to focus on creating a process that would engender transformational change. To enable this, the facilitators we would appoint to support the action learning program had to be of high quality, and the challenge was to set the brief in a way that conveyed very clearly how we wanted to achieve this.

In order for the main project to be successful, we had to have a means to ensure that the facilitators supporting the project were committed to and could practice the principles of action learning that we considered would deliver the outcome sought by the Cabinet Office.

Our experience of appointing facilitators in the past had had varied outcomes. The usual method involved the standard Department of Health or NHS procurement processes. These are detailed and rigorous and are designed to test the market and ensure fairness for potential suppliers. Normally, expressions of interest would be invited, followed by evaluation, invitation to tender, and then an invitation to the individual or company to present to a panel that would then assess the tender and award a contract.

The process itself does not test the expertise of companies and individuals; yet we were concerned about testing the quality of practice, not the quality of company presentation.

At this point we were designing the tendering process and scoping out the design of the actual project. We had to do both concurrently to ensure that there would be coherence between input and output. Because this was a national program, we also had to take account of geographical requirements. Experience had taught us that people will not travel long distances to participate in action learning groups. If urgent work or other matters arose, they would take priority over learning. Thus, we needed to attract high-quality facilitators in a range of locations. We also wanted to ensure that groups developed their work in such a way as to be able to have impact on the health care system. This meant that we had to create the capacity for people to find one another within the NHS and to connect either with others who had similar problems or who were trying to make a system change in their local health economies.

The action learning principles we applied derived from Reg Revans' (1998) classic approach, which proposes that:

- Individuals have responsibility for their own learning;

- People will learn with and from one another;

- The focus is on learning and taking action;

- The outcome is a change either of behavior or some aspect of health care that improves patient experience; and

- The role of the facilitator is to enable learning.

It was this last item that challenged us to think about how we could design a process within the procurement regime that would be consistent with good practice in procurement *and* test quality of practice.

The approach we developed extended the standard business method by proposing that we ask applicants to interact with groups brought together for the occasion. They would work on a case study with the group. The intention was to ask the individuals, be they from companies, consortia, or independent consultants, to spend forty minutes with an action learning group comprised of people from PCTs, some of whom had never engaged with action learning before. The interaction would be independently observed and evaluated. It was ambitious and required a high level of planning and organization. It was also high risk because we already knew that there is wide variation in the application of action learning methods and we needed to be clear about what we wanted to achieve, what sort of practice we were looking for, and how that could be tested and evaluated.

From the outset we met with a lot of questions and some cynicism from providers who objected to the fact that we wanted to meet the practitioners, let alone ask them to demonstrate their practice. There was concern that we were asking too much of the practitioners, that the process would be too stressful for them. There was conjecture as to whether people who had never participated previously in an action learning group could come cold to the process, assimilate the principles of action learning, and make a judgment as to whether what they experienced from the facilitator was, first, a powerful form of action learning and, second, one that would have the impact on the program we were designing. We knew we would have to answer all these points through the recruitment process and in the debriefing to the companies, practitioners, and to our sponsors.

We invited the Revans Institute for Action Learning and Research to independently evaluate the assessment process and to observe and assess the practitioners. We worked closely with the team led by director David Botham. All members of the team were experienced facilitators, and all were engaged in researching action learning at the doctoral level. All had experience of developing and running action learning programs in the public sector. However, this was the first time any of the team had been involved in the kind of process we were designing, and there were mixed views about whether it would succeed.

Having initiated the procurement process, we set aside two days for the assessment of the practitioners. Out of an initial set of fifty expressions of interest, four companies were invited to be assessed. Of these, two were well known (to the NHS) consultancies, one was an academic institution, and one was an independent consultant.

We were very clear with applicants that we would only select from those people who were directly assessed. We would not accept other people from the companies. In all there were thirty-four practitioners. Over the two days, we organized a process that gave each practitioner a forty-minute introductory session with a group. The groups were made up of volunteers from primary care and comprised a mix of chairs, chief executives, and staff from the Nat Pact and Leadership Centre teams. Each set worked with six to eight practitioners.

Initially, the project team had agreed to assess the applicants against a set of criteria derived for the procurement process. We ran into a number of problems with this and the case study.

First was in finding the right content. This could only be an introductory session, and we struggled with how the people involved could assimilate issues and roles in the time available. There would also be bias in that the groups would develop their knowledge through increased familiarization with the topic while each applicant would be fresh to it. What we really wanted to test was the quality of the facilitation as predicated by the Revans approach and the extent to which the facilitator could create a rapport with the group. Managing the assessment and analysis of performance against the suggested criteria did not look robust enough.

Through discussion with David Botham, we came to adopt a new, yet consistent, evidence-based approach. The change we made was to focus "entirely on the ability of the facilitator to create and sustain conscious learning relationships between themselves and the members of the action learning set" (Botham, 2003, personal communication). The applicants would therefore be assessed against questions such as:

- Can I learn from this facilitator?

- Does the facilitator exude experience in the process so that I (and others like me in the PCTs) can feel confident working with them?

- Is the facilitator able to create and sustain a relationship with us so we are learning from and with them and each other? (Botham, 2003, personal communication)

The briefing to the applicants was modified, and they were asked by letter to "focus on establishing rapport with the group. Please bear in mind again that we are looking at interactions between the facilitators and the set members and the capacity to facilitate transformational change at the point of care delivery."

The process design now looked like this:

- Each facilitator would engage with a group for forty minutes;

- The sessions were now content free, that is, there were no prescribed agendas;

- Groups comprised three or four people, most of whom had no experience of action learning, but at least one person in each group did have experience with action learning;

- Each group and facilitator was to be observed by an evaluator from the Revans Institute;

- At the end of each session, there was a period of twenty minutes for group members and the observer to discuss their experience and form a view about the facilitator;

- Separate rooms were made available for each group to meet and prepare; and

- Briefing material was circulated and briefing sessions scheduled prior to and at the beginning of the two days for volunteers (from PCTs and the Leadership Centre) and company representatives.

Facilitation and Approaches

As the groups were observed, it became clear that there were a number of different facilitation styles and approaches:

- *Highly structured:* This was when the facilitator constructed an outline of the sessions prior to meeting the group. This usually took the form of pre-prepared flip charts or handouts, which reflected the intentions of the facilitator and left no room for the group members to offer their views about how the session should be conducted.

- *Lecture:* Again, this was highly structured and consisted of a monologue delivered by the facilitator to the group. At the end of this, group members were requested to accept whatever the facilitator offered rather than contribute to the design of the discussion.

- *Scripted:* This was a variation on the above two approaches but left more room for participant involvement. It seemed that where facilitators were less confident of their skills they tended to be more reliant on a script to help them through the early stages of conversation with their group.

- *Teaching:* Very similar to the lecture, this approach consisted of making a presentation to the group as if the facilitator were presenting to a class or interview panel. Generally, the group members were not invited to participate in conversation until the facilitator was ready.

- *Technique:* This was an interesting variation on the lecture and teaching approaches, in which the facilitator presented a range of techniques that could be used during the course of the session. Rather than focus on the interaction, the facilitator tried to impress the group with a range of business techniques that were guaranteed to generate results in managing change. Typically, these were presented by companies whose tenders had reflected an emphasis on the "tool box" approach to change management.

- *Facilitator-led conversation:* In this approach, the facilitator opened the discussion with a few words and loosely set the context for the discussion. There was little direct reference to action learning, and the group members were soon invited to contribute to the dialogue.

- *Group-generated conversation:* In this approach, the group members were invited to participate as equal partners with the facilitator right from the beginning of the conversation.

There was little difference between the last two approaches, and generally the group members responded positively to facilitators who worked in this way. They treated the group members as equals and they respected the fact that the session was for the benefit of the group, not the facilitator. They also reflected a key principle of Revans' thinking, which is that the group is resourceful and the facilitator is there to act as a guide.

You will recall that we were looking for what we regarded as a sophisticated form of interaction between the facilitator and the group. We wanted to observe a conversation in which the group members felt confident that they could learn with and from the facilitator.

Reactions from the Group

Generally, groups reacted well to those facilitators who presented with little or nothing on paper. The more relaxed the facilitator was, the easier it seemed for group members to move into a conversation and become absorbed in the content offered by their peers. As noted earlier, there was no pre-set agenda, but there was no shortage of material to work on; groups wanted to discuss issues with bosses and peers, challenges of managing a service change, implementation of a new policy, closure of a hospital, managing inter-organizational politics and professional differences, and so on. Those facilitators who invited group members to offer issues for discussion made rare but pertinent interventions. Where facilitators attempted to control or dominate the conversation, the group reacted by either being polite or, as time went on and group members became more relaxed with the process, tolerant of the lack of skill and ruthless in their later analysis.

Which brings me onto the issue of to what extent apparent novices in action learning could assimilate and appreciate the technique to the point at which they felt confident to comment on the skill of a facilitator. The volunteers had been briefed at the beginning of the process. Some were already veterans of action learning, and some had no experience at all. In almost all cases, the first session for each group was very much a fact-finding mission. There was a lot going on for everyone: getting to know one another, settling down, accommodating the observers, and reacting carefully to the facilitators. Immediate reactions varied; those used to action learning offered different reactions from those new to it. The observers moderated reactions by bringing to bear their observations and advising groups to review their perspectives at the end of the process. By the end of day one, we had a full house of expert action learners. It was truly impressive how quickly groups became highly critical, discriminating, and consistent in their assessments. They did this by working closely together, agreeing on what worked well and what did not, and engaging actively in dialogue in the debriefing sessions. They rapidly formed their views of each facilitator to the extent that the evaluators reported that, when sessions went well, participants said the time flew by, and when they did not, one person commented that it was the longest forty minutes she had ever known.

It became apparent that the group members also developed a fine appreciation of the different forms of learning they were being subjected to. This is what enabled the earlier analysis of styles and presentation. A common set of definitions emerged, which gave group members the capacity to differentiate between what they found helpful and what they found less useful. For example, people made comments such as, "This felt like a therapeutic approach," "She was not confident," or "She was clear and had a plan, but was receptive to chaos at the start of the session," "It felt more comfortable . . . good interpersonal skills . . . felt safe . . . right balance and with right tone." Alternatively, some commented, "I felt dismissed as I did not have clarity, felt railroaded . . . not coming away with any learning."

Two things were important. One was the feeling of being treated with respect. These were all senior people with professional and life experience and they did not want to be "taught." Secondly, we had impressed upon them the need to think about the extent to which they felt they could learn with and from the facilitator. This test was applied over and over again and was critical in the analysis of each facilitator's interaction.

The Defining Factors

Of the thirty-four applicants, fourteen were selected.

So what was it that made the difference at the end of the day? The first thing was the personal qualities demonstrated by the facilitator. The groups were not impressed by arrays of management tools and techniques. They wanted to feel valued and respected as equals from the outset. The facilitators who were most warmly received were those who exuded humanity and humility. A consistent reaction from group members was that they found the person warm and open to ideas. These were people who invited conversation, were genuinely interested in the people they were meeting, were secure in themselves such that they did not need to impose their ideas or techniques on others, and were happy to initiate and guide a conversation that could lead to significant learning. It was important that they acknowledged the reciprocity of the learning process and thanked the group members for the privilege of working with them.

Also significant was the way in which facilitators used the technique of action learning as a prop or not. Revans and Botham have always described action learning as a process. It is practiced in many different forms (see Pearson, 2002) and at many different levels. In this case, the most successful facilitators were those who exercised the judgment that "less is more." A little introduction and setting of context were all that were required to enable the group to settle and then move quickly into conversation. The dialogue itself then presented the opportunity for critical thinking and learning without the need for extensive explanation. Group members found that they knew naturally what to do and quickly became impatient with facilitators who spent a long time introducing and explaining action learning.

Finally, two further qualities emerged. These were authenticity and a sense of courage or "being at ease." Again, the "less is more" factor weighed heavily in favor of those who offered the opportunity for an open dialogue. They enabled and guided discussion without dominating and ensured that all group members had the opportunity to contribute or, if not, acknowledged the deficit to the individual and the group.

Analysis and Conclusions

So what was happening here? We saw a number of groups of varied experience brought together to test an approach to learning in a contrived environment designed to test the capacity of facilitators to support and engender learning. What we found was that people were very quickly able to determine what worked well and what did not. Within hours, novice group members were able to describe action learning and explain why a particular facilitator was or was not fulfilling their learning expectations.

One member of the Revans Institute team had been highly skeptical that this would be possible. In his report he stated, "I had previously formed a view that it would take a number of action learning group meetings before anybody could understand what action learning was/wasn't. What was clearly demonstrated during the evaluation process was that, without exception, volunteer group members were all able to interact at varying levels as 'action learners.'"

This process was also enhanced *or not* by the understanding and skills of the facilitators. Key determinants appear to be the attitude and approach of the facilitator in releasing control of the process to the group. The process is, after all, but a guide for the group and the facilitator. However, in most consultancies, there is a high expectation of the facilitator to perform in order to justify his or her presence in the group. Not many contracts would be awarded to people who suggested that the most they would be expected to do would be to make a few pertinent interjections and then let the conversation flow. Yet on this occasion that is precisely what worked well. What defined the successful facilitators from the rest was their maturity, their confidence in action learning, and their ability to trust the process and work with it, not against it. There was nothing contrived about their approach, and yet it delivered the most learning impact for the recipients.

Indicators for Future Approaches

This raises some interesting questions for further exploration. How do you know when you recruit a facilitator to assist with your business development program that he or she will have just the right combination of skills?

In this case study, we were looking to create an environment for innovative thinking and transformational change. We did not want people to harness techniques but to really look at their change issues and do something directly to improve them. We wanted to create a dialogue that would lead to change and for people to feel that they were learning in the process.

What was evident in this case was the need for a high-quality participative conversation, an environment in which people could share and learn and affect the means to bring about change. The choice of facilitator was important, and the means we developed to test this proved worthy of the process and the outcome.

However, it was not without its risks. This was because the whole process relies on identifying facilitators who are highly developed in their skills and also personally secure and mature. Our groups very quickly learned to recognize those who "oozed experience." Strangely, this proved harder to find than we expected. It is also harder to articulate this as an explicit requirement when business thinking and terminology are hard-edged and outcomes focused.

It is tempting to suggest that, in essence, what works well is the skillful interaction of human beings coming together to share issues that they want to address. This is one of the simple, not simplistic, underpinnings of the Revans approach. There are no frills, no gadgets or clever techniques, just plain old-fashioned conversation, managed in a highly sophisticated way. In this sense, what we have done here is to demonstrate with an example how it can work and that it actually does.

References

Pearson, R. (2002). Strategic change management at Merck Hong Kong: Building a high performing executive team using action reflection in learning. In Y. Boshyk (Ed.), *Action learning worldwide: Experiences of leadership and organizational development*. Hampshire, Great Britain: Palgrave Macmillan.

Revans, R.W. (1998). *The ABC of action learning: A review of 25 years of experience*. Salford, England: Salford University.

Catherine Guelbert *is director of organization and leadership development in the National Health Service in London, UK. She has been working with action learning since 1991, gaining her master's in management through action learning in 1993. As well as a practicing leader manager, she is an experienced facilitator and qualified executive coach. She is a member of international networks in action learning and an alumnus of the Windsor Leadership Trust.*

Move It or Lose It
Using Interaction to Engage Adults
Gail Hahn

Summary

This article describes some of the basic tenants of adult learning theory and experiential education. It explains why using engaging interactive learning is important for retention of content with today's learners. It also provides detailed listings of types of interactive exercises or activities, what they are, and how they are used to improve the engagement of the learner in the learning process.

The talking head doesn't cut it any more if we—speakers, trainers, team-building facilitators, teachers, and presenters—want to engage our audiences and increase retention. Adult learners may have different learning styles, but possess several similarities in their need to absorb information and act on it. Although Baby Boomers are used to lectures and "death by PowerPoint" or overhead projector, our Generation X and Y attendees are used to interacting with their learning environments and using their bodies and their minds to synthesize and digest information. If we are to succeed in entertaining and informing our audiences, then we must embrace some generally accepted aspects of adult learning theory and experiential education.

With a degree in recreation and a master's in experiential education, I am forever explaining my background and what it entails to other people, especially my parents, who paid out-of-state tuition for those initials behind my name. Armed with those philosophies, I once again attempt to explain why mixing fun and effectiveness is good business for organizations, speakers, facilitators, and trainers alike.

In a nutshell, experiential education is learning by doing. As Confucius said, "I hear and I forget; I see and I remember; I do and I understand." Another definition, offered by the Association for Experiential Education, is the methodology or philosophy when educators or facilitators purposefully engage with learners in direct experience and focused reflection in order to increase knowledge, develop skills, and clarify values. It is a generally accepted rule that we remember 20 percent of what we hear, 50 percent of what we see, and 80 percent of what we do.

It is of the utmost importance that the presenter ties in the appropriate activity to a relevant point in order to draw out reflection from the participants and make the direct or indirect transfer of learning from that interactive experience to the real world. Interactive activities and group initiatives are by no means just games or time fillers for a program and, if used as such, do a disservice to the participants and the presenter. The activities should be chosen clearly and consciously to reach all styles of learners and create an atmosphere of trust, understanding, and whole-brain learning.

Learner Preferences

Presenters should remember that there are different types of learners in our sessions and that information needs to be presented in a variety of ways to reach each audience member.

- The auditory learners need to hear the information.

- The visual learners need to see the information using props, visuals, slide shows, and handouts.

- The kinesthetic learners need to physically feel and do something with the information by saying it, repeating the information and discussing it, writing it down, or participating in some physical activity to support the learning point.

Learning Domains

In addition to thinking about learning styles, the presenter should also consider how to address each of three learning domains. By working with all three domains, presenters will have greater success enabling participants to understand and retain the content:

- *Cognitive:* To engage the cognitive domain, employ intellectual methods that offer empirical factual knowledge, data, bullet points, and analysis of the information such as thinking, reasoning, remembering, imagining, or learning words. Use handouts with factual data for the left-brainers; give them websites with more content than you will cover for their own in-depth research; give them trends and recent research—the why of covering the content.

- *Affective:* To impact the affective domain, draw in learners emotionally by use of stories, photos, or interactive activities that compel an emotional connection or feeling that imprints in their memories. Tell stories, as people will remember stories more than they remember facts. Be sure the story is clearly linked to your content and that it resonates in some way with participants. As Maya Angelou says so eloquently, "People may forget what you said, but they will always remember how you made them feel." Use photographs in your PowerPoint presentation. Have participants interview each other without talking (using whatever creative means they choose—for example, through writing or exchanging driver's licenses, family photographs, or business cards) and then share their partners' stories with the group as an introduction exercise. Have each person tell why he or she is in the session and what each hopes to learn.

- *Psychomotor:* For this domain, physically engage participants in an exercise by using the mind and the body. Use movement or muscular activity relating to mental processes. Ask participants to walk to a different part of the room to form a group or find their teams; use physical problem-solving exercises such as building a tower of uncooked spaghetti and marshmallows while asking participants to design a logo, slogan, jingle, or advertising campaign around the tower to engage their artistic, physical, and intellectual selves.

Six Laws of Learning

Facilitators should also be aware of the "six laws of learning," how each impacts how learners learn, and what this means for training sessions:

- *Law of Readiness.* People learn best when they have the necessary background, a good attitude, and are ready to learn. They must see a clear reason for learning. (Ask participants to write on a card what they would rather be doing at that very moment, collect the cards, and read some of them to the group, and then throw the cards into a suitcase as extra baggage. Tell the participants that they can now focus on why we are in the room together and why that is important to the group. Allow them to get it out of their system, then ask them why they are there and what they can contribute.)

- *Law of Affect.* A pleasant learning environment and a good feeling associated with the learning allow people to learn and work best. Avoid experiences that create feelings of confusion, anger, frustration, defeat, or futility, which will lessen the retention. (Ensure the room is a comfortable temperature for learning, the sun isn't in people's eyes, the seats are comfortable, and there is no barrier to viewing or hearing the facilitator. Ensure that food, drink, and bathroom needs have been accommodated and that the overall physical and emotional atmosphere is conducive to friendly learning rather than strict and structured. Let the participants know you are there to serve their needs for information and be clear with your directions and expectations. Ensure that participants know in advance what equipment to bring, what not to bring, what to wear, what to expect, what to have read or done before the class, and where and what time the course is being held. Participants are always focused on their personal needs before the team needs or learning objectives. Take care of personal needs first, then move on to the learning content.)

- *Law of Exercise.* Practice and repeat the activity or learning point in order to increase retention. The mind rarely retains, evaluates, and applies new concepts or ideas after just one exposure. Using recall, review, summary, manual drills, or physical applications helps improve retention of the content. (Ask participants to do a pair share of the information that they just learned, then ask them to discuss the major points with their table groups, then ask the table groups or the entire room for highlights. Ask participants to write down the top three "aha" moments they've had in the past hour to lock in the learning. Ask participants to mingle and exchange email addresses and then make a date for them to follow up with each other in a month to see whether they have implemented what they just learned. Ask the group a general question on a key point and give a prize for the first answer or create a game show review of learning points. Keep changing the way participants review and revisit key points in order to lock in the learning by writing, talking, moving, discussing, listening, and tying it to an emotion, a story, a prop, or an exercise that is memorable.)

- *Law of Primacy.* People remember things that come first and that make a strong impression. Creating a positive first experience enhances learning. (Opt for a memorable first impression with a big party sign on the door, music, a celebration cake, a funny costume, a fun icebreaker participants can do while waiting for others to arrive, having a scavenger hunt, or dancing the Electric Slide while waiting to start the program. Attendees will get the idea that this training will be different and will be more willing to take risks and participate in the fun when an upbeat precedent is set from the beginning.)

- *Law of Recency.* Things people learned last will be remembered most. Things people have just completed and that are fresh on their minds will also be retained. Restating, repeating, and reemphasizing enhance the chances of retention. (Create a game-show review; ask audience members for "keepers" they have learned from the day; ask each group to discuss the highlights and then ask each group to announce its version of the highlights; pass around a giant inflatable light bulb or beach ball and whoever gets it states his or her keeper for the day before throwing it to the next person. Keep the most important points at the front of participants' minds by repeating and reviewing and allowing for reflection at the end of the program. Ask participants to write down their action plans for what they just learned—their next steps.)

- *Law of Intensity.* A sharp, clear, exciting, fun, exotic, enthusiastic learning experience teaches more than a dull, boring one. Creating an interactive and engaging session will improve the odds of learning and retention. (Implement activities that involve laughter to cement the learning points with humor to improve retention. Create some louder moments and quieter moments in the session through activities, demonstrations, audience participation, and the use of a variety of interactive activities to mix it up and make it interesting and engaging. Learning can be rowdy and high-energy using out of the ordinary means. Use your imagination and respect the lines of appropriateness.)

Additional Facilitation Techniques

Following are some additional techniques facilitators can use to engage participants and increase learning retention:

- Insert an engaging activity every 8 to 10 minutes to keep participants' attention. Learners today have very short attention spans, as we have been trained by television and computer games that allow for frequent breaks to give us our scores or tell us what we need. Commercial advertisers know this fact very well, as they insert commercials at short intervals to shake viewers awake as they zone out in front of the droning television. People expect action and need it to stay energized, engaged, and informed. Activities can be as simple as raising a hand or standing up, or more involved, such as writing, sharing with a neighbor, a group activity, competition, discussion, demonstration, or reflection through writing or talking.

- Unexpected rewards aid learning; toss out trinkets, prizes, or candy for volunteers and correct answers. Give a big cheer and standing ovation for a job well done after a successful completion of a group initiative.

- A skilled facilitator can create an enhanced transfer of learning from the exercises to the lives of the attendees by using metaphors and isomorphs (a comparison of two things that are similar in form and substance) and by debriefing the specific learning objective, as opposed to a general learning objective. If you include an interactive activity, make sure you have time to process it properly to bridge the transfer of learning and make it relevant.

- Use appropriate sequencing of experiential activities—from simpler to more complex. Facilitators are wise to move from low-risk activities to higher-risk activities or using higher perceived risk activities over actual higher risk activities to encourage the learner to get into the learning zone. Risk includes social risk (looking silly or stupid in front of peers, coming up with the wrong answer or a comment that isn't taken seriously), emotional risk (feeling inadequate, sharing too much, showing limitations, fears, or disabilities), or physical risk (awkwardness, physical touch, close proximity to teammates, physical capabilities). By moving from simpler to more complex activities, you build learners' success and self-confidence. Learners are much more open to sharing and full participation when they are feeling good about themselves, their teams, the facilitator, and the experience.

- Allow enough time for reflection on the purpose of the experience to deepen the understanding, which leads to a greater awareness of the learning, followed by a change in thinking, feeling, or behaving.

- Front load the activity by asking specific questions or making purposeful statements in the activity introduction in order for participants to make a clearer connection to the relevance and meaning of the activity. By consciously making a mental connection between the activity and the transfer of that experience to the workplace, the participants are better able to make that transfer of learning.

- Be aware of the relevance and validity of the activities you choose. People need to know why they are doing a particular exercise and what it has to do with what they will need to know in the future or for the world outside the classroom. Make sure your activities are linked to a purpose and contribute to the content and process of the overall objective. Let your audience know that purpose before beginning an activity.

- Set expectations early, remain objective, and defer feedback when facilitating an interactive exercise. Ensure there is a proper fit between the activity you choose and the audience interest, skills, attention span, size, age, and objective. Do your homework on the group, its challenges, level of interest, desired outcomes, and goals for the session. Prepare your agenda to meet participants' needs and always have more activities ready in case they finish early or already know an activity. Be very flexible in responding to their needs in that moment—whether they need to move inside, move outside, take a break, or end the activity. Be aware of their energy and be ready to change direction or change the course of the program to best suit their needs at that moment.

Activity Stages and Purpose

Following is a list of the major stages for an activity (except for debriefing, which is covered in a separate section that follows this one) and what the purpose of each stage is.

- *Icebreakers:* Warm up the group to each other, to the topic, and to you; learn names; network; learn the needs and energy level of the group; learn the receptivity of the group to creative methods of learning. Are they willing to play or learn how their authentic selves come out and play in an activity?

- *De-inhibitizers:* Active involvement, increased risk, commitment to be silly, cut loose, energize, promote cohesiveness, permission to have fun and be effective.

- *Creative thinking:* Think outside the box, innovation, get unstuck, group or individual problem solving to integrate both sides of the brain.

- *Energizers:* Illustrate key points, enliven, gain attention, shake awake, refocus energy, laughter, tension-breaker, comic relief.

- *Team building, trust, and communication:* Gain buy-in; increase cohesion, trust, and understanding of processes and each other; leadership and followership; listening skills.

- *Decision making and problem solving:* Communicate, cooperate, and compromise during simple to complex activities to demonstrate the process of teamwork; success; frustration; failure or competition versus cooperation or collaboration.

- *Feedback and closing the session:* Review, tie-in to key points, reflection, closure.

Process/Debrief to Create a Transfer of Learning

Debriefing is such a critical element of any activity that it warrants its own section. Following are some tips to make your debriefing as effective as it can be:

- Debrief immediately after the activity is completed while it is still fresh on participants' minds.

- Create a setting conducive to reflection and dialogue—usually in a circle right where they just finished the activity. Participants can be seated or standing, as long as they are not standing for too long without an opportunity to move around.

- Set expectations and ground rules for supportive processing. Get buy-in for the group rules of engagement by offering a few foundational rules (e.g., focus on behavior, not the person, or only speak for yourself and not others), and then ask the group what they can offer as their own guidelines.

- Be observant, use intuition-guided questioning, and encourage without pushing. Draw out the opinions of the participants and let them speak for themselves and take ownership over their experiences. If they own their issues, they are more likely to commit to following through on the outcomes or change their thinking or behavior.

- Be sure that participants understand the ways that the activity is relevant to the real world. Participants often get caught up in the activity or the end result; they don't think about the big picture and how that activity represents some similar situation outside the course. Point out how the activity "matches" and why getting to the end result is relevant—whether it is a direct transfer (a listening skill or specific words to say or sequence of words or behaviors) or indirect (how teams process success or failure).

- Create a solution-focused environment rather than a problem-focused environment when guiding the debriefing process toward the closure of an activity.

- Move from lower-risk to higher-risk questioning:

  ○ *What:* "What" questions are posed in relation to objectives and the substance of group interaction; responses are more often based on thinking than feelings. Examples include: Based on facts, what just happened? What did you see going on? What did you hear the group saying? What other things did you observe during the exercise?

- *So what:* "So what" questions are designed to transform the experience into relevant meaning. Examples include: So what does that mean to you? What difference did the experience make to you or the group? What are the consequences and meaning derived from this experience? So why did we just do this? So what was the purpose of the activity?

- *Now what:* "Now what" questions focus more on feelings than on intellect. They are a higher-risk question designed to elicit feelings. Examples include: Now what are you going to do in reaction to the experience? How will you relate these decisions on similar experiences in the future? Now what is the team going to do differently in the next activity or back at the office? Now what do you do with this information about yourself or your team and how you interact with each other? Now what is next for you?

Conclusion

What you have now are the basic rules of thumb for creating a learning environment that enhances teamwork, trust, communication, fun, effectiveness, and retention. So what are you going to do about reflecting on this information, retaining it for future use, and practicing it so you retain it in your memory banks? Now what do you have to do to merge interactive activities in with your current programs to make them more interesting, educational, energizing, and engaging? For more information on this topic, there are forty-one books, among other resources on experiential activities for your programs, at www.Funcilitators.com/more-resources.

Gail Hahn, MA, CSP, CLL, *is the CEO (Chief Energizing Officer™) of Fun*cilitators™, the author of* Hit Any Key to Energize Your Life *and* 52 Winning Ways to Have Fun at Work, *and contributing author to twenty-one other books. As an energy expert, she facilitates fun and effectiveness around the globe to energize individuals and revitalize organizations through interactive keynotes, team building, and twisted training events. Visit www .Funcilitators.com to enhance motivation, morale, and meaning at work.*

Learn-Ability
A Leader's Most Important Competence
Aviv Shahar

Summary

Requirements of a good leader have changed over the years. This article summarizes research conducted with hundreds of managers and executives to identify a single, most important feature required to lead others through a rapidly changing environment.

Do you have great physical prowess, courage, endurance, shrewdness, decisiveness, faith, confidence, boldness, charisma, or vision? Chances are you would have been able to rise to prominence in the past—but what about today? These characteristics and competencies brought people to power, to leadership positions, and to success in past millenniums; today that wouldn't be enough. Many of these attributes are still important, such as courage, for example, but there is a competence even more critical that you must cultivate if you are to succeed in today's world.

From Noah to King David, from Alexander the Great to Napoleon I, Attila the Hun, Queen Elizabeth I, King Richard the Lionhearted, Julius Caesar, Saladin, great chieftains, religious leaders, freedom fighters, and founders of nations throughout the ages, George Washington, Benjamin Franklin, Abraham Lincoln, Martin Luther King, Jr., Henry Ford, FDR and Eleanor Roosevelt, Winston Churchill, Mikhail Gorbachev, David Ben Gurion, Gandhi, Nelson Mandela, and other national and corporate leaders—each of them possessed great courage and vision that helped them rise to prominence or to power.

A Leadership Strength for the Oncoming Global Shift

We are now hurtling through and toward events and changes that will re-form our world in a dramatic way. Technological, economical, geopolitical, social, and psycho-spiritual changes are unfolding in front of our eyes and in subtle and invisible ways, like tectonic shifts that we cannot quite yet see but we can certainly sense or feel. These changes are about to accelerate and make an even greater leap in the near future.

Every few decades a major shift of global consciousness takes place. Its onset is a bit like being on the shore when the tide comes in. It is so gradual that you don't notice until you realize suddenly that the water has overtaken you. Such is the nature of a shift of consciousness: One day you wake up and you are aware that the world around you looks very different. Singular events like 9/11 and the fall of the Berlin Wall serve as signposts for our collective recognition, but they are even more a symptom of a process that has been steadily underway, rather than isolated causal events.

The coming decades present tremendous risks and remarkable opportunities. Wherever you are and whatever you do, it is not enough just to cope. It is paramount to face these risks successfully and, at the same time, wisely embrace the opportunities to participate and lead the way forward in the extraordinary developments that are already reshaping our world.

With the help of hundreds of executives and managers who have participated in our leadership seminars, we have identified a single feature as the most crucially important competence necessary to lead others in a rapidly changing business and socio-political environment. This capability has become a key competence and quality standard for every person aspiring to excel, especially for a leader who hopes to survive at the top in the 21st Century. It is this quality that allows leaders to thrive and reshape the environment in which they operate. This competence is *learn-ability*.

Learn-ability is the ability to learn. In talking about learn-ability as a leadership competency, we say that high-level learn-ability is a high capacity to harvest and/or distill meaningful knowledge and to apply it in an impactful way to optimize leadership effectiveness and performance.

In a world of rapid change, learn-ability is the essence of leadership. You may be leading an organization of 100,000 people or leading yourself and your family; or perhaps you are the leader of a project, a city, a university; or you are the president of a country. Your ability to learn and adapt and offer the benefit of that learning process to others is the essence of the leadership process.

Peter Drucker (2001) taught us that the only two functions of a business are *marketing* and *innovation*. Learn-ability is the key competence for both. Marketing is about learning and understanding the needs of your clients and then learning how to educate the clients about the value, benefits, and enrichment they receive from your products, services, and experiences.

Learn-ability is also the engine of innovation. It is the ability to learn from one attempt to another, to harvest the experience of success or of failure, and to utilize and apply that knowledge in a relevant way in new fields and situations, and to new problems. Further, it is the ability to recognize patterns and similarities, to understand new needs, and to appreciate new combinations at the interfacing thresholds of diverse fields and dynamics.

Learn-ability is the propelling locomotive of entrepreneurism. Don't stop at thinking that entrepreneurism's driving core is creating capital or gaining power. Wealth creation, individual ownership, free society, and market economy are the enablers of entrepreneurial energy. They offer the means and the expression for entrepreneurs. But if there is a spiritual core to entrepreneurism, it is learning—the development and the inner and outer growth of individuals, society, and human kind at large, the core competence we call learn-ability.

Learn-ability is natural. In fact, it is the very nature of life: the whole universe is a learning system that allows and embraces change, development, innovation, and evolution. The question is, What prevents and blocks this natural ability? The answer is that educational systems that don't support natural learning prevent it. Management that doesn't encourage and promote learn-ability loses out on its precious innovative and creative power and prevents it.

Learning at 32,000 Feet and Higher

When I travel, I have the most amazing learning experiences. I often find myself on a long flight with someone sitting next to me who is willing to engage in a fascinating and intense conversation while nearly everyone else on that flight is asleep. I wonder whether most people realize the person sitting next to them may carry an insight, a lesson, an experience, or wisdom that could be vital for them. I have found that every person who sits next to me has had something to teach me, something exactly right for what I needed at the time. Being able to see the world through someone else's eyes and experiences stretches me to new understandings, ideas, and learning.

These conversations have taken place with a tooling engineer for the aerospace industry, a cosmetics specialist, an accountant, a sales manager of computer games, a woman who built a cleaning service business, a Romanian entrepreneur, a philanthropist, a nine-year-old girl, a distinguished biotechnology scientist, a civil engineer, a woman who suffered from cerebral palsy, a Native American business leader, a manager of a nuclear shipyard, an investment analyst, a Lebanese living in England, a Hasidic Jew, and a Catholic theologian priest from Uganda. You can say I am completing my Ph.D. in psychology, management, and comparative religion all at 32,000 feet and higher, courtesy of the airline industry.

The civil engineer taught me about the organizational skills of large-scale projects. The civilian executive from the shipyard explained the Department of Defense initiative to cut its budget by 25 percent, why it's not likely to succeed, and what is needed for the initiative to work. He also explained about the danger of the coming knowledge drain with the imminent retirement of a generation of managers. The nine-year-old reminded me of the fears of a nine-year-old. The investment analyst and I discussed how to structure my portfolio, whether we have a debt bubble and a real estate bubble, and what the fundamentals driving the bull market in commodities are.

The biotechnologist elaborated about the evidence for collective intelligence at the cellular and genomic level and what we might be able to learn from that about organizational intelligence. It was a difficult and painful experience when the Lebanese man seated beside me insisted all the way from Milan to Chicago that his son will never live in peace with my son and that Jews have no business in the Middle East. But at least we spoke for five hours somewhat peacefully. The Catholic priest gave me an inside view of the Vatican, the struggles of the church, and his feelings about the election of the Pope. He bravely answered my questions about the challenges of celibacy and the validity of experiencing the power of the Holy Spirit outside the framework of the church.

The beauty queen and cosmetic specialist told me what she would do with my face in the event I was called to have my fifteen minutes of fame on national television. But don't tell the airline industry about all my free learning. They might start charging me airfare plus tuition just because I decided to use my air travel to continue my learning and education. The person sitting next to me is usually infinitely more interesting than magazines, my BlackBerry and, on many occasions, even the in-flight movie.

Learning Inclinations

It's important to know your personal learning inclinations and preferences. I am amazed when I discover in my seminars that most people don't realize that they have a learning style and inclination. Are you a reader, a listener, an experimenter, an observer, or a teacher who learns by teaching? Are you a head learner, a heart learner, an instinctive and intuitive learner, or a hands-on learner? I am a conversationalist and I love learning through conversations with other people. Put me anywhere with anyone and I will take their jewels. But I don't steal jewels to take them away; I try to clear off the dust, shine it up, and give it back to them with added value and awareness. When people say to me, "I have never had a conversation like this" or "This is the most significant conversation I have had in many years," and so on, it is not because I impressed them with my wisdom, but because they impressed me with the treasures hidden in their experience that they didn't know they possessed.

Experience shows that learn-ability can be nurtured, cultivated, and grown. When my wife and I married twenty-four years ago, we thought we knew each other because we had been together for three years. The truth is we could only have known each other to the level each one of us knew ourselves. But at twenty-four you cannot know what your needs, feelings, world view, preferences, food allergies, struggles, and comfort zone will be at thirty-four or forty-four. So we have had to discover all of the above, each at his or her own time and pace. One of the reasons so many relationships hit a brick wall is because people suppress the learnable dimension by holding onto frozen dreams, instead of realizing that a relationship is a learning journey.

We worked at it. We worked at it hard and we worked at it soft, and we made learn-ability central to our lives. We discovered that it made every year a bit better because we were able to take in more about life, about ourselves, about each other, and about how to keep opening up the future. Last year was the best year of our life together, and this year is shaping up to be even better. I'm convinced it is because both of us have developed the practice and discipline of learn-ability, which refreshes, redefines, and invigorates the love that drew us together in the beginning.

Learn–Ability: A Practice and Discipline to Nurture

What are the ten practices and disciplines of learn-ability?

1. Curiosity

Having an intense curiosity and active inquiry about everything is the first marker. You demonstrate genuine interest in the experiences and perspectives of other people. You choose to and have the capacity to listen and observe with great inquisitiveness and distill the learning value of the experience. Curiosity is a form of deep and passionate engagement with your environment, in which you are swept up in the fascination of discovery and learning. Look at the learning process of a toddler and you will see that type of thirst for discovery. The practice of curiosity is an openness that seeks to embrace diversity and new insight without minding who or what is the source.

Case in point: Moshe Feldenkrais (1972, 1981, 1985) applied his intensely curious mind and engineering background to heal his knee after an accident. He then used his Judo experience combined with profound observational skills from an engineer's perspective to develop a new understanding and appreciation of the versatile movement and interconnectedness of the human body. This led him to create a revolutionary system of awareness through movement and functional integration. Feldenkrais has helped thousands of people regain mobility and eliminate pain. The essence of his practice is continual curiosity and the subtle neural re-activation and re-learning that it causes.

2. Adventurism

The spirit of daring to try new things and plunge into unfamiliar situations. It's deciding that you love the spontaneity of the unexpected more than you love the comfort of routine. Adventurism is when discovery overrides security and you choose to go up the road less traveled. You are ready to take risks with the knowledge and confidence that all will be well, that the way will be found, and that the learning you need to help you make this leap is right here inside the endeavor. This trust in one's own *learn-ability* and in the resources available in every situation is the reason that development and growth always find people who love adventure.

Case in point: Richard Branson thrives on adventures. He started 250 companies driven by the passion to do new things and to be true to his vision. Virgin Atlantic was started after market research comprised of two phone calls. Branson distilled enough learning from these two calls to be convinced that there was room for a new airline. In his heart Branson is an adventurer; his drive to discover new possibilities and opportunities is his modus operandi of learning in action through entrepreneurial business. (See www.virgin.com/aboutvirgin/richardbranson/whosrichardbranson.aspx)

3. Adaptability

The capacity to swiftly recognize and acclimatize to change without losing your core purpose and convictions. With this quality, you have the ability to see things for what they are and to overcome the denial reflex. Adaptability also means the capacity to let go and the flexibility and readiness to embrace new conditions and unfamiliar situations. This isn't simply coping with change, but welcoming change with an inherent cheer and optimism that is moved to discover how to make the best out of every new set of circumstances. As toddlers we were all extremely adaptable. It is much later that we develop inhibiting self-views and entitlements that stifle the chameleon-like capacity we were all born with to naturally and rapidly adjust to changing environments.

Case in point: The Dalai Lama was raised in a secluded world based in centuries of tradition and during his childhood was expected to fulfill a specific role according to a time-honored custom. The Chinese invasion of Tibet shattered this world forever. After escaping to India, he adapted his cause and the leadership of the Tibetan people and transformed himself to take on a much bigger role on the world stage. He maintains the integrity and central ideals of the Tibetan way while communicating to the West and the world at large a universal message. The Dalai Lama is an avid learner and demonstrates extraordinary adaptability.

4. Kaleidoscoping

The capacity to recognize relationships and patterns. Those with this quality practice an active inquiry that seeks to understand the core principles that are the basis of all systems. Kaleidoscoping is the ability to compare and correlate seemingly unrelated fields and apply concepts from one to another, such as using the terminology and anatomy of weather systems in organizational behavior and the life cycles of the forest in the marketplace. You discover that building an investment is the same as building trusting relationships—they follow the same principle; they both need ongoing deposits. The infrastructure and activity of a beehive can teach us about promoting a culture of efficiency and excellence in execution. Kaleidoscoping is also the capacity to handle complexity and discover meaning in new combinations, connections, and interrelationships.

Case in point: Thomas Friedman's (2006) *The World Is Flat* is a story of connecting the dots that describes a set of dynamic trends that together form a newly appearing kaleidoscopic picture. Friedman travels the world and moves in and out of politics, the economy, technology, and the demographic and psycho-graphic dynamics to gather clues about emerging patterns. He meets with thought leaders and trend setters as he continues to figure out the interrelationships hidden inside the shape-shifting kaleidoscoping landscape. Friedman's unique brilliance is his ability to perceive what others don't and to tell the story in a way that helps us see and appreciate the unfolding and evolving world paradigm.

5. Humor

The capacity to enjoy contradiction, to thrive in the face of impossibilities and recognize their funny implications. Humor arouses interest, keeps attention, helps you connect with people, relieves stress or tension, disarms hostility, and facilitates communication in difficult situations. It helps relate facts and figures, makes information more memorable, and emphasizes points and ideas. Humor helps teams to come to a collective understanding that a situation is safer and less threatening than it would first appear. Humor shows that you don't take yourself too seriously and makes people happy. It is said that "If they're laughing, they're listening." If they are laughing, they are also engaging and learning about themselves and the situations they are in. Laughter reduces the output of negative stress chemicals in the brain and dramatically improves cognitive and creative thinking (see www.helpguide.org/life/humor_laughter_health .htm). Humor is an envoy for a special brand of learning and is often the fastest and most memorable learning experience you will find.

Case in point: Many political leaders are gifted with a special wit such that they are able to use to communicate their teachable points of view. For example, Benjamin Disraeli, former British Prime Minister, said, "Like all great travelers, I have seen more than I remember, and remember more than I have seen" and also, "Talk to a man about himself and he will listen for hours" (www.brainyquote.com/quotes/quotes/b/benjamindi 108147.html). Levi Eshkol, former Israeli Prime Minister, said, "Put three Zionists in a room and they will form four political parties" (http://thinkexist.com/quotes/levi_esh kol/). And from Ronald Reagan: "I am not worried about the deficit. It is big enough to take care of itself" (http://politicalhumor.about.com/cs/quotethis/a/reaganquotes.htm).

6. Commitment

Great tenacity and extraordinary commitment and conviction. It is the "sticking-to-it" power that kept Edison persevering through his many attempts, which he did not see as failures but as learning how not to create a light bulb. *Learn-ability* involves discipline and passion that keeps you focused and promises great follow-through, as demonstrated by the Curie couple when they were mixing tons of pitchblende on the way to discovering radium.

Case in point: Lance Armstrong's commitment to be the best made him an avid student of physics and physiology, and he spent hours in the wind tunnel to learn and experiment with every aspect of bike-riding, including the equipment and the subtle shifts of his body position, to find the elusive perfect form. He developed the science of a year-long training cycle and preparation calculated to build top form exactly on time. Armstrong took a scientific approach to dismantle the power equation and discover a way to climb a mountain far more efficiently by standing and spinning lower gears at a much higher cadence. Finally, he learned to use his teammates and the pelleton to optimize his efforts throughout the Tour De France (www.trainright.com/info .asp?action=display&uid=413).

7. Imagination

Being able to see things before they happen and visualize possibilities before they are realized. Imaginative people have the innate or developed capacity to conceive of a way, a product, a process, or a service and what it can do. Imagination is the ability to envision a scenario and foresee the arising of a new relationship, a Spielberg-and-Lucas-type capacity to create a new world of possibilities. The imagination we speak of includes being able to stay with a question or a problem for a long time in a contemplative fashion until it opens up and gives way to new answers and intelligence. Imagination is a "practice of mind" that enables learn-ability.

Case in point: Walt Disney started his Laugh-O-Grams cartoon shorts in 1922, which led him to imagine and create everything we now associate with Disney. From the development of his great animation works to his ideas for an amusement park, where he envisioned his employees spending time with their children, leading to the creation of Disneyland and EPCOT (Experimental Prototype City of Tomorrow), Walt Disney learned by imagining and taught us all to imagine. Disney's life's work was the demonstration that what you can imagine you can create. He showed us that the path from imagination to actualization is one of insatiable learning (www.justdisney .com/walt_disney/biography/long_bio.html).

8. Reframing

The capacity to create new context. People who can reframe are able to shift from one paradigm to another and to formulate new questions that open untapped resources and lead to new possibilities. I will take the liberty to reword the famous Einstein quote: "When we are able to reframe the questions and problems we are faced with in a new context and level, we are more than half the way to finding a solution." Reframing is about developing a habit of honesty and forgiveness. I cannot reframe the setback of yesterday into a learning opportunity before I am prepared to forgive my own or another's mistake. We are speaking here about the mindset in which a mistake is only a "missed take"—an opportunity you did not use. A take that you attempted and missed simply clears the way for another better or more informed take. Reframing is when you are able to understand the situation you are in and the issues you are looking at in new ways.

> When I go into the forest, I look down and see the broken trunks and the rotting leaves and branches. I then look up and see the new green growth against the sky. When I focus on the former, I think that the forest is dying. The latter tells me the forest is continually growing. The truth is that the forest is both dying and re-birthing itself. So is the case with all life pursuits where I can choose to focus on what is dying, on what is being born, or on the cyclicality of both, which then affords me a perspective in which to reframe my endeavors.

Case in point: FDR's leadership was propelled by his ability to reframe the issues of the day and identify opportunities and hope in the midst of despair and depression. His ability to reframe the national conversation ("The only thing we have to fear is fear itself") was in part based on having had to reframe his own personal tragedy and despair with paralysis to find the learning and hope available for him and for others who suffered from polio. Today we often have a cynical view about the political spin of this or that side. But there is a more profound dimension that a true leader manifests by which the reframing is an inside-out inspiration that helps us all reframe our own experiences and perceptions. True leaders teach us to see our reality differently and therefore re-commit ourselves with new meaning, purpose, and context.

9. Collaboration

Learning is a collaborative process. It is the connective process from one portal to another, from your portal to the environment's portal—and the possible interaction therein. We depend on one another and are unable to cope and answer alone the demands put on us. It's much like one dendrite in your brain reaching out to connect with another because it cannot contain the charge. It builds a circuitry, which we experience as new thought, learning, and discovery. This is similar to the anatomy and dynamics of a diverse team that unleashes collective ingenuity that was not possible for any one player alone. Collaboration involves and enables learning because first we learn how to connect and work together. Then there is what we discover collectively, which is greater than the sum of our individual parts. The capacity to be a participatory learning agent extends beyond partnering with other people to include working with other cultures, other problems, and other fields. We speak here of the learn-ability that is liberated on a movie set when each of the actors is fully in character, no longer separated, and the scene takes on a life of its own.

Case in point: The power of the Internet is in the interactive learning space it has become. We are continually learning how to optimize and use the opportunities it brings to us. eBay's success is an example of a community of collaborative learning. Meg Whitman promotes eBay as a community that thrives on mutually beneficial and collaborative educational transactions. Adaptability is a key competence if you are to succeed in this reciprocal and mutually instructive environment.

Case in point: Jack Canfield and Janet Switzer (2007) assert in *Success Principles* that the success principle that most high achievers credit with bringing them success is the mastermind group: "Many of the greatest minds in human history have gathered around themselves advisors, experts, fellow scientists, and others to brainstorm, get feedback, ask for guidance, and receive the combined benefit of the spiritual energy that comes from more than one mind working on solving a problem and creating an opportunity."

10. Generosity

You only know and have something for real when you've given it away. The best way to learn is to teach. The best way to develop yourself is to coach others to develop. Coaching others to learn and grow means that you give of yourself generously in terms of time, energy, knowledge, resources, and the sharing of your passion. You then become a learning conduit of knowledge, wisdom, and experience. Generosity of spirit permeates how we are and what we do and what we can learn. It allows us to be compassionate, kind, and resourceful in our interactions. Generosity promotes learn-ability as it fosters trust, open communication, creativity, knowledge-sharing, idea-sharing, and passion and inspiration-sharing. Being generous is both a spiritual capacity and a practice and discipline, as exemplified in the idea that teaching another to fish is a greater act of generosity than giving that person a fish. The greater generosity is the learning, coaching, and mentoring process that helps others to develop the tools, means, and systems to solve problems, innovate, and make life better for themselves and for others.

Case in point: Bill Drayton's Ashoka brings together people driven by a vision, spirit of generosity, and long-term commitment to systemic social change. Drayton created an organization that provides valuable resources and opportunities to help spread pioneering social innovation. Ashoka is a community of learning without borders that helps its "fellows" learn from each other's successes and challenges and keeps them on track to achieve their goals. Ashoka pursues a vision to transform the lives of young people and their impact on society by enhancing their skills, leadership, and engagement in their communities. Drayton created a network that teaches the power of entrepreneurial social change, learning, and development (www.ashoka.org/).

Key Practices

In the following paragraphs, three key practices managers can use to promote organizational learn-ability are described.

1. Storytelling

At Emeritus Assisted Living, John Cincotta, the director of marketing, promotes a weekly ritual of sharing a success story. Every week he receives emails with stories of special successes from throughout the 180 buildings the company manages. The story includes what has happened, what behavior promoted the exemplary service that resulted in a new resident's moving in, and what was learned. The stories are distributed with additional humorous and motivational comments throughout the company. Storytelling has become central to promoting organizational learning at Emeritus.

As another example, at our leadership retreats, we often conduct a "From you I have learned" exercise. Each participant tells a story about a person who has had a formative impression on him or her. When the person finishes telling the story, he or she ends with saying, "and so from [this person], I have learned about courage/how to say no/how to pick myself up and have another go/how to forgive," and so on. People tell stories about a parent, a grandparent, a teacher, a manager, or a friend. It's a powerful exercise because people learn to distill and articulate a specific learning from their experiences and they learn even more from each other's stories.

As we work through this life-centering story exercise, people are surprised with the value that lives inside the significant stories of their lives. They also are surprised by how much wisdom is available to them when they learn to reframe their experiences.

2. Celebrating Failures

Growing numbers of organization are adopting the ritual of celebrating failure. As Richard Farson and Ralph Keyes (2002) suggest in *Whoever Makes the Most Mistakes Wins*, failures may not only be inevitable on our road to success, but might actually help us attain it. The point is in learning to acknowledge the new experimentation, the daring, and the wisdom distilled from the failure and risk-taking innovative culture it promotes.

3. Optimization Meetings

Hold weekly "optimization meetings" with your team to harvest learning. Meeting agendas can include the following:

- What was the best thing that happened this week? What was my/our greatest accomplishment/success?

- What did we learn from this?

- What is the deeper lesson inside the learning?

- What was the biggest challenge this week?

- What did we learn from it?

- What is the deeper lesson inside the learning?

- How can we use and apply these lessons? In what other places can we leverage these insights?

Learn–ability Survey

The following survey can be used to assess your own level of learn-ability. For each item, circle Yes or No. Scoring and interpretation information follow the survey.

1. In the last six days, I encountered and looked up the meaning of at least one new word.   yes   no

2. I explore new sources of information.   yes   no

3. I have a habit of debriefing and reflecting on what happened and how I experienced or felt about it.   yes   no

4. I deliberately expose myself to different viewpoints and opinions.   yes   no

5. In the last twenty days, I have tried to do something I have never done before.   yes   no

6. When I experience a setback, I focus on the learning I can embrace from it.   yes   no

7. I seek out new experiences and adventures.   yes   no

8. When others speak, I listen attentively without forming a response in my mind half-way through their sentence.   yes   no

9. I have learned to befriend the discomfort of new situations.   yes   no

10. I can recall a recent situation in which I laughed at myself and my behavior.   yes   no

11. I open conversations with a stranger (on a flight/in the book store/anywhere).   yes   no

12. I regularly ask myself: What is another way to look at this problem?   yes   no

13. I consult with and listen to my instinct and intuition when making decisions.   yes   no

14. I keep a pad nearby to write down new ideas and thoughts.   yes   no

15. I have a "box" of unsolved questions/problems that I have been thinking about and working on for years.   yes   no

16. I am interested in what other people think and feel.   yes   no

17. Sometimes I stay up at night trying to puzzle out a question.   yes   no

18. I get up in the morning with anticipation for new experiences and learning.   yes   no

19. I have registered a new patent in the last seven years.   yes   no

20. Understanding what is being talked about is more important
    for me than saving face and pretending I know.   yes   no

21. I welcome robust discussions on contentious issues.   yes   no

22. I go out on reflective walks in nature.   yes   no

23. I try to envision and create possible future scenarios on a
    variety of personal and societal issues.   yes   no

24. When I don't know what to do, I don't get too stressed.
    I know new insight and intelligence will turn up soon
    enough.   yes   no

25. I am not afraid to fail; the only true failure for me is
    to not try.   yes   no

Calibrate your level of learn-ability according to the number of "yes" responses:

    20 to 25   Outstanding: High degree of learn-ability
    15 to 19   Good degree of learn-ability
    10 to 14   Degree of learn-ability can be improved
    6 to 9   Low level of learn-ability; you mostly avoid new learning
    0 to 5   Almost no learn-ability exhibited

Increase Your Learn-Ability

Following are twelve things you can do to cultivate and develop your learn-ability:

1. Practice thinking with analogies. Once a day, explain something through an
   analogy. Thinking with analogies will lead your mind into new relationships,
   connections, and opportunities.

2. Read about great pioneers, inventors, and innovators. When you read about
   Madam Curie or Steve Jobs, it cannot help but inspire you to your next level
   of learning and discovery.

3. Keep a pad nearby. When new ideas turn up, write them down. This trains your
   mind and thinking process that you have a value for new ideas. Because you
   have alerted yourself to this attitude of wanting more ideas, more will begin to
   appear.

4. Surround yourself with people who love learning and discovery. This is extremely important—the energy of conversations with people who love learning and discovery is very contagious.

5. Before you go to sleep, write down three things you learned today, three things you want to do better tomorrow, and a question/problem you want to learn more about or solve. By doing this for forty days, you will establish a mindset that will begin working automatically for you.

6. Spend a day trying to see the world through the viewpoint of someone else. This requires discipline, but here is a way to do it. Stop five times during the day for a few minutes to imagine and write in your journal how what you have just seen and experienced would be seen and experienced by a nine-year-old, an Eskimo, a billionaire, your spouse, your great-grandfather, a 12th-Century person, or a person living in 2100. This will expose you to considerations and thinking outside your box—your frame of reference.

7. For a full day, don't use the word "I." (Every time you do use the pronoun "I," put a dollar away for your favorite charity.) You will discover a new relationship with your environment.

8. Explain to a nine-year-old in his or her frame of reference the complex issues and problems you are grappling with. Needing to explain to a nine-year-old will force you to simplify your thinking and focus on the core principles involved.

9. Once a week, start a conversation with a total stranger. Practice the skill of appreciating another person's viewpoint, experiences, needs, and hopes. After the conversation, write down five new things you have learned. This will teach you to harvest new learning through observations and listening.

10. Take one day a month and give yourself a break from needing to be reasonable. Do what you feel like, follow your gut, be spontaneous, do the unreasonable and harmless things you want to do. At the end of the day or on the following morning, ask yourself: What have I learned?

11. Spend fifteen to twenty minutes in the morning reflecting and thinking about your purpose, your values, and your goals. Reflect and write about the new learning and development that you anticipate for the day. As you create for yourself a space of reflection in the morning, you will find that the small amount of time you take to center yourself before you start the day pays back ten-fold. This process gives you more stability, stamina, and focus.

12. Frame problems and questions in a way that empowers you with the responsibility and mandate to find answers. Stop blaming others or yourself; stop framing issues in a way that puts the onus on everyone and everything else. Concentrate on those things over which you have some control. Frame the issues and problems you deal with in terms of the part that you can control. This is a huge shift of mindset that will empower and accelerate new learning for you.

References

Canfield, J., & Switzer, J. (2007). *The success principles.* New York: HarperCollins.

Drucker, P. (2001). *The essential Drucker.* New York: HarperCollins.

Farson, R., & Keyes, R. (2002). *Whoever makes the most mistakes wins.* New York: Simon & Schuster.

Feldenkrais, M. (1972). *Awareness through movement.* New York: Harper & Row.

Feldenkrais, M. (1981). *The elusive obvious.* Cupertino, CA: Meta Publications.

Feldenkrais, M. (1985). *The potent self.* San Francisco, CA: Harper & Row.

Friedman, T. (2006). *The world is flat.* New York: Farrar, Straus, & Giroux.

Aviv Shahar *is the founder of Amber Network. He is an author, a speaker, and a coach. He has extensive experience in coaching leadership development, executive effectiveness, and creative and strategic thinking. Mr. Shahar has trained and coached top managers from an array of companies, including Hewlett-Packard, Emeritus Assisted Living, Northrop Grumman Corp, GAP Inc, Frito-Lay Inc., Bank of Tokyo-Mitsubishi, Berkeley National Labs, the U.S. Department of the Interior, and the U.S. Department of Defense. He brings to his work over twenty years of experience in management, philosophy, and education, which he synthesizes into the whole-person-development methodology in his seminars, retreats, and workshops. His writings have been published in the Pfeiffer Annuals, the AMA Best of the Best, T+D, and* The Futurist.

Customer Dynamics
Utilizing Customer Feedback to Improve Your Organization's Performance
Carol Ann Zulauf and Karl E. Sharicz

Summary

Many organizations go through the process of obtaining customer feedback, but few take full advantage of the data provided. After a brief introduction to organizational dynamics, this article will explore customer dynamics—how to obtain and use customer-feedback data to improve your processes and make your organization more successful.

The Big Picture

Every organization has very significant dynamics operating within it. These dynamics are ongoing, continuous, and influence what goes on in the organization. How you, as a leader, no matter what your position in an organization, work with these dynamics determines the success and effectiveness of the decisions made and the outcomes that result in your organization.

You may be asking, "How does one recognize these dynamics?" Good question! The really good news is that working with the dynamics in your organization starts with the *patterns* that are observable in your organization. What do you see occurring—or not occurring? Start with your most vexing issues, problems, or challenges. Ask yourself or your team, "How significant is this? How long has it been a problem? What have we done before to address this issue?" Some "bigger" questions that should also be asked include:

- What is working successfully in our organization and how can we build on that?

- What is our reality with our team, with the results we are getting, with our customers, with our other stakeholders?

- Where are we going as a team, as a department, as an organization?

- What skills, competencies, knowledge, networks, and relationships will get us there?

- Where is the best place to start to make the best interventions with the challenges that we face and to build on the successes we already have?

From Organizational Dynamics to Customer Dynamics

Every organization has embraced and implemented, to varying degrees, customer satisfaction or customer loyalty initiatives. Much can be written and talked about on these two initiatives alone! Some baseline data (Reichhold, 1996) on customer loyalty and retention includes the following:

- A 5 percent improvement in customer retention rates will yield a 25 to 100 percent increase in profits.

- Firms that earned superior levels of customer loyalty and retention also earned consistently higher profits—and they grew faster as well.

- Customer loyalty is inextricably linked to employee and investor loyalty, and major improvements in the one often require improvements in the other two.

- On average, U.S. corporations now *lose half their customers* in five years.

Let's take a closer look at what this data means in terms of *customer dynamics*.

Customer Feedback

Measuring a customer's satisfaction with your products or services or their loyalty to your organization, by itself, will net you little more than an expensive report card. Unless you are prepared to use the resulting customer feedback as a source of strategic information that converts intelligence into corrective actions, you cannot expect your process to provide bottom-line results for your organization.

As has been stated by numerous authors on the topic, a vast majority of companies collect customer feedback in some fashion. However, only about half of those who collect customer data go on to communicate that information to the remainder of the organization, and only a small percentage of those actually make any process improvements and validate the effectiveness of the improvements made. This statistic will be discussed further in this article under the section, "Changing the Dynamics in Your Organization." Organizations doing more than simply measuring customer feedback clearly have a competitive advantage. It has also been stated and generally accepted that you cannot expect to gain customer loyalty without having first established a loyal and customer-centric organizational culture. This interrelationship can be depicted by the causal influence analysis shown in Figure 1.

The relationship among these key components is very strong (Reichhold, 1996).

Survey Design

In this section, we'll look at several broad-based survey designs for obtaining customer feedback. Effective surveys are designed with specific desired outcomes. If yours is a service-oriented business, then a transactional survey is more likely to provide you with the feedback that will allow you to make the necessary interventions to help sustain and build a service business. Transactional surveys measure a service event, as a point in time, and look at a customer's expectations and measure the degree to which your organization either met or did not meet expectations. A regular frequency of transactional

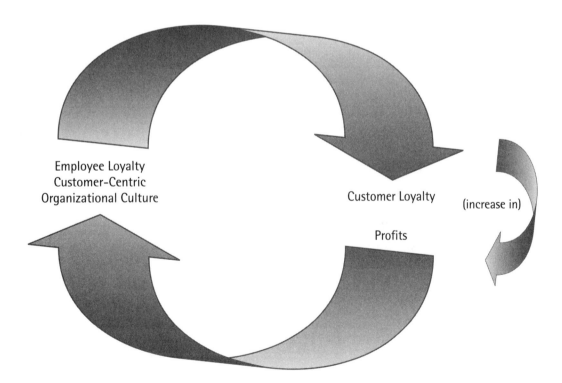

Figure 1. Causal Influences of Employee Loyalty and Customer Loyalty

surveys over time will provide you with a trend analysis to determine whether you are improving, declining, or remaining the same. If yours is a product-oriented business, then you're likely better off using a relational survey. Relational surveys measure the perceptions of customers in relation to their use of your products over time. These surveys can be repeated at intervals as well, but do not require the shorter frequencies of a transactional survey. Last, there is what we call the "translational" survey, the hybrid between the transactional and relational surveys. If your business involves both products and related services, this survey type can be used to help you achieve both objectives.

Measurement Systems

Measurements can be either quantitative or qualitative. Quantitative metrics are the easiest to obtain and distill. The most common quantitative measurement systems involve either a 5-point or 10-point scale. Customers can be asked to rate their satisfaction with certain experiences posed as a question, or they can be asked how much they either agree or disagree with a statement provided to them. Two examples are given below. These examples employ the 5-point scale, where typically the customer is given a choice of descriptive answers rather than numbers.

Statement Sample

1. Please rate your satisfaction with the overall value of the services provided relative to the cost.

    -   Exceeded Expectations

    -   Above Expectations

    -   Met Expectations

    -   Below Expectations

    -   Did Not Meet Expectations

2. In comparison with similar service providers you have used, how would you rate our overall service?

    -   Much Better

    -   Better

    -   The Same

    -   Worse

    -   Much Worse

By comparison, when a 10-point scale is employed, typically only the number of the scale is given so that the customer is asked to rate on a scale of 1 to 10, with 10 being the highest and 1 being the lowest.

The main advantage of using a 10-point scale is that smaller differences can be more readily detected. Other than that, both scales are adequate and generally acceptable. It is desirable to design surveys that will yield key and critical information that can be acted on by employing the shortest possible set of questions or statements. This may require considerable and interactive development time and validation through pilot-testing. Customer surveys of no more than twenty questions are typical, usually taking approximately ten minutes to complete.

Survey Deployment

The two most common ways to conduct customer surveys are by phone or via the Internet. Phone surveys typically yield a higher success rate than web-based surveys, simply because the customer has been immediately and actively engaged through a phone call. Web surveys rely on effective communication, plus a customer's inclination and motivation to act independently. Both methods are effective; however, if you are using an independent and impartial third-party to conduct phone surveys (and this is highly recommended), the higher costs of this method may be prohibitive. Web surveys also have the advantage of automatic tabulation and in many cases auto-analysis and dynamic and instantaneous up-to-date reporting.

Survey Analysis

There are many ways to tabulate, organize, and analyze survey results, and a complete assessment of this topic is well beyond the scope of this article. In general, there are some key metrics that are used by many, if not all, of those conducting customer surveys. The primary metric is the overall score or weighted average. Assuming a twenty-question transactional survey was conducted among three hundred customers and employed the 5-point scale, for example, an overall score of 3.7 out of 5.0 would indicate that the overall performance of the organization was generally above expectations, but not quite at the 4.0 level and above, where customer loyalty factors come into play. Interventions and actions followed by re-measurement and analysis among a similar subset of customers would reveal the effectiveness of the intervention. Another often-used metric comes from a question designed to determine the customer's likelihood of remaining a customer. In this case, the percentage of customers who are either "extremely likely" or "likely" to keep doing business with you are added together. A total of 75 percent would indicate that you have reached a minimum level of customer loyalty. Recently, a far more predictive question based on a customer's willingness to recommend you to others has emerged as one of the most important metrics in a customer survey. In his pioneering book, *The Ultimate Question*, consultant Frederick Reichheld (2006) describes the "net promoter score" or NPS. According to Reichheld, NPS is calculated as the percentage of "promoters" minus the percentage of "detractors" and provides the single most reliable indicator of a company's ability to grow. On the 10-point scale, for example, customers rating you either a 9 or a 10 would be considered promoters. Any customer rating you a 1 through 6 would be considered a detractor. Taking each into account and subtracting your detractors from your promoters yields the NPS. The NPS of the average U.S. company is less than 10 percent. World-class organizations have NPS scores in the 60 to 80 percent range. Depending on the survey design, you can determine an NPS for individual services or products offered by your organization.

Changing the Dynamics in Your Organization

If your net promoter score is typical of what the average U.S. company is receiving— less than 10 percent—and your objective is to become a world-class organization, then very strategic interventions need to be made in your organization.

As indicated earlier, many organizations measure customer satisfaction, but fail to implement process changes and then re-measure to determine the effects of the intervention. Clearly, this is a prime place to begin to change the dynamics in your organization. Careful analysis and synthesis of your actual data need to be undertaken. For example, what are your customer response rates? What are your customers saying? What are your strategic goals when it comes to customer satisfaction, loyalty, retention? What are your measures and data on employee satisfaction and loyalty? Can you get at that data? One significant experiential application that can begin to uncover how engaged and loyal your employees are is to start to work with their "mental models"— the assumptions and beliefs that drive their behaviors and decisions. An example of this experiential application follows:

Mental Models Experiential Application

Instructions: In teams of three or four people each, identify the following:

1. Describe a mental model that you have that captures how engaged you feel with the work you do with customers and the interactions you have with customers.

2. How does this mental model link to the actions you take and the decisions you make when interacting with those customers?

For example:

Mental Model: "I did exactly what the customers asked for, but they don't seem satisfied at all."

Actions Taken: "I find that what customers ask for doesn't always match up to what their expectations are. So what I really need to do is to dig deeper into what their actual needs and expectations are."

Your Mental Model:

Your Actions/Decisions:

Action Management

The insights generated from the mental model application can be used to start to make significant interventions and changes to become more of a customer-centric culture. These insights, data, and information can then be linked to customer loyalty and service information. Customer service issues will become more apparent, especially those that require more immediate attention. For this reason, it is essential to have an integral "action management" system in place to attend to those customers who may be on the verge of defection to the competition. The elements of an effective action management system would include alerting those within the organization where product and service delivery takes place, having certain checks and balances that follow the process of responding to the customer and correcting the deficiencies, and, finally, having a method of ensuring that the customers' issues have been properly addressed by their own admission.

Implementing an Action Management Plan will start to create employee and customer loyalty best practices within your organization. Some of these best practices will encompass:

- *An engaged employee base.* Engaged employees are highly committed to the organization and it shows in their interactions with customers by going "above and beyond" in a very sincere way, not forced because they "have to." Having engaged employees will also lead to having employees develop solid and reliable business relationships. And having a relationship with customers is the foundation to repeat business.

- *Developing managers in the organization who are engaged, fair, have high emotional intelligence capabilities, and are trustworthy and willing to work with their employees.* Research from the Gallup organization has stated that the quality of the local manager determines whether an employee (as well as the customer) stays or leaves (How Do You. . ., 2006).

- *Inculcating a customer-centric culture that starts at the top of the organization.* The endorsement of top management is essential to the success of any customer service improvement effort.

- *Incorporating employee and customer-focused initiatives at the strategic level of the organization.* These metrics are just as critical as a focus on financial performance.

Continuous assessment, intervention, and changes in the organization need to be made to ensure that the strategic focus and operational practices are being implemented to attain the vision of employee and customer loyalty in order to reach the end result: repeat customers who feel they receive value for what they pay for and who enthusiastically and willingly recommend you to others. An internalization of these practices will cause what we call the "Success to the Successful" system dynamic within your organization.

References

How do you assess employee satisfaction and retention? (2006, September 28). Session at the American Society for Healthcare & Environmental Services Conference, Nashville, Tennessee.

Reichheld, F. (2001). *The loyalty effect.* Cambridge, MA: Harvard Business School Press.

Reichheld, F. (2006). *The ultimate question.* Cambridge, MA: Harvard Business School Press.

Dr. Carol Ann Zulauf, *an associate professor at Suffolk University in Boston, also runs a consulting practice, specializing in leadership, systems thinking, and customer dynamics. Her clients span high-tech, government, healthcare, education, financial, and consumer organizations. Dr. Zulauf's prior work experience includes a senior training position for Motorola, Inc. Her publications include* The Big Picture: A Systems Thinking Story for Managers *by Linkage, Inc. She is a frequent presenter at regional, national, and international conferences.*

Karl E. Sharicz *is a marketing manager with SimplexGrinnell, a Tyco International company, and focuses on customer loyalty measurement and management systems. His career history includes training management roles within several high-tech manufacturing organizations, and he holds a master's degree in adult and organization learning from Boston University. Previously, Mr. Sharicz spent several years in the applied biosciences, where he published many articles dealing with chemical analysis techniques and made presentations to professional associations.*

Contributors

Jean Barbazette
President, The Training Clinic
645 Seabreeze Drive
Seal Beach, CA 90740–5746
 (562) 430–2484
 fax: (562) 430–9603
 email: info@thetrainingclinic.com
 URL: www.thetrainingclinic.com

Zane L. Berge, Ph.D.
UMBC
1000 Hilltop Circle
Baltimore, MD 21045
 email: berge@umbc.edu

Beverly J. Bitterman
5307 Winhawk Way
Lutz, FL 33558
 (813) 964–1260
 fax: (813) 961–7062
 email: beverly@beverlybitterman.com

Robert Alan Black, Ph.D., CSP
Cre8ng People, Places, & Possibilities
P.O. Box 5805
Athens, GA 30604
 (706) 353–3387
 email: alan@cre8ng.com
 URL: www.cre8ng.com

Brooke Broadbent
521 Windermere Avenue
Ottawa, Ontario
K2A 2W3
Canada
 (613) 862–4459
 email: coach@brookebroadbent.com
 URL: www.brookebroadbent.com

Mary J. Buchel, MA, SPHR, CPF
Buchel & Associates—Strategies
 Unlimited
835 Satinwood Court
Brookfield, WI 53005
 (262) 821–0456
 email: mbuchel@wi.rr.com
 URL: www.buchelassociates.biz

Dennis Collins
General Manager
Lincoln Financial Media
20450 NW Second Avenue
Miami, FL 33169
 (305) 521–5279
 email: DpcWiz@bellsouth.net

Kathleen Finch
5075 Raymond Avenue
Burton, MI 48506
 (810) 743–7041
 email: kathyfinch@sccglobal.net

Peter R. Garber
Manager, Employee Relations
PPG Industries, Inc.
One PPG Place
Pittsburgh, PA 15272
(412) 434–2009
fax: (412) 434–3490
email: garber@ppg.com

Donna Goldstein, Ed.D.
Development Associates International
3389 Sheridan Street, Suite 309
Hollywood, FL 33021
(954) 893–0123
email: DrDonna@DrDonnaGo.com
URL: www.DrDonnaGo.com

Leonard D. Goodstein, Ph.D.
4815 Foxhall Cresecent, NW
Washington, DC 20007
(202) 333–3134
email: lendg@aol.com

Catherine Guelbert
1, Lower Marsh
London SE1 7NT
UK
0797 635 2003
email:
catherineguelbert@btinternet.com

Gail Hahn, MA, CSP, CLL
CEO (Chief Energizing Officer)
Fun*cilitators
9026 E. Minnesota Avenue
Sun Lakes, AZ 85248
(866) Fun.at.Work (386–2896)
fax: (530) 326–2979
email: Gail@Funcilitators.com

George Hall
Adjunct Professor,
Business Administration
University of Phoenix
40 Fox Hollow Road
Downington, PA 19335
(484) 341–8008
email: gchall@email.uophx.edu

Aynsley Leigh Hamel
12 Breezy Tree Court, Apt. B
Timonium, MD 21093
(410) 961–6440
email: ahamel113@msn.com

Nancy B. Hastings, Ph.D.
365 Education
Wayne State University
College of Education
5425 Gullen Mall
Detroit, MI 48202
(313) 577–8349
email: nbhastings@wayne.edu

Cher Holton, Ph.D.
The Holton Consulting Group, Inc.
1405 Autumn Ridge Drive
Durham, NC 27712
(919) 767–9620
fax: (866) 500–7697
email: cher@holtonconsulting.com

Shruti Jain
(987) 321-2992
email: sj3@rediffmail.com

Homer H. Johnson, Ph.D.
Department of Management
School of Business Administration
Loyola University Chicago
820 N. Michigan Avenue
Chicago, IL 60611
(312) 915-6682
email: hjohnso@luc.edu

Narendra Kardam
(931) 337-6079
email: prof.nkardam@gmail.com

Nikhil Kulshrestha
(989) 144-3738
email: nikhilperfect@yahoo.com

Deborah Spring Laurel
917 Vilas Avenue
Madison, WI 53715-1509
(608) 255-2010
fax: (608) 260-2616
email: dlaurel@laurelandassociates
.com

Vincent A. Miller
923 State Street
St. Joseph, MI 49085
(269) 983-1280
email: earlybrd@qtm.net

James L. Moseley, Ed.D.
395 Education
Wayne State University
College of Education
5425 Gullen Mall
Detroit, MI 48202
(313) 577-7948
email: Moseley@wayne.edu

Udai Pareek
Distinguished Visiting Professor
Indian Institute of Health Management
  Research
1, Prabhu Dayal Marg, Sanganer Airport
Jaipur 302011
India
+91 141 2791431
fax: +91 141 2792138
email: udai@iihmr.org

Dr. Edwina Pio
AUT Business School(Management)
AUT University, Private Bag 92006
Auckland 1142
New Zealand
+64-9-921 9999, ext. 5130
email: edwina.pio@aut.ac.nz

Greg Robinson
Challenge Quest, LLC
P.O. Box 396
Pryor, OK 74362
(918) 825-4711
email: greg@challengequest.com

Mark Rose
11729 Cedar Valley Drive
Oklahoma City, OK 73170
(405) 323-1522
email: mark@challengequest.com

John A. Sample, Ph.D., SPHR
Sample & Associates
2922 Shamrock South
Tallahassee, FL 32309
(850) 443-5429
email: sampleassociates@
comcast.com

Dianne Hofner Saphiere
Cultural Detective
Nipporica Associates LLC
8425 Cherokee Lane
Leawood, KS 66206
   (913) 901–0243 or (913) 901–0244
   email: Dianne@CulturalDetective.com

Aviv Shahar
President
Amber Network
15363 NE 201st Street
Woodinville, WA 98072
   (425) 415–6155
   email: Ambercoaching@aol.com

Karl E. Sharicz
Consultant
Sharicz & Associates
20 Briggs Street
Quincy, MA 02170
   (617) 573–8089

Mel Silberman, Ph.D.
President
Active Training
303 Sayre Drive
Princeton, NJ 08540
   (609) 987–8157
   fax: (609) 987–8156
   email: mel@activetraining.com

Avinash Kumar Srivastav
Associate Dean (Research)
ICFAI Business School
64, Sri Krishna Avenue, 13th Cross,
   6th Main
JP Nagar, 3rd Phase
Bangalore 560078
India
   +91 80 26582279 / 26593416
   fax: +91 80 2658 1160
   email: aksrivastav@ibsindia.org

Sivasailam "Thiagi" Thiagarajan
4423 East Trailridge Road
Bloomington, IN 47408
   (812) 332–1478
   email: Thiagi@thiagi.com
   URL: www. thiagi.com

Sherene Zolno
Proaction Associates
25900 Pillsbury Road, SW
Vashon, WA 98070
   (206) 463–6374
   email: szolno@comcast.net

Dr. Carol Ann Zulauf
Associate Professor
Suffolk University, Boston
20 Briggs Street
Quincy, MA 02170
   (617) 573–8089
   email: czulauf@ mindspring.com

Contents of the Companion Volume, *The 2008 Pfeiffer Annual: Consulting*

Experiential Learning Activities

**Change Topics

Editor's Choice

Inventories, Questionnaires, and Surveys

Articles and Discussion Resources

How to Use the CD-ROM

System Requirements

PC with Microsoft Windows 98SE or later
Mac with Apple OS version 8.6 or later

Using the CD with Windows

To view the items located on the CD, follow these steps:

1. Insert the CD into your computer's CD-ROM drive.

2. A window appears with the following options:

    Contents: Allows you to view the files included on the CD-ROM.

    Software: Allows you to install useful software from the CD-ROM.

    Links: Displays a hyperlinked page of websites.

    Author: Displays a page with information about the Author(s).

    Contact Us: Displays a page with information on contacting the publisher or author.

    Help: Displays a page with information on using the CD.

    Exit: Closes the interface window.

If you do not have autorun enabled, or if the autorun window does not appear, follow these steps to access the CD:

1. Click Start -> Run.

2. In the dialog box that appears, type d:<\\>start.exe, where d is the letter of your CD-ROM drive. This brings up the autorun window described in the preceding set of steps.

3. Choose the desired option from the menu. (See Step 2 in the preceding list for a description of these options.)

In Case of Trouble

If you experience difficulty using the CD-ROM, please follow these steps:

1. Make sure your hardware and systems configurations conform to the systems requirements noted under "System Requirements" above.

2. Review the installation procedure for your type of hardware and operating system.

It is possible to reinstall the software if necessary.

To speak with someone in Product Technical Support, call 800-762-2974 or 317-572-3994, M–F 8:30 a.m.–5:00 p.m. EST. You can also get support and contact Product Technical Support through our website at www.wiley.com/techsupport.

Before calling or writing, please have the following information available:

*   Type of computer and operating system

*   Any error messages displayed

*   Complete description of the problem.

It is best if you are sitting at your computer when making the call.

Pfeiffer Publications Guide

This guide is designed to familiarize you with the various types of Pfeiffer publications. The formats section describes the various types of products that we publish; the methodologies section describes the many different ways that content might be provided within a product. We also provide a list of the topic areas in which we publish.

FORMATS

In addition to its extensive book-publishing program, Pfeiffer offers content in an array of formats, from fieldbooks for the practitioner to complete, ready-to-use training packages that support group learning.

FIELDBOOK Designed to provide information and guidance to practitioners in the midst of action. Most fieldbooks are companions to another, sometimes earlier, work, from which its ideas are derived; the fieldbook makes practical what was theoretical in the original text. Fieldbooks can certainly be read from cover to cover. More likely, though, you'll find yourself bouncing around following a particular theme, or dipping in as the mood, and the situation, dictate.

HANDBOOK A contributed volume of work on a single topic, comprising an eclectic mix of ideas, case studies, and best practices sourced by practitioners and experts in the field.

An editor or team of editors usually is appointed to seek out contributors and to evaluate content for relevance to the topic. Think of a handbook not as a ready-to-eat meal, but as a cookbook of ingredients that enables you to create the most fitting experience for the occasion.

RESOURCE Materials designed to support group learning. They come in many forms: a complete, ready-to-use exercise (such as a game); a comprehensive resource on one topic (such as conflict management) containing a variety of methods and approaches; or a collection of like-minded activities (such as icebreakers) on multiple subjects and situations.

TRAINING PACKAGE An entire, ready-to-use learning program that focuses on a particular topic or skill. All packages comprise a guide for the facilitator/trainer and a workbook for the participants. Some packages are supported with additional media—such as video—or learning aids, instruments, or other devices to help participants understand concepts or practice and develop skills.

- *Facilitator/trainer's guide* Contains an introduction to the program, advice on how to organize and facilitate the learning event, and step-by-step instructor notes. The guide also contains copies of presentation materials—handouts, presentations, and overhead designs, for example—used in the program.

- *Participant's workbook* Contains exercises and reading materials that support the learning goal and serves as a valuable reference and support guide for participants in the weeks and months that follow the learning event. Typically, each participant will require his or her own workbook.

ELECTRONIC CD-ROMs and web-based products transform static Pfeiffer content into dynamic, interactive experiences. Designed to take advantage of the searchability, automation, and ease-of-use that technology provides, our e-products bring convenience and immediate accessibility to your workspace.

METHODOLOGIES

CASE STUDY A presentation, in narrative form, of an actual event that has occurred inside an organization. Case studies are not prescriptive, nor are they used to prove a point; they are designed to develop critical analysis and decision-making skills. A case study has a specific time frame, specifies a sequence of events, is narrative in structure, and contains a plot structure—an issue (what should be/have been done?). Use case studies when the goal is to enable participants to apply previously learned theories to the circumstances in the case, decide what is pertinent, identify the real issues, decide what should have been done, and develop a plan of action.

ENERGIZER A short activity that develops readiness for the next session or learning event. Energizers are most commonly used after a break or lunch to stimulate or refocus the group. Many involve some form of physical activity, so they are a useful way to counter post-lunch lethargy. Other uses include transitioning from one topic to another, where "mental" distancing is important.

EXPERIENTIAL LEARNING ACTIVITY (ELA) A facilitator-led intervention that moves participants through the learning cycle from experience to application (also known as a Structured Experience). ELAs are carefully thought-out designs in which there is a definite learning purpose and intended outcome. Each step—everything that participants do during the activity—facilitates the accomplishment of the stated goal. Each ELA includes complete instructions for facilitating the intervention and a clear statement of goals, suggested group size and timing, materials required, an explanation of the process, and, where appropriate, possible variations to the activity. (For more detail on Experiential Learning Activities, see the Introduction to the *Reference Guide to Handbooks and Annuals*, 1999 edition, Pfeiffer, San Francisco.)

GAME A group activity that has the purpose of fostering team spirit and togetherness in addition to the achievement of a pre-stated goal. Usually contrived—undertaking a desert expedition, for example—this type of learning method offers an engaging means for participants to demonstrate and practice business and interpersonal skills. Games are effective for team building and personal development mainly because the goal is subordinate to the process—the means through which participants reach decisions, collaborate, communicate, and generate trust and understanding. Games often engage teams in "friendly" competition.

ICEBREAKER A (usually) short activity designed to help participants overcome initial anxiety in a training session and/or to acquaint the participants with one another. An icebreaker can be a fun activity or can be tied to specific topics or training goals. While a useful tool in itself, the icebreaker comes into its own in situations where tension or resistance exists within a group.

INSTRUMENT A device used to assess, appraise, evaluate, describe, classify, and summarize various aspects of human behavior. The term used to describe an instrument depends primarily on its format and purpose. These terms include survey, questionnaire, inventory, diagnostic survey, and poll. Some uses of instruments include providing instrumental feedback to group members, studying here-and-now processes or functioning within a group, manipulating group composition, and evaluating outcomes of training and other interventions.

Instruments are popular in the training and HR field because, in general, more growth can occur if an individual is provided with a method for focusing specifically on his or her own behavior. Instruments also are used to obtain information that will serve as a basis for change and to assist in workforce planning efforts.

Paper-and-pencil tests still dominate the instrument landscape with a typical package comprising a facilitator's guide, which offers advice on administering the instrument and interpreting the collected data, and an initial set of instruments. Additional instruments are available separately. Pfeiffer, though, is investing heavily in e-instruments. Electronic instrumentation provides effortless distribution and, for larger groups particularly, offers advantages over paper-and-pencil tests in the time it takes to analyze data and provide feedback.

LECTURETTE   A short talk that provides an explanation of a principle, model, or process that is pertinent to the participants' current learning needs. A lecturette is intended to establish a common language bond between the trainer and the participants by providing a mutual frame of reference. Use a lecturette as an introduction to a group activity or event, as an interjection during an event, or as a handout.

MODEL   A graphic depiction of a system or process and the relationship among its elements. Models provide a frame of reference and something more tangible, and more easily remembered, than a verbal explanation. They also give participants something to "go on," enabling them to track their own progress as they experience the dynamics, processes, and relationships being depicted in the model.

ROLE PLAY   A technique in which people assume a role in a situation/scenario: a customer service rep in an angry-customer exchange, for example. The way in which the role is approached is then discussed and feedback is offered. The role play is often repeated using a different approach and/or incorporating changes made based on feedback received. In other words, role playing is a spontaneous interaction involving realistic behavior under artificial (and safe) conditions.

SIMULATION   A methodology for understanding the interrelationships among components of a system or process. Simulations differ from games in that they test or use a model that depicts or mirrors some aspect of reality in form, if not necessarily in content. Learning occurs by studying the effects of change on one or more factors of the model. Simulations are commonly used to test hypotheses about what happens in a system—often referred to as "what if?" analysis—or to examine best-case/worst-case scenarios.

THEORY   A presentation of an idea from a conjectural perspective. Theories are useful because they encourage us to examine behavior and phenomena through a different lens.

TOPICS

The twin goals of providing effective and practical solutions for workforce training and organization development and meeting the educational needs of training and human resource professionals shape Pfeiffer's publishing program. Core topics include the following:

Leadership & Management

Communication & Presentation

Coaching & Mentoring

Training & Development

e-Learning

Teams & Collaboration

OD & Strategic Planning

Human Resources

Consulting

What will you find on pfeiffer.com?

- The best in workplace performance solutions for training and HR professionals

- Downloadable training tools, exercises, and content

- Web-exclusive offers

- Training tips, articles, and news

- Seamless on-line ordering

- Author guidelines, information on becoming a Pfeiffer Affiliate, and much more

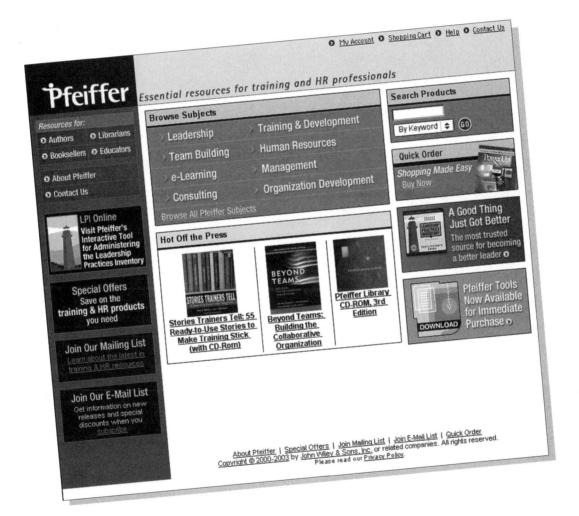

Discover more at www.pfeiffer.com